CHASING ALEXANDER

CHASING ALEXANDER

A MARINE'S JOURNEY ACROSS IRAQ AND AFGHANISTAN

CHRISTOPHER MARTIN

Hardback ISBN 978-1-7372598-1-7

Ebook ISBN 978-1-7372598-3-1

Library of Congress Control Number: 2021911296

Published by Notional Books

notionalbooks.com

This book is dedicated to the memory of:

James Swink †
Joseph Bovia †
Joshua Twigg †
John Bishop †
Timothy Jackson †
Stephen Coty Sockalosky †
Frank Zaehringer III †
Joshua Cullins †
Terry Honeycutt Jr †
Dakota Huse †
Michael Geary †
Garrett Misener †
Maung Htaik †
Jacob Tate †
Joseph Giese †
Abraham Tarwoe †
Cory Bay
William Hannibal
Jeffery Blake Murphy

† Killed in Action

PROLOGUE

Turning left at the end of the barbed wire, we rocketed out onto the road, our Humvee spraying sand and rocks behind us. I struggled to calm my breathing as cars and buildings and Iraqis flew past my back seat window. Another long burst of machine gun fire crackled above the roar of the engine.

"We're about fifteen minutes out," said Sergeant Cochran in the front seat. "Nassar says the fire is slowing down, but they still want our help."

I rubbed my thumb on my rifle safety and turned back to my window. *This is it*, I thought, *my first firefight*. I bounced my knee and scanned for roadside bombs.

"What's that sound?" Erickson asked. He was sitting to my left and glanced at me with concern in his eyes. I cocked my head and listened. He was right—there was a faint beep coming from somewhere in the Humvee.

"Holy shit!" he yelled. "Is that a fucking bomb?" Erickson asked, as his eyes went wild.

"No," Cochran said, as he twisted in his seat and reached back behind him. "It's not—"

Boom! There was an enormous blast, and the Humvee filled with sand and smoke. I couldn't see anything in front of me, and my hearing was gone, replaced by fuzzy static.

Oh my god, I thought. *We just got blown up.*

1

MARCH 2007

Alexander the Great was born in Pella, Macedonia, in July of 356 BCE. His father, Philip, was the king of Macedon.

The legend of Alexander begins when he was twelve. Philip had acquired a great horse, but it was too wild to be tamed. Many men tried and failed to saddle the horse, but Alexander realized that the horse was frightened of its shadow. He guided the horse away from the sun and mounted it, to the astonishment of the men watching him. He named the horse Bucephalus, and they rode together for the next eighteen years.

Around this time, Alexander had a new tutor, the philosopher Aristotle, who taught him math, literature, and philosophy. Alexander's favorite book was the Iliad. He carried a copy of it everywhere and slept with it under his pillow.

I grew up in a small town in central Pennsylvania, in the shadow of Penn State University. A town filled with professors' kids, farmers, and suburbia. Nestled between two soft ridgelines, I compared Happy Valley to the Shire in the *Lord of the Rings* books. It was safe, idyllic, and utterly devoid of adventure.

When I was young, I was a husky kid with thick glasses. I had bifocals in fourth and fifth grade, and I always did my homework. At school, I raced through tests and reading assignments so that I could glance up and see if I was the first one to finish. I was that kid.

A few years later, in middle school, I got contacts and started lifting weights. I joined the football team. Instead of racing through tests to finish first, I started acting out in my advanced classes. It was easy to be a bad kid in advanced geometry. As I moved through high school, I cared less and less about school, and by the time I was a senior, I was lost.

My parents pushed me to apply to colleges, but I dragged my feet. All I wanted to do was drink beer. More school sounded soul-crushing, but I had no way of articulating that. My grandfather was a professor and my mom was a teacher, so not going to college was never an option.

In my senior year, I had more Cs than Bs, and more Ds than As. Fortunately, I ended up graduating with good enough grades to get into Penn State after applying on the very last day.

It would be generous to say I attended Penn State. I was enrolled, sure, but I only showed up to class three times a semester: syllabus day, the mid-term, and the final. During the day, I went to the library, sat in an easy chair near a tall window, and raced through books. I devoured biographies of Napoleon, Augustus Caesar, and Alexander the Great. I lost myself in the adventure and ancient glory of the *Iliad*, and Livy and Arrian's histories. Sitting in that easy chair, alone and struggling in school, I'd escape to two thousand-year-old battles.

Then I would get dressed for work. I'd throw on my green work polo and some jeans, and go wash dishes for eight hours. Standing in the back corner of the kitchen, I blasted food off plates and dried silverware with small white towels. My partner at the sinks was Frank, a fifty-year-old, whose mother took care of him. Sometimes he would snack on the half-eaten food that came in. As I scrubbed burned pots and scalded my hands, I would daydream about Alexander and leading thousands of men across the world.

At the end of the night, I'd head home, my shirt soaked and speckled with food. Changing quickly and spritzing myself with cologne to hide the smell, I'd race downtown to find my drunk friends and try to catch up as best I could. Whenever I was talking to a girl and she said I smelled funny, I tried not to take it personally.

After a year, I ran out of biographies. I was also starting to run out of friends. It's hard to hang out when you're always depressed and have to work at night. I was lost and alone, just a fat kid who tried to keep people from noticing him. Reading stories about ancient conquerors had helped me escape into someone else's life—a life that was exciting and important, a life far away from my lonely existence.

During my unhappy mornings and afternoons, when I ran out of biographies, I sat in my easy chair at the library and started reading the newspaper. The war in Iraq was usually splayed across the front pages, with pictures of burning Humvees and grimy young men in front of palm trees. It was the fall of 2006, and the war was going poorly. But the more I read the newspaper, the more interested I became in the war. At that point, the first personal accounts of the war were being published. I read every book about Iraq I could get my hands on.

I read about the army pushing into Baghdad, the Marines clearing houses in Fallujah, and helicopter pilots flying missions over the Green Zone. It was enthralling. It had all the adventure and danger and heroism I vicariously felt in the history books, but I could turn around and read about it in the news. I was connecting the places, stories, and events from these books with what was happening in the news every day. It was incredible. It was a new escape from a life that I hated.

. . .

On a weekend off the next spring, I was sipping bottles of cheap beer with a friend on his balcony. We started talking about the war.

"Can you imagine, man?" I asked.

"Nah, forget that noise. I'm not dying for George Bush," he said, as he peered down at the building's parking lot.

I leaned forward in my chair and rolled the bottle between my hands. "I'm just saying, imagine someone is waiting for you inside a house. And you have to kick in the door and get them before they get you." I shook my head. "It's wild."

"Pfft," he blew air between his lips. "I could never do that."

Then it clicked. It was like a bubble popped in my mind. *I could do that*, I thought. The idea of fighting in Iraq hadn't occurred to me before. I assumed I would get a degree, get a shitty job, buy a house maybe. The idea of fighting in a war was only something that existed in my books and newspapers. But it finally clicked. I *could* do that.

I started reading and researching my options. I ditched my library easy chair for a scarred desk. Every day I filled up the desk with books, notes, and printouts. The hours flew by as I traced the US military through the previous hundred years.

I was starting to think I wanted to join the Marine Corps. Their emphasis on leading from the front reminded me of Alexander leading every charge. I started daydreaming about leading a squad down a dusty street somewhere in Iraq. It felt exciting. It felt important. It felt like there was a purpose beyond washing dishes, skipping class, and feeling sorry for myself.

The more I read about the Marine Corps, the more I realized I wanted to be a Marine. They were the toughest, the hardest. If I was going to pick up a rifle and head off to war, I wanted to be with the best.

. . .

I went to talk with a recruiter. A handsome black Marine in a crisp uniform sat down at a table with me. He said, based on my time in college and my intelligence scores, I could do anything I wanted. All options were open for me: intelligence, aircraft maintenance, crypto-graphic communications, everything. I told him I only wanted to be in the infantry; I wanted to be a grunt. He offered me a pamphlet with a list of non-combat jobs and told me I could make a ton of money if I did intel, got out, and worked for a contractor.

"I'm not going to do it if I can't be a grunt," I told him. He sighed and said okay.

If I was going to do this, I wanted to go the whole way. I wanted to be like the men in the books I read, leading the charge into the teeth of battle.

A week or two later, I had lunch with my dad and I told him I was thinking about enlisting. He froze, his fork hovering over his plate. His speared piece of omelet quivered.

"You're thinking about joining the army?" he asked.

"Well, the Marines, but yeah."

He put his fork down, closed his eyes, and rubbed his head. "But..." he started, then stopped. "But what if you get sent to Iraq?"

I knew this would come up, so I made up something about wanting a desk job, doing intelligence work. He didn't like the idea. I knew he wouldn't. That's why I lied. I wanted to join the infantry. I wanted to be in it, in the trenches, on the front lines, not in an office.

In my mind, I wanted a mission. I wanted an adventure. I wanted to wade into the tides of history, to soak in the events, and to make a splash, however small, of my own. The last thing I wanted was to sit behind a desk, push paper, or fix airplanes. All those biographies of Alexander had fixed this heroic vision of warriors in my mind. That was the kind of man I wanted to be; I wanted to be like Alexander. The only place for me to do that was on the front lines, even if I had to lie to my family about it. My parents were horrified that I wanted to enlist. So I told them I was going into military intelligence, to make it easier for them, and for me.

For the next few weeks, every family dinner was a stressful affair. Strained silences and untouched food filled the background of tense conversations about our days, that weren't really about our days. My dad would open his mouth to say something, pause, and close it again. The words were too hard to say.

And I didn't say anything, because I didn't want anyone to talk me out of enlisting. I was twenty years old; Iraq and the possibility of death were a million miles away. Leaving my small hometown and uninspiring job felt like a miracle. My life had taken a new trajectory, a new path, one beyond the quiet desperation of middle-class American life, one that was exciting and noble and uncertain.

I stood a little taller whenever I told people I was joining the Marines. They asked if I was worried about going to Iraq, but I was more worried about boot camp.

2

JULY 2007

During Philip's reign, he had perfected the usage of a new weapon, the sarissa, a twenty-foot-long spear. The ancient Greeks fought shoulder to shoulder, in a tight formation called a phalanx. Their shields overlapped, protecting each other, while they used their spears to attack the enemy. Philip's sarissas were twice as long as the spears of the other Greeks, allowing the Macedonians to attack and destroy other armies with ease.

By the time Alexander was young, Philip had conquered nearly all of Greece. Alexander took after his father, and even as a teenager, he was a skilled warrior and leader, winning honors for his prowess in battle.

In 336 BCE, Philip was planning to invade the Persian, or Achaemenid Empire, the largest empire the world had ever seen at that point. Founded by Cyrus the Great, the Persian Empire stretched from modern Turkey to Egypt to Pakistan.

Philip was in the process of launching an invasion across the Aegean into Turkey when he was assassinated by one of his bodyguards. After that, Alexander was crowned king at age nineteen.

The bus creaked as it navigated the winding roads. It was late, after midnight, and there was little moonlight. All I could see out the window was the occasional tree, Spanish moss hanging off its branches.

When we left the Savannah airport to drive to Parris Island, some of the other recruits were energetic. They stood in their seats and boasted about high school sports teams and girlfriends. I strained to hear a kid with a Brooklyn accent talking about his brother's time on the island. The gist of his advice was to keep your head down and not to volunteer for anything. I could do that.

I don't think I said a word to anyone. Most of the recruits were quiet. I tried to keep calm as the pit of my stomach churned. Incredibly, some recruits were sleeping, their heads bouncing against the window as the bus jostled over potholes.

As we drove deeper into the night, the tension started to build, and the recruits said less. The kid next to me kept his face pressed to the glass, trying to see what was ahead of us.

"Oh shit, we're here," someone up front said. Electricity flowed through the bus as whispers rippled down the rows. Street lamps glowed in the humid night air. We slowed down and rolled past a large sign welcoming us to Parris Island Recruit Depot. As I craned my neck to see out the window, I felt a wave of panic wash over me.

Can I do this? I wondered, as I inspected the athletic young men around me and compared their muscular arms to my pudgy gut.

The bus made its way through the empty streets of the base. I watched the squat palmetto palm trees as we rolled past. The air brakes whooshed as we slowed down and stopped in front of a wide brick building. I started to hyperventilate and looked around wildly as the overhead lights turned on, obscuring our view out the windows. Fear widened the other recruits' eyes.

The bus door opened up. A slightly built Marine in green camouflage climbed aboard. His Smokey the Bear hat was slung low, hiding his face in the shadow. He stood at the head of the bus, put his hands on the front seats, and leaned menacingly into the aisle.

"Welcome to Parris Island Marine Corps Recruit Depot," he growled. "When you address me, you will call me 'sir'. Do you understand," he said—it wasn't a question.

"Yes, sir," some of the recruits muttered.

"I said, you will address me as sir; do you understand!" he shouted.

"Yes, sir!" more of the bus replied in a disjointed harmony.

"When I tell you to move, get off the bus and line up on the yellow footprints." I held my breath as he scanned up and down the rows. "Move! Now! Move, move, move!"

We stood and started shuffling off the bus. The Marine stood next to the driver and loomed over us as we exited.

"Faster, you disgusting things!" he yelled at the recruits in front of me. They pushed into each other as they rushed to exit the bus. I made eye contact with the Marine. His eyes were bulging, and thick veins throbbed on his neck.

"Faster, *faster!*" he screamed, inches from my face. I felt myself recoil as I hustled down the bus steps.

Outside, painted on the blacktop, were four columns of yellow footprints. I ran over and stood on my spot, heels touching, feet forty-five degrees apart.

The air was warm and thick with humidity in the July night. Sweat dripped down my back as I stood there trying not to move, terrified I'd do something wrong. Once we were all lined up, the Marine walked over to us. He pointed to the doors on the brick building.

"These silver hatches over there are symbolic of your journey to become United States Marines. You will only walk through them once, upon your arrival to the island. When I tell you, you will form a single file line and enter. Do you understand." Again, it wasn't a question.

"Yes, sir!" we replied.

"Good. Now move! Move, move, *move!*"

As we filed towards the building, I stared in awe. The doors had the Marine Corps symbol on them, and above them was a sign that read, "Through these portals pass prospects for America's finest fighting force, United States Marines." A shiver of excitement went down the back of my neck.

We filed into a room with several phones on the wall. We were instructed to call home, and read the script next to the phone. Nothing more; nothing less. No, "I love yous," no "I'll miss yous," or "I'll see you soons"—only the script.

I picked up the phone and dialed my parents' house. My mom answered. It was late, and I could hear the stress in her voice.

"This is recruit Martin calling to tell you I have arrived safely at Parris Island," I began.

"Chris, are you—" she tried to cut in, but I talked over her.

"Please do not send any food or bulky items to me in the mail."

"Chris, wait—" she pleaded, but I kept going, my fear of the raging Marine behind me hurrying me up.

"I will contact you in seven to nine days by letter with my new address. Thank you for your support, goodbye for now."

As I finished the script taped to the cinder block wall, I could hear her try to say "I love you." Pulling the handset away from my ear, I hung up the phone and looked at it, just for a moment.

That was the last time I would talk to my mom for the next thirteen weeks. The longest stretch of silence in my life, but before that could sink in, the Marine leading us around yelled for the next recruit to step up.

Over the next few days, we processed into the military. We spent most of our time standing in lines—standing in lines to fill out paperwork, to be vaccinated, and to pick up gear. When a supply Marine handed me my camouflage uniforms, or "cammies," I stared at them in awe. I rubbed the green-and-brown uniforms between my fingers with reverence. I wasn't a Marine yet—I had to earn that title—but at least I would dress like one. Then the supply Marine handed me green T-shirts with double white stripes on the front.

"Here you go, fat body, your special shirts," he said, as I took the shirts. I felt my face flush as I tried to suck in my gut. I shoved the shirts deep into my seabag.

As we carried our seabags and backpacks full of clothes and equipment back to our squad bay, I could see recruits further along in training. Their uniforms were crisp, and they marched in beautiful precision. I turned and watched my group. We didn't look anything like them. Our group had stragglers back a hundred yards, dragging their gear behind them. My arms burned as I shifted my bags, and sweat blurred my vision. I felt pathetic.

The next day, I went to the optometrist with a few other recruits and got fitted for my military regulation glasses. I needed thicker, harder plastic lens, glasses that would double as eye protection.

"Your prescription is so strong, it's going to take a while for your BCs to come in," the doctor told me.

"BCs, sir?" I asked, as I slipped my civilian glasses back on.

He laughed. "We call them birth control glasses. They're so goofy, no one has ever gotten laid wearing them."

"Oh," I managed, as I walked out the door, on my way to the dentist.

The next day, it was time to meet our drill instructors. We gathered around the front of our squad bay, sitting on the concrete floor. Rows of metal-framed bunk beds stretched out behind us. I was excited. I knew things were about to change for the worse, but I was tired of filling out paperwork. I wanted to train. I wanted to be tested.

Three men marched out of the back room. They were dressed in khaki shirts and olive-green pants, and colorful ribbons covered their chests. I sat up a little straighter; we all did. The drill instructors marched up to us and stopped.

The one in the middle was tall and thin, with inky black skin. The men flanking him were shorter: a wiry black man and a muscle-bound Latino. When the tall, thin man spoke, he had gold teeth that flashed in the fluorescent light.

"I am Staff Sergeant Robinson, your senior drill instructor," he said. He stood there, with perfect posture, his hands behind his back. The other two didn't move at all. They stared straight ahead. Robinson introduced the other two as Sergeant Jones and Sergeant Castillo. They would be our drill instructors, Robinson explained. It was their job to turn us into US Marines. My heart started to beat faster. I knew what was coming next.

"At my command, stand on the yellow line in front of your bunks," Robinson said. I pushed my palms into the cold concrete floor, ready to spring into action.

"Move!" Robinson yelled, and the room exploded in a hurricane of movement. We all stood at once and ran to our spots in front of our bunk beds, while the drill instructors nipped at our heels. My arms trembled as I stood there, trying my best to keep still. Castillo, the muscular Latino, ran up to me and put his face an inch away from my ear.

"Open your fat, disgusting mouth!" Castillo screamed, spittle splashing on my cheek.

"Aye, sir!" I yelled.

"Louder!" he yelled, in a deep, gravelly voice.

"Aye, sir!" I yelled louder.

"Scream!"

"Aye, sir!" I screamed, my vocal cords straining and burning as I tried to get louder.

Castillo sneered at me, turned around, and sprinted over to another recruit. He held his hand out, pointing at a gangly white kid with acne, and screamed at him.

Recruits and drill instructors screamed all around me. Robinson had us run from one end of the squad bay to the other, and back to our spots on the line. We did push-ups, jumping jacks, and screamed louder and louder for the drill instructors.

Nothing we did was fast enough, loud enough, good enough.

————

"Lights, lights, lights!" the firewatch screamed as he flipped the light switch the next morning. My heart raced as I sat up in my bunk bed and reached down for my glasses before I ran to get on the line. I stood there, barefoot on the cement floor, my heels touching over the yellow line that ran the length of the squad bay. The other recruits scurried around me as the drill instructors stalked around. I blinked under the fluorescent lights.

"Put your left sock on right now!" Robinson yelled. In unison, we all reached down, grabbed a sock, and started hopping around trying to put it on.

"Three, two, one!" Robinson said.

"Done, sir, done!" we yelled back, and stood, ramrod straight on the line, one foot socked, one foot bare.

"Bullshit. Take your sock off right now! Four, three, two..." Robinson counted down over our rush of frantic fingers as we took our sock back off.

"One!"

"Done, sir, done!"

"Good. Now put your left sock on! Five, four, three..." Robinson counted us down again as Castillo and Jones walked up and down, watching us like sharks.

"Get outside! Now! Move, move, move!" Robinson said, and we ran to the door. We pressed together in a crush of arms and green T-shirts, shaved heads and yellow reflective belts as we smashed ourselves through the metal doorway and into the predawn. Running down the steps, the humidity hit me. The air was wet and viscous. We jumbled together in formation, from tallest to shortest. Orion peered down at us from over the treetops.

We lined up, nut to butt, and shuffled through the line at the chow hall, squirting great globs of hand sanitizer into our palms. I held my tray with both hands, my elbows pinned to my sides. The server noticed the white stripes on my shirt, and poured out some of the eggs in her ladle before putting the rest on my plate.

I made my way out of the line, and sat down at a small table where I set my tray down, placed my hands on my knees, and waited. Staring straight ahead, I tried to watch the rest of the recruits out of the corner of my eye. They were slowly filling up the tables. My stomach quaked and rumbled.

When we were all seated, Robinson walked around us, slapping errant hands and pushing slouched shoulders. He walked to the center of the room and stood there, hands on his hips, gold teeth sparkling.

"Eat!" he said, and we rushed to pick up our spoons and forks. I shoveled eggs into my mouth with my right hand and shoved toast in with my left. I crammed, chewed, and swallowed as fast as I could. I only drank water to wash down my food more efficiently.

"Get up! You're done!" Castillo yelled, as he stormed into the room. I dropped my fork on my plate, eggs still speared on the end. I watched the recruit across from me, his eyes bugging out as he shoved half a cinnamon roll into his mouth. Castillo saw it, too.

"Spit it out! Spit it out, you fat, disgusting thing!" Castillo roared in the recruit's ear, as he stood over the recruit. The recruit opened his mouth and let the roll fall out. It was slimy but mostly intact.

We stood with our trays and joined the crush at the door. Green shirts, yellow belts, and empty stomachs surged outside as we dumped our trays of food into the trash.

.   .   .

The sun was coming up. Pinks and purples washed the horizon as we ran. We ran and did pull-ups from rows of red-painted bars. We ran and did push-ups in the wet grass. We ran past great sandboxes and under steam pipes and across bridges, while we breathed in the rotting smell of lowland mud. We ran and ran, and ran some more, a sea of green shirts, yellow reflective belts, and heaving lungs bobbing along through the twilight.

The sun climbed above the horizon as we ran back up the steps to our squad bay. Standing on the line, we undressed one item at a time: shoes, then socks, and then clothes. We stood there naked, heels together, eyes straight ahead.

"Five, four, three," Robinson said, and we sprinted up to him, our flip flops clapping beneath us, "two, one!" We pressed together, nut to butt, towels in one hand, soap in the other. In a long line, we shuffled into the bathroom and the showers. Castillo had turned them all on. Every other one was hot; the others, cold. We shuffled together under the shower heads, shaved heads and soapy crotches and broken flip flops slipping and sliding across the tile floor.

We sat in a cold auditorium and listened to lectures on the history and lore of the Marine Corps. We learned about men like Chesty Puller, Dan Daly, and Smedley Butler, and places like Hue City, the Chosin Reservoir, and Iwo Jima. We learned the Marines' ranks, customs, and traditions.

I took notes on how the rank system works. On the enlisted side, we recruits were at the bottom of the totem pole, then came privates and lance corporals. They were the foundation, the worker bees of the Marine Corps. Then came corporals and sergeants, the middle management, they supervised the privates and lances. Above that were the staff enlisted, staff sergeants, gunnery sergeants, and up and up. They were the head honchos of the enlisted world. Parallel to the enlisted side were the officers. They all had gone to college and led units, but the staff enlisted advised them. Lieutenants worked with staff sergeants, captains worked with first sergeants. There were levels and levels above that, but the different names and rank insignia were making my head spin.

There was a whole new vocabulary we needed to learn. Windows were now called portholes and walls were bulkheads, a nod to the Marines' naval heritage. Pens were ink sticks, running shoes were go-fasters, and our hats were covers. The strangest one was that T-shirts were shirts, but our long sleeve camouflage shirts were called blouses. I did my best to write it all down but the air conditioning and exhaustion made it hard to stay awake. My head bobbed into my chest as I nodded off, then snapped back up as I furiously blinked my eyes.

Marching over to a large pavilion in the afternoon, Robinson taught us a song.

"What makes the grass grow," he shouted out.

"Blood makes the grass grow!" we screamed back.

"Who makes the blood flow," he commanded.

"Marines make the blood flow!" we answered.

"And what are you born to do?"

"Born to fight, trained to kill, ready to die but never will!" we sang in unison.

"Again!" Robinson yelled.

At the pavilion, we staged our rifles and took off our camouflage blouses. The floor of the pavilion was covered with shredded tires, creating a soft, rubbery surface. A Marine with a black shirt and camo pants stood out in front. He directed us through basic martial arts moves: how to stand, how to punch, how to kick. We would uppercut or rear hand strike and yell, "Marine Corps!"

After the basics of fighting, the instructor taught us how to stomp on someone's skull with the heel of your boot, to inflict the most damage. He taught us to strangle someone in the fastest and most efficient way. We fixed bayonets to our rifles and ran through an obstacle course, stabbing rubber human targets with faces, while we screamed "Kill! Kill! Kill!" and "Marine Corps!"

When we were finished, we put our blouses back on, and marched back to the barracks to get ready for dinner.

———

One damp morning, we linked up with the other platoons in our class, and marched over to the obstacle course. I eyed the log structures apprehensively. The course was a series of telephone poles that had been cut into square arches, with some double pull-up bars, and a rope to climb at the end. It looked like fun. This was the kind of thing I had enlisted to do, not march around all day.

Castillo and a drill instructor from another platoon demonstrated how to complete the obstacles. Their shirts were tight, and you could see their broad back muscles flexing as they climbed over the walls and log arches. Castillo climbed the rope without his legs, to demonstrate how not to do it, and to show off a little.

We waited in a line, four recruits wide, and a few hundreds long. I watched the other recruits navigate the obstacles, looking for any tricks I could use to get through this.

The first obstacle was a pull-up bar that we had to climb over. The drill instructors had demonstrated two ways of doing it. The first way was to jump up and swing your legs over your head, doing a backward roll over the bar. The visibly athletic recruits were doing it that way. They landed gracefully, grabbed a handful of wood chips, and yelled, "Marine Corps!" There was no way I could do that.

The other, easier way was the chicken wing. You jump up, do a pull-up, and swing an arm over the bar, trapping it in your armpit. Then you hook an ankle on the bar and use your other leg to swing your body around and over. Even the huskiest recruits were able to do that in pretty short order. *That's what I'll do,* I thought.

When it was my turn, I took off at a jog and leaped for the bar. I caught it, pulled myself up, and chicken-winged the bar. *Easy enough,* I thought. But when I tried to hook my ankle over the bar, I couldn't do it. I didn't have the strength. Hanging there, I caught sight of the other recruits blowing past me.

It's okay, I told myself. *You got this.* Using the wooden log at the end of the bar, I walked my feet up and hooked my ankle over the bar. I still felt confident, but I was relieved. I lifted my other leg and swung down hard. The momentum flipped me over the bar much faster than I expected, and I nearly fell off. Instead, I dropped to the ground, grabbed a handful of wood chips, tossed them in the air, yelled "Marine Corps!" and jogged to the short line in front of the second obstacle.

This one had a small horizontal log to step on. From there, you jumped and grabbed a metal bar, and using your momentum, you were supposed to swing your legs out and hook your ankles onto two other metal bars running parallel to each other. Then you had to use those bars to slide down to an elevated log, where you climbed up and jumped onto a higher log beam, rolled over it, and down on the ground. Fresh off my success on the first obstacle, I was ready. I was having fun. This was much better than sitting in class.

I stepped up on the log, crouched, and jumped. I grabbed the smooth metal bar and swung my legs out, stretching for the parallel bars. But I missed them. My feet weren't close enough to grab hold of the bars. I swung back and dropped to the ground. I shook my hands out and hopped back on the log.

Alright, I thought, *just a little more momentum.* I jumped again, caught the bar, and kicked my legs as hard as I could, but I still couldn't reach the next set of bars. This time, I dropped back down and moved back to the end of the short line for the obstacle. I needed to reassess what I was doing.

Watching the other recruits, I wasn't sure what I was doing wrong. They made it look easy: jump, swing, grab, and go, a whole stream of bald, young men in green smoothly navigating the obstacle. I thought I wasn't being smooth enough. No need to kick; let my momentum do its thing.

When it was my turn again, I stood on the log, shook my shoulders, and rolled my head. *Relax*, I thought. *Everyone else can do it; so can you.* I jumped and swung, and didn't come close. I could feel the panic rising in the back of my throat, mixing with embarrassment creeping up my cheeks. A little voice in the back of my mind suggested that maybe I couldn't do it.

I dropped down and stared at my hands. The calluses at the base of my fingers were puffy and red from swinging on the bar. Rubbing my hands together, I tried to give myself a pep talk, but I noticed the line for the first obstacle was gone. There were only a handful of recruits waiting in line behind me now.

Castillo appeared next to me. "Get up there," he growled in his gravelly voice.

"Aye, sir," I yelled, and got back on the log, ready to try again. I jumped, swung, and missed. Hanging from the bar, I could see all the other recruits up ahead. Everyone else had finished the obstacle, except for me. My face went red with shame.

Castillo shook his head and told me to do it again.

When I dropped down from the bar, I looked at my hands again. I had torn a callus. A bloody red spot was under my middle finger. I didn't care; I had to finish this.

I got on the log and tried again. And again. And again. No matter how hard I tried, I couldn't reach the parallel bars. I was all by myself. I dropped down from the bar and observed the other recruits. Most of them had finished the entire obstacle course. They were standing in formation, silently watching me struggle. As I hopped back on the log, I could feel their eyes on me. I had never felt so inadequate in my whole life.

I stood on the log and wiped my hands on my pants. Calluses on both hands had torn off, and I had blood all over my hands, trickling down my forearms. Castillo, feeling pity, or maybe embarrassment, told me to go get in formation. I hung my head and jogged over. I had failed my first attempt at the obstacle course. Not only had I failed, I only finished one obstacle. My face burned as I stood in formation.

· · ·

Later that day, when we got to the chow hall for lunch, I squirted extra hand sanitizer into my palms. I needed it, so my hands didn't get infected. But I wanted it to hurt. I wanted to blend the shame and the pain. I never wanted to forget that I couldn't do it. So I rubbed and ground my hands together, and the torn calluses opened back up. Blood and hand sanitizer mixed together and burned. I rubbed the clear gel deep into my wounds and grit my teeth in pain. I wanted to kill the part of me that couldn't hack it.

That night, after dinner, Robinson pulled me and two other recruits up to the front of the squad bay.

"You three didn't finish the O course today," he said. "I'm going to give you all a page eleven. It's a note in your file. It won't follow you to your units, but it's paperwork for us here. Got it?"

We got it. I felt awful. Not only couldn't I finish the course, but I was also getting bad marks in my file. I knew boot camp would be hard, but it had only been two weeks and I was barely holding on.

He filled out the other recruits' page elevens first. When it was my turn, he asked me if I had climbed a rope before.

"This recruit didn't get to the rope climb, sir. He failed on the second obstacle," I said.

Robinson's eyes widened, and he shook his head. "That was you, huh. I was hoping that nasty recruit wasn't one of mine. You need to get your strength up." He filled out some paperwork, had me sign it, and slipped the paper into a folder with my last name on the tab. Glancing up, he made eye contact with me.

"Go away, nasty," he said, as he closed my folder. I jogged back to my bunk, and stood in line, wondering what failures tomorrow would bring.

At night, we would sing the *Marines' Hymn*. Lying on top of our blankets, the whole platoon would belt out, "From the Halls of Montezuma to the shores of Tripoli." Our heels together, arms at our sides, lying down in the position of attention. "We fight our country's battles, in the air, on land, and sea." Pride coursed through my tired body as we got louder. "First to fight for right and freedom, and to keep our honor clean." No matter how poorly I had performed that day, I always felt the goose bumps run down my neck. "We are proud to claim the title of United States Marines." I wanted to claim the title of Marine. I wanted it more than anything I had ever wanted. So I lay there and sang and willed myself to try harder.

––––––––

Right before lunch, on a particularly hot August day, we were practicing marching. The South Carolina sun pressed down on us, oppressive and suffocating.

"Lef' face . . . March!" Robinson called out. But instead of a smooth ninety-degree turn to the left, someone turned to the right. Robinson yelled at us to run back to the starting point and start over.

"Right oblique... March!" Again, someone missed the cue and kept marching straight, causing a pileup. Robinson blew a gasket. He threw his clipboard across the parade deck and said he was leaving. Castillo stood in front of our formation, looking over his shoulder as he watched Robinson leave. I felt the sun beating down on my back, my uniform already soaked through with sweat.

Robinson was our protector of sorts. He was focused on turning us into Marines. Castillo hazed us until he was told to stop. You could feel the platoon tighten up as Castillo turned back to the platoon. He smiled at us.

Fuck, I thought as I closed my eyes.

Castillo ran us over to one of the giant sandboxes. He said we were going to bake some sugar cookies. We stacked our rifles and put our covers in our cargo pockets. We formed up in the sand and the baking began.

"Push aye, sir! Jumping jacks aye, sir! Sit-ups aye, sir!" We worked out under the blazing sun. My muscles strained, and my lungs burned. We had been on the island for a few weeks, but we hadn't been hazed like this. When we did push-ups, I did my best to grab a second of rest on the ground, but almost immediately we were up again, doing burpees, or jumping jacks.

Up and down we went in a blur of arms and sand and sweat. Seconds turned to minutes, which turned into an hour. Every few minutes, Castillo would have us lie on our backs, and roll around in the sand. The white sand stuck to our sweaty clothes and bodies. It covered our shirts and pants, and got inside our ears, eyes, and mouths. Only when Castillo felt we had had enough, he put us back in formation. We stood there, a heaving, sweaty, sand-covered mass.

"See what happens when you're nasty?" Castillo said. I tried to blow some of the sand out of my mouth when I exhaled. When we picked up our rifles, I could feel the sand packed inside my torn calluses.

———

I was raised Catholic, but I stopped going to mass when I was confirmed. Maybe it was the freedom to not go, or maybe it was the horrific sex abuse scandal coming out of Boston. Either way, outside of weddings and funerals, I hadn't set foot in a church in two or three years. But I attended mass at Parris Island religiously.

On Sundays, we had four hours where we could attend religious services. It was our only free time all week, and it was a peaceful respite from the constant nerve-fraying stress. No drill instructors; no push-ups. You could even talk to other recruits when you were waiting for the bus back to the squad bay. It was a short break from the grind of boot camp, but it made a world of difference.

The Catholic priest was a Navy chaplain. The Marine Corps doesn't have religious leaders, they're borrowed from the Navy. Marines pride themselves on only training combatants. That said, the chaplain was exactly the kind of man I expected. He was tall and broad-chested, with a silvery flattop haircut. He would read off all the sports scores: college football, NFL, MLB, even NASCAR. It was a small act of kindness for an auditorium of people missing home, giving them something that they cared about and could connect with. I liked and respected the chaplain.

The Sunday after we made sugar cookies, I counted down the minutes until mass. Things kept getting worse. The day-to-day of boot camp was brutal, but after failing the obstacle course, my confidence in myself was gone. I needed a chance to escape and steel myself for the week ahead.

After the readings, but before communion, Catholics offer a list of people or things to pray for. On Parris Island, they prayed for all the Marines, soldiers, sailors, and airmen who had been killed in Iraq and Afghanistan during the previous week. Normally, I didn't pay it too much mind, but this week the list was huge. It was August 2007, and the surge in Iraq was at its peak. A lot of people had died.

As I sat there, listening to the names of the fallen, it finally sank in. *I could die in Iraq.* It sounds insane to say that the thought hadn't crossed my mind. It had, but I was a young man. I thought I was invincible, until I was struggling in boot camp with an infantry contract and a ticket to the Anbar province.

My vision started to collapse. Despite the air conditioning, cold sweat ran down my forehead. I saw an image of my mom, sitting in my church back home, sobbing. My closed casket in front of the altar. A folded flag limp in my mom's lap.

Jesus, I thought, *what have I done to my mom?* I was headed to Iraq, and I was the slowest, weakest recruit in my boot camp class.

I came to mass looking for relief, but I found despair. As we knelt for the consecration, I bit my lip to keep from crying. Here I was, on a one-way track to war, and I couldn't even finish the obstacle course.

On the bus ride back to the barracks, I thought about Alexander and about the kind of man I wanted to be. My vision of myself as a heroic warrior was fading further and further away. The obstacle course had crushed my confidence that I could make it, that I could ever be a Marine. I wasn't born into a warrior family like Alexander. I wasn't a prince waiting to be king. Instead, I was a chubby kid from a middle-class family.

What would Alexander do? I asked myself. The answer came to me immediately. He wouldn't whine to himself in the back of a bus; he would take charge. He would push harder, faster, more ferociously than everyone else. No slacking off, ever. If I was going to make it through and survive in Iraq, that's what I needed. I needed to be harder, tougher, if I was going to merge the man I wanted to be with the man I was. I needed to be like Alexander.

3

SEPTEMBER 2007

As news of Philip's death spread throughout Greece, many of the Greek city-states under Macedonian control considered rebelling against the new king. The city of Thebes kicked out the Macedonian troops stationed there. Alexander feared Thebes would be the first of many cities to revolt, so he took a small army and marched down to confront them. In what would become a trademark of his, Alexander completed the march much faster than the Thebians believed possible and caught them by surprise. Shortly after arriving at Thebes, Alexander ordered his army to massacre the citizens and burn the town, to send a message to any other cities that were thinking of rebelling. His harsh tactics worked; the other city-states pledged their loyalty to Alexander.

We still marched every day, but we started doing other things too. We went to the pool for water training. It was mostly treading water in boots and kids who had never learned to swim floundering.

Then there was the gas chamber. We filed into a small concrete building where a small camp stove burned and filled the room full of tear gas. A few recruits had their gas masks on incorrectly and started coughing and drooling or puking on the floor. I pulled my mask straps down so tight I lost feeling in my scalp.

And the rappelling tower. We stood in lines next to a fifty-foot-tall tower as we tied ropes around our legs for a harness. I tried to slow my breathing and keep my hands steady as we walked up the rickety metal stairs. Some of the other recruits were laughing and excited. This was the kind of thing they came to do. I did my best to not look down.

As I took my position at the top of the wall, I hung my heels over the edge. The instructor smiled at me encouragingly as I leaned back. My legs shook, and I leaned back, and back, and back until I was upside down.

"What are you doing?" the instructor yelled at me, his face peeking over the wall. "Keep going! You have to let out more rope!" I eased up with the hand at the small of my back and slid down the wall a little way, my head bouncing off the wooden slats. Looking up, I could see the ground, and safety. I let out more rope. My legs twirled above me as I bounced and slid down the wall until I came to rest on my shoulders. As I got to my feet, an instructor on the ground stared at me.

"I've been doing this for a while, but you've got to be the dumbest person I've ever seen," he said. I was so relieved to be down that I gave him a toothy smile.

"Yes, sir," I said, as I jogged away, my limbs singing with life and relief.

———

After a month at Parris Island, we went to the rifle range. We packed up all our things and rode buses out to decrepit, musty barracks. They were smaller than our old barracks, the bunk beds crowded together in a concrete room. Pipes and air ducts crisscrossed the ceiling. There was an opening somewhere that let the humid air pour in, so everything was always wet: the floor, the beds, our clothes. The moisture was inescapable.

During the day, the rifle range was tranquil. We spent our first-week "snapping in". A marksmanship instructor taught us the firing positions. He demonstrated how to hold our rifles, how to aim, how to breathe. It was relaxing. We lay in the warm grass and practiced aiming at trash cans with targets painted on the side. I tried to imagine a man with a gun instead of the bull's-eye. Maybe singing "Blood makes the grass grow" and yelling "Kill!" all the time was starting to get to me. The rifle range was a pleasant change of pace, until the evening.

Every evening the hazing got ratcheted up. Robinson was no longer our protector; now he was worse than Castillo. We would come back from dinner and watch the drill instructors tear the squad bay apart. They knocked the bunk beds over, flipped the mattresses, and dumped our footlockers on the floor. Our evenings were spent in a haze of screaming and putting our meager possessions back in order.

One afternoon, I got pulled into the squad leaders' group to help bring our laundry back. The squad leaders were the best recruits in the platoon. Our clothes were washed in sacks the size of tables. Instead of picking up the laundry and heading back to our squad bay, Castillo ran us up and down the concrete stairwells, while we tried desperately to drag and push and carry the enormous sacks.

"Four, three, two, one!" Castillo croaked at us. We were supposed to drag the bags to the third floor of our building, but we didn't make it. We were only a handful of steps away. So we took the bags back down the stairs, across the yard, and up the stairs of a neighboring barracks. And back again. My arms strained, and my fingers were frozen into hard curls.

When we finally dropped off the laundry, Castillo ordered us into a closet. He had us do jumping jacks and burpees in the small space and we smacked each other with every arm swing. We were all exhausted, so instead of smoothly jumping up and down, we would do a jumping jack and stop to suck wind.

Castillo raged at our sloth. As the blood pounded behind my eyeballs, I felt a switch flip. I could do one more. I jumped and clapped my arms above my head, collapsed back down, and jumped again. And again. Everything condensed into a singular desire—I just wanted to do one more, then one more, and one more again.

"Y'all see that?" Castillo asked the group. I kept staggering through my jumping jacks, while everyone else bent over and tried to catch their breath. "Looks like Martin wants to be a squad leader! Imagine that! A fucking fat body taking your spot. Do you want to be a squad leader, Martin?"

"Yes... sir!" I yelled in between breaths. I wanted to beat Castillo. I wanted to be a squad leader, to be a Marine. I kept staggering through my jumping jacks, jumping harder and harder as I watched the squad leaders slack off.

"What the hell?" Robinson stuck his head in the closet. I made eye contact with him as I did another jumping jack. "Get out of here. We have shit do," he said, his gold teeth sparkling.

We still made time for marching. In the spare hours between dinner and lights out, we would march under the orange-and-rose setting sun. We were smoother now, faster. Left faces and right obliques, about faces and mark times—our steps were crisper, louder. Columns of camouflage and rifles and confidence.

Most mornings, we still went running. My green shirts were looser now, and my uniforms baggy. I hung from pull-up bars and rhythmically pumped out reps. I could do sit-ups now, over a hundred of them. As we ran past the sandboxes, under steam pipes, and over bridges, I'd pull ahead of recruits. Green T-shirts, yellow belts, and accomplishment, huffing and puffing in the dawn light.

When the day came to fire our rifles, the morning was beautiful. There were great billowing clouds with rays of sun coming up behind them, like a Renaissance painting. The marksmanship instructors and range safety officers smoked cigarettes and drank coffee as we listened to their safety briefing. I breathed in the rich, earthy smells of tobacco and burnt coffee.

We took our positions on the firing line, and the safety officers passed out the sparkling brass rounds. I loaded them into my magazines with care. I knew what to do, how to hold my rifle, how to breathe, how to shoot. But it still stirred something inside me to know they were live rounds. It felt a little nerve-wracking, holding a loaded rifle, and a little exciting too. My stomach pulled in as I grinned and crammed in earplugs.

As I lifted my rifle to my shoulder, I felt something new. A wave of excitement and power swept over me. This was an M-16 assault rifle with a loaded magazine. It felt heavier, more serious in my hands, as I pulled it into my shoulder. We weren't marching or attending lectures now; we were on the firing line. It felt good. It made me feel powerful.

I fired slowly, methodically marking shots and taking smooth breaths. Sitting, standing, kneeling. Breathe in, find the natural point of aim, keep tight, exhale, pause, fire. The sun warmed my back, and the earplugs silenced all my troubles.

Popping in a magazine, I racked a round. I sighted in and pulled the trigger, the recoil thumping into my shoulder, the air smelling of cordite. Bull's-eye.

After we finished on the firing line, we were patted down by the drill instructors to ensure we weren't bringing any ammunition back. Later that night, when we got back to the barracks, we stripped naked and did jumping jacks, to make extra sure that we weren't hiding anything.

———

After we finished at the rifle range, our training started winding down. We moved back to our old barracks. Our marching was brilliant: crisp turns and loud stomps. We were looking sharp. Most evenings, we trimmed, ironed, and polished our dress uniforms in preparation for our final inspections. We practiced for written tests and physical fitness tests. But we had something bigger on our minds.

The Crucible—the final challenge of boot camp. A fifty-four-hour marathon of forced marches and runs, boxing, and obstacle courses. If we finished it, we would come back and earn our place as Marines.

We got up early, much earlier than usual. Not that anyone slept much. The excitement was palpable. The entire training class formed up outside: hundreds of recruits with bulky backpacks and rifles slung over our shoulders. I stood light on my feet, near the front of the platoon's formation. This was the hardest part of boot camp, but I was looking forward to it. I wanted to be tested, to be challenged. To earn the title of US Marine.

Cypress trees swayed in the breeze. We jostled quietly, shifting from foot to foot, adjusting pack straps. Apprehension and confidence floated through the ranks. Platoon by platoon, we set off into the night, a silver moon lighting up the sky.

The Crucible took place on an abandoned airfield near the southern part of the island. As we marched through the night, we passed streets with names like Belleau Wood and Yorktown. Walking through straight rows of pine trees, I thought about all the thousands of men who had come through here before me. Men who had fought in the trenches of the Great War, and who waded ashore in the Pacific. Who trudged through the snow in Korea, and who sat silently in the jungles of Vietnam. Even those who that very day rolled down the streets of Fallujah. And now I was doing it. I felt honored and humbled to be following in their footsteps.

Once we arrived at the staging area for the Crucible, we split into small squads. Luckily, my group had Robinson as our leader. It wouldn't have been the same to have some random drill instructor that none of us knew.

Our first challenge was a recreation of a Pacific landing. We had to low crawl, face down in the sand, through a long course, dragging ammo cans and water jugs under barbed wire. Flares exploded in the sky, turning the night to day. A god-awful soundtrack was pumped in. It was full of gunfire, men screaming and choking, explosions, and metal clanging. I thought about the warriors that had done this. It was awful, crawling on your belly, sand running down your shirt, and filling up your boots. I tried to imagine the terror of machine guns and mortars raining down on me.

After that, we went to an enormous obstacle course. I stood looking at a ladder built of telephone poles that stretched thirty feet in the air. I took a deep breath and climbed onto the first rung with my partner. The next rung was about chest height. I wrapped my arms around it, swung myself onto the crossbeam, and stood up, using the side as a brace. My legs started to shake as I climbed to the next rung.

You can do this, I said to myself. I took a deep breath, and put my glasses in my pocket. Problem solved. I could barely see the log in front of me, let alone anything more than a few feet away. I kept climbing and climbing, and reached the top. Swinging my legs over, I switched sides and scrambled down.

When I hit the ground, I felt exhilarated. I never could have done that a few months ago. But before I could reflect on how far I had come, it was off to the next obstacle.

. . .

Our first night, we slept in a small building with a concrete floor and a metal roof. Four hours was all we had. I took my boots off and immediately fell asleep.

The second day started the same: lots of marching and running. We ran to the casualty evacuation—or evac—station and started patrolling down a wooded path, looking for a downed helicopter pilot. Once we hit the end of the trail, a recruit was selected to be the pilot. We had to carry him back to the start of the trail. He wasn't the largest recruit in our squad, but he was heavy enough that not everyone could carry him.

Jogging down the path, we traded turns carrying the wounded pilot. Soon, Robinson started picking other recruits to be casualties.

"You're shot in the arm. Can't carry on that side. You're shot in the legs; you have to be carried. You're dead."

Soon, everyone was helping someone else. I had a recruit slung over my shoulders and held the corner of a tarp carrying another recruit. We couldn't run anymore; now we were shuffling along.

Boom—more casualties. Eventually, only another recruit and I were left unscathed. We would each carry someone about ten yards, set them down, jog back, and grab someone else. My arms burned, and my legs ached, and sweat poured down my back. We raced as best we could, dragging and carrying the other recruits down the trail as Robinson counted down our time left.

With an unnerving air of calm, Robinson told us to stop. We didn't finish the evac; we ran out of time. He told us to start jogging, and we ran past the next station. He said since we didn't care about evacuating our wounded brothers, we were going to pay for it.

We ran around until he found a long, muddy pool that smelled like rotten eggs.

"Start low crawling," he said. No anger, no fury, only a command. We wiggled into the gray muck. I could feel the cold water pouring into my shirt and soaking through my pants. We crawled through it again and again. I pressed my body as deep into the mud as it could go. I was disciplined; my mind was stronger than the cold. If this was what I needed to do to become a Marine, I would sleep in this mud.

Soon, I was completely covered in the stinky, gray filth. My rifle looked like it had been dug up and my hands were numb with cold, but I kept crawling. I wanted more. I wanted it to be harder.

Robinson told us to get up and get in formation. We jogged over and formed up, stinking water pouring out of our pockets and helmets. He glared at us.

"That Marine to your left and right is the only thing you need to care about. I don't care if you're tired, if you're hungry, hell, if you're shot; you keep pushing for them. Got it?"

"Yes, sir!" we said. I felt his words burn into me.

"Good. Let's go."

We ran down a small root-filled trail off the main path to an obstacle course in the woods. It was almost relaxing. Running through the woods with my friends, hopping small walls, walking on balance beams, swinging across monkey bars. At one point, we passed the shore of the island. I scanned the horizon. Colorful beach houses were barely visible on the opposite coast. Not long ago, I would have wanted to be there, sitting in the sand, drinking a beer. But at that moment all I wanted to do was strive, to push myself, to see what else I could do.

It was like flexing a hand I didn't know I had. I could do it, all of it. I could climb walls and race through obstacle courses and push myself further than the other recruits. I wasn't the fat kid in the platoon anymore. I was leading from the front.

Eventually, we came to an eight-foot-tall wall. Loaded up with gear and rifles, it was too tall for some of the shorter recruits to jump up. I ran up to the wall, and squatted down with my back braced against the boards.

"Step on my thighs and climb over," I said. It worked perfectly. One after another, our small squad climbed up and over the wall. Someone kicked their leg back as they climbed over, and their boot cracked me in the face. Immediately blood started pouring out my nose. The next recruit paused and stared at me.

"Don't stop," I said. "Keep going." He climbed on my legs and hopped over. I wiped the blood off my face with my muddy sleeve. It hurt, but it felt great. I felt like a Marine.

We rallied together on the other side of the wall and hustled through to the end. Robinson wasn't angry; apparently we had made decent time.

Later that night, as we gathered in our hut to sleep, we got the news that one of the recruits in our platoon had fallen off an obstacle and broken his shoulder. He would have to leave the platoon and spend time recovering in the medical unit. We were horrified. Once he was healed, he would start over in a new platoon, and do all of this again. Poor guy.

I had the first firewatch shift. I was exhausted. Pacing in between the rows of sleeping recruits, I could feel myself falling asleep. Thankfully, it was the first firewatch shift, and not one of the middle two shifts. Three consecutive hours of sleep is better than three broken up.

When it was my turn to lie down, I didn't even take my boots off. I simply collapsed onto the floor, pulled my blanket up, and fell asleep.

The lights came too soon. Still dressed in my grimy clothes, I sat up and put my glasses on. As we groggily packed up our blankets, the clever recruits pulled out coffee packets they saved from their Meal, Ready-to-Eat or MREs, our packaged field rations. I watched five recruits pour the instant coffee grounds in between their lips and gums.

"It's like dipping. It hits your bloodstream faster," one told me. I passed, and instead swished the crystals in my mouth with some water. It was bitter but fortifying.

We formed up outside to start the nine-mile march back. As I shouldered my pack, my feet felt funny. They were tender from all the running and walking, but something felt different. The bottoms of my feet felt almost fuzzy. I brushed it off. As we marched into the darkness, I could see Orion winking down at us from the sky. I smiled.

The march back was miserable. Recruits started by suffering in silence, wearily dragging along the dark roads. But soon, the whimpering started. Feet hurt, shoulders hurt, and sand rubbed our legs raw. I watched a recruit gracefully pissing as we walked. He whipped it out and started taking a leak while walking. As we closed in on the barracks, my feet were killing me. I was limping more than I was walking at this point.

Almost there, I kept telling myself. It was a mantra. *Almost there, almost there, almost there.* Eventually, the barracks appeared as the sun was coming up. As we pulled in, the relief was amazing. Putting your pack down after a long hike is a glorious feeling.

After we dropped our packs and rifles, we got into formation around a statue of the Iwo Jima flag-raising. With the sun coming up, and steam rising off our sweaty shoulders, we had done it. We had earned the title of US Marine.

The senior officers gave speeches about our accomplishment, while the drill instructors went through the ranks, personally congratulating us. They addressed us as Marines and handed us a small metal Eagle, Globe, and Anchor, the symbol of the Marine Corps. I watched out of my peripheral vision as some recruits broke into tears. Tears of joy, I supposed. When Jones shook my hand, I didn't feel elation, I didn't feel rapturous. I was tired, hungry, and my feet were killing me. It wasn't the transformative experience that I had hoped it would be.

In the end, the Crucible wasn't challenging enough; I wanted more. More pain, more difficulty, higher stakes—I wanted to fight and prove to myself that I could follow in the footsteps of great warriors like Alexander. The Crucible wasn't enough to make me the man I wanted to be.

When we got back to our squad bay to shower and get cleaned up, I had trouble taking my boots off. It took Castillo and a medic, both pulling together, to wrench my boots free. Under my socks, my feet were swollen, wrinkled, and pale white. The medic told me I had trench foot, and that I needed to change my socks regularly and keep my feet dry. He seemed impressed that I had been able to finish the hike at all. That meant more to me than the ceremony.

————

The next few days passed in a blur. After thirteen weeks on the island, the fact that we were leaving took a while to sink in. Everything started to take on a new sense of urgency. We practiced our drill for the final competition. We cleaned our gear to get ready to turn it in. Everyone's stuff was caked with mud, clay, and leaves from the Crucible. It was a strange change to be addressed as Marines now, instead of "disgusting recruits". We no longer got hazed. We were treated like the privates that we were. Privates don't get much respect, but it's more than recruits get.

There was a ceremony for the meritorious promotions to Private First Class, or PFC. All the squad leaders and a handful of other exemplary men received the honor. I was already a PFC, thanks to the handful of college credits I had before I enlisted.

The day before graduation was Parents' Day. We had a few hours to show our families around the island. I was lucky my dad came down from Pennsylvania. Not everyone had someone show up.

I was excited to have my dad meet Castillo. The drill instructors were in their dress uniforms, looking sharp with starched shirts and chests full of ribbons.

But when I introduced my dad to Castillo, he was drunk. It was a crushing disappointment. I wanted my dad to meet the fearsome drill instructor that tormented me for months. To see how I had changed beyond the weight loss, the posture, and the bearing. In that moment, I wished I could show my dad Castillo yelling at me as I hung from the obstacle course bars, Castillo turning us into sugar cookies, Castillo cramming us into a supply closet as I did more jumping jacks than the squad leaders. I wanted my dad to see how this man had pushed me beyond what I thought I could ever do, how he had burned away my fear and self-doubt, how he had turned me into a Marine. Instead, my dad met a guy who smelled like vodka and wanted to talk about pickup trucks.

Castillo stood at the front of the squad bay. It was late, past ten. I had never been up so late on the island. We usually hit the rack right after the sun went down, but this was our last night. Castillo was still a little drunk. He was digging through a box of MREs, looking for something to eat. His dress uniform was still immaculate, though. His pants were crisp, shirt seamlessly tucked in, ribbons perfectly horizontal.

"Hey, Marines," he called out. "If you're still up, come see me in the drill instructors' hut."

I looked around. Most of the platoon was sleeping. It felt weird to go to bed when I wanted to. The six or so of us that were still up glanced at each other. No one said anything. We stood in unison and followed a swaying Castillo into the hut.

Castillo leaned against the wall and slid down to the floor. We formed a loose semi-circle around him, sitting cross-legged out of muscle memory. He ripped open the brown MRE packet with his teeth and began poking around inside the pouch.

"Who wants to hear about Iraq?" he asked.

I felt my curiosity rising. No one said anything at first. Having a real conversation with Castillo still felt taboo. After a moment of silence, I said, "I do."

Castillo was popping M&Ms into his mouth by the handful. He nodded.

"Martin, you're a grunt, aren't you?"

"Yes, Sergeant," I said, beaming a little.

"Good. You're tough." He paused, and burped. "How much weight did you lose here?"

"About forty pounds."

"Ha shit. Damn, well..." he trailed off, as he began flipping through the box of MREs again. He must have been looking for more

M&Ms. "Ahhh," he said, as he pulled a new MRE out and ripped it open. He pulled out a chocolate peanut butter packet and smiled. "This is the best shit ever," he grinned. "Oh, okay, Iraq." He squeezed the whole packet into his mouth. "I was in the initial push, you know, to Baghdad."

"Cool," someone behind me said.

"Yeah, it was cool, if you think shitting your brains out and getting shot at is cool."

I didn't know if getting shot at was cool, but I thought Castillo was cool for having been shot at. He had his Combat Action Ribbon proudly displayed on his dress uniform. Neither Robinson nor Jones had one. I wanted one; I wanted that ribbon on my chest.

"What's it like, Sergeant?" I asked.

He fixed his blank stare on me for a second, and quickly dropped his gaze to the floor between his outstretched legs. "It's not good. I don't like it." He rubbed his nose but kept looking at the floor. "I was in Motor-T. I was driving a 7-ton when our convoy got attacked. Just sitting there, getting shot up while we tried to turn around." He was quiet for a while.

When he finally lifted his head, he appeared a little surprised to see us. Glancing around the room, he said, "You all have been trained well. Staff Sergeant Robinson did a good job. Follow your training and you'll be alright."

The next day, we graduated from Parris Island. The ceremony was enjoyable. After thirteen weeks of being treated like scum, having people celebrate your achievement felt awkward, but I appreciated it. It felt strange to smile.

After the ceremony, my dad and I loaded up his car, and drove off the island.

4

NOVEMBER 2007

With Greece pacified, Alexander set off to achieve his father's dream of an invasion of Persia. In 334 BCE, he set out across the Dardanelles, the narrow waterway between Greece and Turkey, never to return home.

He stopped at the ancient city of Troy, to pay respect to the heroes of his favorite book. Soon after, his army faced its first major test during the Battle of the Granicus River, where they fought Persian troops and Greek mercenaries. Alexander led his elite Companion Cavalry unit in a charge to split the Persian army. They formed in a triangle, with Alexander at the tip riding Bucephalus, and crashed into the Persian lines. Alexander nearly had his head caved in by an axe blow, but was saved by his friend Cleitus the Black.

In the end, the Macedonians won a punishing victory, sending a message to the Persian king, Darius, that Alexander was there to fight.

After a week or two at home, I set off for Camp Geiger and the Marine Corps School of Infantry East. I flew to the tiny Jacksonville, North Carolina airport, where it was clear there was a new class starting: half of the plane had fresh high and tight haircuts. At the baggage claim, everyone had the same issued camouflage bags. It was a mess sorting out whose stuff belonged to whom.

I took a cab to Camp Geiger. As I pulled into the base, there was an old helicopter dramatically mounted on a slab of concrete. Next to it was a large sign with an American flag that read "Pardon our noise, it's the sound of freedom." I got chills. This was exactly where I wanted to be.

The check-in process was chaotic at best. Instructors were yelling at clueless Marines, who turned into supplicant recruits at the first hint of confrontation.

"Where the hell do you think you're going?" one sergeant yelled.

The Marine snapped to parade rest, hands behind his back, and screamed out, "Aye, Sergeant!"

"Jesus, no. I said, where are you going?"

"Aye, Sergeant!"

"Christ, just, go over there and wait in that line."

"Aye, Sergeant!" the private said, and jogged over to a line of confused-looking Marines.

Our first week, on a cold November morning, we formed up for physical training. It was dark and frigid, and the wind crept inside me, chilling me deeply. We stood outside in formation by platoon, all of Charlie Company assembled. Despite our sweats, gloves, and hats, it was miserable. To escape the wind, we huddled together in a tight formation, like penguins rubbing together to keep warm. One of the instructors came out of their office.

"Okay, Char-lee," he drawled. "Everyone hold up your hands so I can see your gloves." We did. He shook his head.

"Looks like some of you decided not to wear any gloves this morning. Everyone, get back inside and take off your gloves." Our collective groan floated away on the wind as we raced up the stairs of the barracks to put our gloves away.

Once we were formed up again, a different instructor came out.

"Charlie Company!" the squat Marine bellowed. "Hold up your beanies so I can see that you all have them." We pulled our tan-colored hats off and held them up.

"Oh good, numbnuts over there don't want to wear a hat this morning. Go put 'em back." Again, we broke formation and ran up the stairs to put our hats away. Tensions were starting to flare among the freezing Marines. People started yelling and shoving each other in the stairwells and in between bunks.

"Make sure you have all of your shit before you go back outside," some intrepid guy yelled.

"Fuck you!" someone else yelled back, as we ran down the stairs.

We continued to play this game. Someone was wearing a hoodie instead of their issued sweatshirt, so the sweatshirts had to go. Someone had their sweatpants drawstrings hanging outside of their pants, so those had to go as well. Eventually, we were standing outside in the cold in only our T-shirts and shorts. The freezing wind was terrible on our naked arms and legs. Our ears tingled, and eyes watered.

At that point, all the instructors came out. They were only wearing shorts and T-shirts, too.

"Well, good work, Charlie. Now we're all cold. Let's go," a staff sergeant said, and we jogged off, shaking and shivering, into the darkness.

Most of our days centered on academics. We had classes about weapons systems, small unit tactics, and radio operations. It still wasn't what I, or anyone else judging by the grumbling, had signed up to do, but at least it was interesting.

The other Marines in Charlie Company seemed tougher, harder

than the guys in my boot camp platoon. The instructors picked a bowlegged black Marine to be our group representative, because he had been arrested for assault and they figured he could keep us in line. It felt like everyone else was bigger, strong, and faster than me.

When we took breaks in between classes, a quiet guy named Longman did push-ups on his fingertips in the hallways. He had a soft Massachusetts accent and a thick shock of black hair. During the Crucible, he had broken his foot, but instead of telling the drill instructors and risking having to do it all again, he walked the nine miles back and didn't tell anyone.

In the classroom, I found myself competing with a guy named Kelly from Ohio. With his broad shoulders and strong jaw, he was a dead ringer for Tom Brady. As we sat in overly warm classrooms, many of the other guys daydreamed or drifted off, but Kelly and I took notes and studied at night.

And when we had to clean up or organize the classrooms, a sarcastic guy from Pennsylvania named Dolph always took charge. He had sandy hair and tended to frown instead of smile, but he always made sure everything was done correctly. That he did it without looking like a brownnoser, or seeking any credit for it, earned him respect from everyone.

At meals, we talked to Marines in other training companies. They told us they were allowed to smoke cigarettes after classes and watch movies on their laptops at night. We didn't have any of that. No nicotine except on weekends, and we trained until the lights went out.

After dinner, we would file into our squad bay and practice the combat crouch and combat glide until our legs shook and burned. We took apart and reassembled guns for hours. We cleaned the barracks from top to bottom every other day. On the days that we didn't clean well enough, the instructors would splash laundry detergent on the walls, floors, and lockers. Our head instructor, Sergeant Shampainor, would throw the empty detergent bottle down the center of the squad bay and quietly say, "Do it again."

Shampainor had a medium build, with a thick mop of black hair. All of his uniforms were bleached white by the sun. His cover flopped over and had a bent brim, and he had these nervous ticks. He would glance over his shoulder every few moments, and his eyes never stopped moving. They bounced from the person he was talking to, to the windows, to over his shoulder, to the sky, and back to the person he was talking to. A real twitchy guy. Rumor had it that he had killed an insurgent in Fallujah with a knife.

There were rumors about all of the instructors. The School of Infantry was a place where a lot of grunts were sent to cool off for a while. These guys had done a few tours through Iraq and now needed to decompress. Another instructor had won an award for killing a team of insurgents single-handedly. Yet another won an award for fireman carrying a wounded Marine through Fallujah when it was too dangerous to send Humvees to pick him up. All of our leaders had hard-won combat experience, and we loved them for that. They were the crusty, salty, dangerous men we all aspired to be. If blood makes the grass grow, these guys were professional gardeners.

––––––

After a few weeks of classroom instruction, Charlie Company headed to the field for our first round of infantry training. We were focusing on basic rifleman skills. The Marine Corps prides itself on an ethos that every Marine is a rifleman first. Even the non-infantry Marines went to Marine Combat Training school for a month or so, before heading on to their official job school. For us grunts, though, this was our official job school. We would stay here for advanced training and receive our specific infantry job. As we headed to the field, I kept my fingers crossed, hoping that I wouldn't screw up.

By this point, it was early December. Every morning, we would roll out of our tents into crisp, frost-covered fields. Most of the mornings were beautiful, the golden sun illuminating the brown leaves and icy grass.

We spent hours practicing the fine art of buddy rushing. In teams of two, we would sprawl out on the ground at the initiation of "contact" or receiving fire from an imaginary enemy. As my buddy lay down suppressing fire, I would pop up and take a few quick steps forward. "I'm up, he sees me, I'm down" was the mantra. I would plop down, and fire off suppressing rounds, while my buddy moved. That's it—the foundational building block of Marine infantry skills. Add more people to scale up: four people in a fireteam, thirteen in a squad.

I was surprised at how tiring it was. With all the gear—bullet-proof vest, helmet, ammo, water, loaded magazines—it was thirty or forty pounds. Wearing that while doing a burpee every few feet, for hundreds of yards, wears you down. We practiced in a frosty field for a few hours, then headed to a range to do it for real.

As I loaded my magazine with live rounds, I was nervous. I tried to keep my hands steady as my breathing quickened. I had never fired my rifle outside of the close controls of the Parris Island rifle range. Now we would be moving around over uneven terrain with other people. I wondered if people ever got shot during training.

My buddy and I patrolled forward until we heard the instructors bellow, "Contact!" I hit the dirt behind a little hill and peered through the scope on my rifle. There were targets in the distance, green silhouettes of men popping up from small berms.

Crack. Crack-crack. I fired off a few rounds, the recoil jostling my vision as the smell of gunpowder filled my nose. The green man went down.

I glanced over at my buddy, who was scanning the area for more targets.

"Moving!" I yelled over to him.

"Move!" he hollered back, waving me on with his non-firing hand. I popped up and said to myself, *I'm up, he sees me, I'm down*, as I took a few steps towards another tiny crease in the ground. I plopped down and sighted in on the target as it popped back up. While I took a few shots, I heard my partner yell "Moving!" So I opened up on another target as he took a few steps forward.

I was in the zone. It was simpler than I imagined. I shot while he moved, and vice versa. A glance over let me know when he was set, and I would take off. We finished the course quickly. As we jogged off the range, an instructor motioned us over to him.

"Hey, idiots, don't just lay down. Look for some cover next time. Check?" he said.

"Aye, Sergeant," we answered, and jogged back to the group of Marines that had already finished the range. I couldn't stop smiling. As we took off our helmets, steam rose from our sweaty heads into the cold morning air.

"That was awesome!" I said to the assembled group. Smiles and nods all around. Here we were, firing rifles, running around in the cold, and learning how to be warriors. It was everything I wanted it to be.

We spent the week moving from range to range. We did buddy rushing ranges, a light machine gun range, and a grenade launcher range. We even got to see the instructors fire an anti-tank missile. It was deafening and knocked over a tree. Everyone cheered when the tree came crashing down.

———

After the week was over, it was time to pick our jobs.

In the Marine Corps, there are specialized jobs within the infantry. The riflemen are the basic grunts. The guys you see in movies, the bleeding edge of combat units. On paper, the other infantry Marines support the riflemen. Those other jobs include mortarmen, machine gunners, and rocket launchers. Those support jobs have separate platoons and companies, called Weapons Platoons and Weapons Companies.

The infantry is grouped into threes. There are three fireteams of four in a squad, and three squads in a platoon. Then in a rifle company, there are three rifle platoons, plus a weapons platoon, with light machine guns, mortars, and rocket launchers. In an infantry battalion or unit, there are three rifle companies, and a weapons company, with the heavy machine guns, mortars, and rocket launchers.

Regardless of whether a Marine is a rifleman, mortarman, or machine gunner, they're all infantry, they're all grunts, but the riflemen are the centerpiece.

We formed up as a company out in front of our barracks. The instructors told us that our class would train for four jobs: riflemen, machine gunners, mortarmen, and assaultmen—the rocket launchers. The instructors for the latter three lined up in the center of the formation.

"If you want to be in the weapons platoon, line up out here," the company gunnery sergeant said. I watched as a handful of people jogged over to the mortarmen and assaultmen lines, while a deluge of people ran to the machine gunner line. I stayed put; I wanted to be a rifleman.

The machine gunner instructor laughed at his fellow weapons platoon instructors, and then started walking up and down the line, looking over all the Marines that wanted to learn from him. He started to point at people.

"Too small; get out. Too thin; leave. Too short..." And on he went, trimming down the group until it was the tallest, beefiest, most muscular Marines left.

"No one else wants to be a mortarman, huh?" Shampainor yelled out, looking at the three or four people who had volunteered to join him. He pulled out a clipboard. "You can be an idiot and be a gun bunny," he pointed to the machine gunner line. "But you can't be a moron and be a mortarman. When I call out your name, get in line." He had a list of our intelligence scores.

"Holy shit, who are Clark and Martin?" he called out. I stepped out, along with a squarely built Marine with freckles. "You two have almost perfect scores," Shampainor said.

"Yes, Sergeant," we replied in unison. I could feel disappointment welling up in the pit of my stomach.

"Well, get over here," Shampainor said. We jogged over to the small line. I was furious. Seventy-five percent of Charlie Company were going to be riflemen, and I got called out to do something I had no interest in doing.

Shampainor continued down the list. Each name he called out saw a reluctant man shake his head, and jog over to join us. Outside of a small group, no one wanted to be a mortarman.

From there, we separated. My new squad was all mortarmen, and we followed Shampainor everywhere. In the mornings, we sat in a small classroom and learned about indirect fire, mortar emplacement, and fire direction. In the afternoons, we would stand in fields of golden sunshine and practice on the small mortars, the 60mm guns. Shampainor had us compete, seeing who was the fastest and most precise. Mortars shoot at targets that they can't see, so we used a series of sticks in the ground to aim the cannons. I missed the rifleman training. While we were learning about angles, the riflemen were out in the field, sleeping in holes and having mock battles.

———

Right before we started working with the big guns, the 81mm mortars, we had our last hike of the training cycle: twenty kilometers, a little over twelve miles. This was our first hike as mortarmen, and now we had to carry our extra gear. The bipod and cannon for 60mm mortars each weighed about fifteen pounds, while the baseplate weighed about ten. Our squad would have to rotate the gear amongst ourselves during the hike. About twenty Marines carrying eighteen pieces of extra gear, it was going to add up.

Before we started moving, I leaned into Dolph and Kelly, pulled a white bottle out of my cargo pocket, and gave it a shake.

"You guys want some ibuprofen?" I asked.

Kelly raised his eyebrows. "Don't mind if I do," he said, as he held out his hand. I shook a few brown pills into his palm.

Dolph frowned. "I don't need that, ya pussies," he said, as he hoisted the bipods on to the top of his pack.

"Alright, man. Suit yourself," I said as I tapped a pair of pills into my hand before sliding the small bottle back into my cargo pocket. I knew I was going to need it. I had a goal for the hike—I wanted to carry an entire mortar system.

I wasn't fat anymore, but I was still the chubby guy with huge glasses. Many of the Marines in Charlie Company were muscle-bound natural athletes. There were guys who could do twenty-five pull-ups or run three miles in under sixteen minutes. I couldn't do any of that. But I could walk. I could keep putting one foot in front of the other, no matter how painful it was. I needed to prove that even if I wasn't the fastest or strongest Marine, I could be the toughest.

Hikes are brutal. All your gear, your pack, rifle, and body armor, all hang off your shoulders, and they ache like you've subbed out Atlas. Everyone trudges along in silence, no talking for hours. But the worst is the mental aspect. You never really know how much further you have to go. You walk, one foot in front of the other, struggling with the pain. And that little voice comes to you, and says, *Just quit. This sucks. Why not stop for a while?* And the most important thing in the world is to never listen to that voice. Find a landmark and tell yourself, *I have to make it to that tree, that telephone pole, that road crossing.* And when you get there, pick out your next target while you keep the voice at bay.

We set out into the night. At first, we trudged through the training area, past the long rows of barracks, and into the woods. I was carrying a mortar cannon and kept my ears tuned to anyone asking for help. Before we got to the first rest point, a smaller guy called out.

"Can anyone take these bipods from me?"

"I can!" I called back. I dropped into the open center of the column and walked back to him. Once we met, I took the bipods off his shoulders as we were walking. Jogging back to my spot in the column, I pulled off the cannon and turned to Kelly.

"Hey, man, help me put this together." We struggled to connect the bipods to the cannon as we walked. This was starting to seem like a dumb idea.

"Fix it at the rest area," Kelly said. With that, he placed the bipods over my shoulder, and I carried the cannon cradling it in my left arm while I kept my other hand on my rifle.

After a few miles, the company was called to a halt.

"Packs off! You've got five minutes to drink some water and fix your gear!" one of the instructors yelled. I dropped my pack and quickly assembled the bipods and cannon. Shampainor was walking down the middle of the trail, counting all the pieces of mortar gear.

"Three cannons, four bipods, two baseplates." He scratched the list in a small notebook.

"Four cannons. Martin, do you have bipods too?" he asked.

"Yes, Sergeant," I smiled as I took a swig of water.

"Okay. Five bipods," he said and continued down the line. Not the reaction I was hoping for. I looked around as I drank some water from my canteen. I needed to get a baseplate from someone.

"Hey, Haley, how you doing with that baseplate?" I asked the slight guy from Tennessee who was a carbon copy of Johnny Depp.

He pushed his glasses up. "You're not getting my baseplate, Martin," he drawled. I pursed my lips and lifted my chin. Someone else then.

"Two minutes!" came a cry from upfront. I stood up and repeated the call as it went down the line. Time to gear up. I hoisted my pack back on, and nestled the combined cannon and bipods in the space between my helmet and pack. As I tightened my straps, I saw a struggling Marine. His pack was a mess, straps hanging every which way, the whole thing tilted to the side. *Perfect*, I thought.

"Yo, man, you want me to take that baseplate while you get your pack on?" I asked.

He looked up, his helmet cocked at an awkward angle. "Oh sure. Thanks you," he replied. I slowly bent over, one hand on the mortar equipment, and grabbed his baseplate off the ground. I slid the chest strap from my pack through the middle and clipped it shut. He was straightening out his straps.

"I can take that back now," he said.

"I'll just hold on to it for a while," I fibbed. "Let me know when you're ready to have it back." He looked relieved.

There, I had it—a 6omm mortar, forty extra pounds, forty more pounds than any rifleman was carrying in the back of the formation. I rubbed my tongue on my teeth and grinned. Now I had to finish the hike.

We marched off into the night, down pine tree-lined trails and through sandy marshes, across backroads and past highways, the bipods and cannon balanced on my pack, while the baseplate swung gently from my chest. I kept my hands on my rifle.

At our next stop, I set up my mortar. I wanted everyone else in the platoon to see, to know I had it. As I sat on my pack and sipped water, I watched the whispers and pointing. *Good*, I thought, as I tossed down a few more ibuprofen. Kelly took a few more, and so did Dolph this time.

We were at the halfway point. We turned the formation around by walking down the center of the column, Charlie Company stretching back through the woods. We walked past the machine gunners, big guys carrying big guns. Next came hundreds of riflemen. Their gear was dirtier than ours, their uniforms a little more faded. Ours were still new-looking.

As we trudged on, the straps from my pack dug into my shoulders. I did little hops, trying to temporarily take the weight off. The baseplate kept clanging against my rifle, banging my knuckles until they bruised and bled. I kept popping more ibuprofen while we walked.

I started picking out a tree up ahead. I'd hunt for a good tree, one with a smooth, round trunk, and I'd tell myself, *Just make it to the tree, and you can pass off some gear*. And I'd walk and stumble and drag myself to the tree. Then I'd find another tree. My world was shrinking. All that mattered now was the next tree. As long as I had a tree to get to, I couldn't pass off my mortar. Despite the January cold, sweat poured down my back and off my face. Drops of sweat fell on my hands and mixed with the blood from my knuckles.

I was having trouble walking when we finally cleared the forest. My legs were chafed, and I could feel the blisters covering my feet. As we marched through the training area, I counted the barracks up ahead. I was delirious as we approached, I couldn't wait to drop my gear. My spine felt like it had shrunk a few inches.

When we formed up in front of our barracks and dropped our packs, I assembled my mortar and beamed. I'd done it. No one else wanted to do it, could have done it. But I did.

Later, in the showers, a machine gunner I didn't know came up to me. "Hey, you the mortarman that carried the whole thing?" he asked.

I was rubbing a bar of soap over my blistered feet. "Yeah. Why?"

"That's badass. That hike sucked. I can't imagine carrying extra stuff just because," he said, as he washed his chest.

"Thanks, man," I replied, as I did my best to hide my pride. I wasn't there yet, but I was inching closer to the kind of man I wanted to be.

———

One evening, we were out in front of the barracks, practicing on the 81s. Even though it was January, no one had gloves on, and our hands stuck to the frozen metal. As the sun pushed our shadows taller, a cluster of helicopters flew by, heading out from the other side of New River Air Station. I listened as the sound of freedom flew overhead. Through the *whunk-whunk-whunk* of the rotors, Shampainor perked up.

"Hey, mortars! On me." We hopped up from the guns and jogged over, rubbing our freezing hands together. "You see those helos up there?" Shampainor asked, as they flew south. "You know who flies those metals cans?"

A couple of guys mumbled "Officers" or "Marines."

"Yeah, fucking officers," Shampainor retorted. "Lieutenant colonels and majors that have been in the Corps longer than most of you have been alive." He glanced over his shoulder in that nervous, always alert manner of his. It was hard to tell what he was getting at. "I know you all hate me." A murmur of dissent arose like a limp cloud. Shampainor was a pain, and hate was a matter of degree. "Shut up," he barked. "If you don't hate me, I'm not doing my job." This was new.

He looked around, checking to see if anyone was in earshot of our little cluster. "Listen," he began with uncharacteristic softness, "those officers up there flying them helos, they don't mean shit. Sure you gotta salute them, and say 'sir' and all that, but the thing is, they work for you." I shifted my weight, uncomprehending. The entire time I had been in the Marines, it was made abundantly clear that we were at the bottom of a very tall totem pole.

"The Marine Corps doesn't give a damn about pilots. All that matters is the infantry. Those flyboys up there, they're your ride, they're your air support, and they exist to support you. Period. I know you're just a bunch of privates, but you're grunts, or you will be. And every last one of you is going to Iraq. You're gonna go kick in doors and get a look under the Reaper's hood. Those colonels flying around don't have shit on that." The cold air never gave anyone goose bumps like this.

"Everyone in the Marines is either in the infantry, or only around to support it. Admin, air wing, even fucking tanks, and arty—none of them run the show. We do." Shampainor thumped his chest. "And even me, sergeants, squad leaders, team leaders, we're here to back up that lance corporal walking point down some shithole street in Fallujah. That's what this whole thing is about, that grunt, walking point. Everything we do is to back him up. So I keep you fuckers out here late, practicing gun drills, and we train in the barracks at night, and I fucking jerk your chain around to get you ready. Trust me, I've been there. Your time is coming, and if I open the *Marine Corps Times* and see any of your ugly faces in there, then I let you down. Not gonna happen."

A sense of awe and power pushed the cold out of my fingers. This was why I wanted to be a Marine. This was why I wanted to be a grunt. I wanted to be that guy walking point. Excitement and pride raced through my blood. I would have run through a hail of bullets for Shampainor if he had asked me to. He twitched and glanced at the surrounding rooftops. "All right, circle jerk over. Get back on the guns."

5

FEBRUARY 2008

Alexander and his army moved down the western coast of Turkey, where they liberated a series of small towns. One of the towns they stopped in was Gordium, home of the Gordian Knot. Legend had it that whoever could untangle the complicated knot would become the king of all Asia. For years, no one could undo the knot, no matter how hard they tried.

When Alexander arrived in Gordium, he attempted to untie the knot, but like everyone else, he was unable to. So he drew out his sword, sliced through the rope, and then untangled the knot.

On a wet February afternoon, we loaded into buses on Camp Geiger and started the drive to Camp Lejeune, where we would join our unit. Almost everyone in Charlie Company was heading to the same battalion.

A Marine from our new unit was talking to the bus driver about Iraq. I strained to eavesdrop on their conversation, but I only caught snippets, something about driving off-road and banging his face on his machine gun.

Close to the entrance to Lejeune, the fences surrounding the base had flags and banners and cups pushed into the chain-link. The cups spelled out "Welcome Home Sgt Jones!" The banners said similar things. It was clear a unit had recently gotten back from a deployment.

As we drove through the gate and on the base, I started to get nervous. We had heard that the real hazing happens in the fleet, as regular Marine units are called. Lance corporals fresh off their third deployment to Iraq would haze us constantly. Corporals with wild PTSD would keep us up for days, reenacting their time in Fallujah. We were all expecting the worst.

As the buses pulled up to our barracks, Marines were already unloading our bags on the sandy ground. But in an anticlimactic turn of events, our new platoon was out training for the week; it was only us new guys, or boots, for now. So we spent the next few days getting situated. We were issued bed linens, rifles, and night-vision goggles, and filled out paperwork. It was boring. I wanted to meet the platoon.

A few days later, after we picked up our gas masks, there was a buzz in the barracks. The platoon and the rest of Weapons Company were finally back from the field. We were all excited to finally see these mysterious fleet Marines we would be serving with. Excited, and nervous, that the hazing was about to begin in earnest.

We were brought to a small office, not much more than a desk and a couch. A Marine in dirty, muddy, green camo, with leftover smears of camouflage paint on his face, was sitting in there. He had a buzzed head and was scrubbing his rifle with a toothbrush. When he smiled up at us, he had a gap-toothed grin. He introduced himself as Lieutenant Szwebjka, our platoon commander, and took us to meet the platoon.

The 81s platoon was in the lounge next door, cleaning their rifles. It was a small, motley crew: maybe ten corporals and sergeants and ten privates and lance corporals. Us boots filed into the room and stood at parade rest, hands behind our backs.

"Gents, these are the new 81s Marines," Szwebjka said. "I expect that you'll welcome them to the platoon."

"Kill," a Marine cleaning a small machine gun said, waving a gangly arm in our general direction. In the fleet, people said 'kill' for all kinds of reasons—as an acknowledgement, as a motivational burst, even as a sarcastic aside. On a normal day you might hear people say 'kill' fifty or more times.

I surveyed the room, trying to judge the dynamics. Were these combat-hardened grunts? Were we about to be hazed into the dirt? Some of the sergeants looked hard, but everyone else had new uniforms. They were dirty but new and soft-looking. Not many had Castillo's flinty stare or Shampainor's twitches.

"Well, don't just stand there," one of the sergeants said. "Keep doing whatever you were doing." With an "Aye, Sergeant," we filed out of the lounge and got back to checking into the battalion.

Over the next weeks, we spent time getting to know the platoon. The junior Marines were all boots, like us. They had arrived in the last few months. Only a few of the corporals and sergeants had ever been to Iraq or Afghanistan.

One corporal was a beefy, blonde Wisconsinite named Skewes. He was fresh from recruiting duty but had been in Iraq before. He was temporarily running the Fire Direction Center (FDC), while the two sergeants who were normally in charge were at Mortar Leaders Course, a job school for advanced mortar skills.

Skewes was a fresh-faced, all-American Midwesterner, with an American flag tattooed on his arm and a surprisingly earnest personality. He was friends with another corporal, Gleason, a tall, thin Texan with a burning intensity. Gleason was stronger and faster than almost everyone else in the platoon. Between that, and his encyclopedic knowledge of guns, radios, and tactics, he should have been a Green Beret instead of a Marine.

The platoon continued to expand. A few new sergeants joined us. One was an instructor from the Marine officer school at Quantico;

some others had left the Marines but reenlisted. We got a few more boots too. Another infantry class dropped, rounding out the lower ranks. We were up to about fifty Marines in the platoon.

Our days were based around cleaning: cleaning the hallways of the barracks, cleaning our rooms, cleaning the community showers and bathrooms. When we weren't cleaning, we stayed in our rooms, hiding from any passing corporals with a broom looking for an unsuspecting private. So far, the fleet had none of the hazing, or even training, that I had expected.

Once the new boots were in our platoon, Skewes held tryouts for the FDC. There were only three people interested in trying out: Kelly, me, and a tall blonde Marine, who had been in the fleet for several months before Kelly and I got there. I figured the FDC was the path to advancement. Everyone was on the gunline, handling the mortars, but the FDC told them what to do. It wasn't a leadership position per se, but it was a position of distinction.

The four of us met in the lounge one day before lunch. Skewes explained the basics of FDC.

"A forward observer calls in where they want the rounds to land, and the FDC figures it out so that the gunline can shoot at it," he said. He had a fat lip of Skoal, that he kept pressing on with his tongue. "We use these plotting boards to do that." He held up a disc about the size of a pizza box. It had a wheel of clear plastic graph paper bolted to another piece of plastic graph paper. He spun the wheel to show how easily it turned.

"I'm going to show you how to set up your boards, then we'll go through a handful of practice missions," he said, and spit into an empty water bottle.

We spent the next several hours in that hot, dry room, setting up and wiping down our plotting boards. We used colored map pens to write in the mortar's firing directions, observer positions, and GPS grids. It was unusual, working off two different graphs, but Kelly and I quickly got the hang of it. The blonde Marine figured it out, too, but wasn't as quick.

Skewes would call out an adjustment, "Down 150, left 200," and we would be off to the races. Turn the disc to the observer's angle of direction, and move your plot three squares down and four squares left. Spin the disc back to the mortar directions, and grab the ruler to check the distance. Flip through a thick book of firing tables and look up the distance to find the elevation for the mortar. Jot it down on the edges of the plotting board, and glance up.

As soon as I lifted my eyes from the plotting board, I peeked at Kelly. He was already looking at me. *Shit, he beat me.* Barely, though, judging by the way he was setting down his ruler. Skewes pushed the wad of tobacco to the other side of his mouth. Eventually, the blonde guy finished.

Skewes took our plotting boards and checked our answers. In the FDC it's rare to get an exact match on your work. Instead, it needs to be within a small margin of error. Kelly and I were inside it, and other guy was a bit outside.

"Well, it looks like Kelly and Martin are the new FDC boots," Skewes said.

————

After Kelly and I made it into the FDC, we started training exclusively with Skewes. He prided himself on being strong and in shape, so every morning we would do wind sprints and pull-ups, push-ups, and sit-ups. Some of the other teams in the platoon barely trained, but we were out every morning, running in boots and our flak jackets. I liked having Skewes as a team leader. He had deployed; he had been in the fire. He would mention things like, "When I was in Iraq, I lost twenty pounds," but he never told us any stories. None of us boots were privy to the stories from the battlefield.

During the days, we practiced our FDC skills. We learned how to plot polar, grid, and shift missions. We learned about phosphorus smoke screens, suppression of enemy air defenses, continuous illumination, center and off-center plotting. We learned how to talk to the observers. "You, this is me. Fire mission over" was constantly running in the back of my mind. Kelly and I were getting better. The unspoken competition between us pushed us harder and faster.

Skewes loved it. He didn't believe in cheating, but if he didn't come in first in something, he wanted a rematch. It was a fun little team we had: a couple of guys from Big Ten country, talking trash about football.

Kelly and I moved into a room with a pair of newer Marines. Already in his mid-twenties, Shen was older than most of us. He was a Chinese immigrant, and rumor had it that he knew exactly two words when he showed up at boot camp, "Yes, sir." God only knows how he made it through Parris Island. The other guy was Abbott, a skinny kid from upstate New York. He was soft-spoken and had unusually large hands that hung off his thin arms like shovel blades. Kelly and I had gotten to the unit a whole two weeks before Shen and Abbott, so of course, we took the bottom bunks, because of our seniority.

Time rolled on. Kelly and I practiced with our plotting boards, while the rest of the platoon practiced on the mortars. We ran in the mornings, and cleaned our rifles in the afternoon. The corporals and sergeants taught classes on grenade launchers, Humvee tactics, and how to clear insurgents from a building. Some mornings, Szwebjka ran us around the barracks while we carried sandbags. In the afternoons, we mopped the hallways while we listened to the distant boom of artillery rounds.

We were always mopping the hallways. One time we found an electric floor buffer, like the ones that high school janitors use. It worked amazingly well. You could see your face in the tile floors after we used it. We could also ride it down the hallway. One afternoon, as we were timing each other to see who could ride the buffer the fastest, the company gunnery sergeant caught us.

"Holy shit!" he yelled at us. "What the fuck are you war dogs doing?"

We jumped up and stood awkwardly at parade rest.

"Just buffing the floor, Gunny," someone said meekly.

"Jesus Christ, don't you know the tiles are made of asbestos?" he asked. We looked down. Our pants and boots were covered in a light dusting of white powder.

"Someone get a goddamn hose in here and wash all that shit out before we end up in a cancer commercial," he said, as he walked away.

———

After work, I mostly hung out with Kelly, Dolph, and Longman, but I was quickly becoming friends with some other guys. Cocagne, pronounced "cocaine," was a tough-as-nails Michigander, with a gruff voice and a slight tilt to his walk. He was one of the best Marines in the platoon, but couldn't stay out of trouble and kept getting busted back down to private. Blackwood was a laid-back ex-football player from Alabama. He had the slinking grace of an athlete, but was particularly talented at laying low in the barracks to avoid cleaning duty.

We had guys from the Rust Belt and the Bible Belt, the suburbs, the cities, and the country. During the week, we'd run and train and complain about the sergeants. On the weekends, we would pack into cheap hotels and chug cases of beer, and in the morning, we'd wake up in bathtubs, under sinks, and on the floor. Everyone came from somewhere different, but on some level, we were all the same. Everyone wanted more than life back home offered, wanted more than an easy life. We wanted to be tested, to be challenged, to stand in the crucible of combat and see if we could take it.

One morning when we formed up for roll call, three new guys were standing off to the side. Two of them were smoking cigarettes and laughing, while the other cracked jokes in a Southern drawl. I stood next to Kelly in formation as I watched Skewes walk over and join them. Listening in, I could hear them talking about the Mortar Leaders' Course. *These must be the other members of the FDC*, I thought.

After we were all accounted for and were dismissed to clean the barracks, Skewes pulled Kelly and me over. He introduced us to Sergeant Cochran, a squat Michigander with glasses, and Sergeant Tuttle, a tall, lanky Oregonian with thick, black eyebrows. They were going to be joining us in the FDC. They had both been to Iraq, and Cochran had been to Afghanistan as well. They had an easygoing attitude when talking in front of low-ranking Marines. Not a bad thing; it was clear they were sergeants, and Kelly and I were not.

The other Marine walked up while Kelly and I stood at parade rest.

"Whoa, watch out for these two. I can see the bloodlust in their eyes." He chuckled and smiled. "Hey, I'm Corporal Carnahan, but you can call me corporal."

Kelly and I smiled. We might still be privates, but we weren't inside sweeping the floors. We were in the inner circle, standing with the team leaders and squad leaders. Even if we weren't allowed to talk, at least we were in the room.

Tuttle and Cochran agreed with Skewes that mortars weren't used in Iraq anymore. We needed to train on the mortars, but our focus was on basic infantry skills: room clearing, foot patrols, and mounted patrols in Humvees. Szwebjka had a little ditty for this: "Jack of all trades, master of mortars." The sergeants all made fun of Szwebjka's saying, and like the little brothers we were, us privates copied them.

After our morning runs, the communal shower was full of mortarmen and machine gunners, with a line of towel-wrapped men waiting. As people started to get cold standing in line, someone would yell, "Yo, hurry it up," and a mortarman would grab a handful of soapy crotch and say, "Hey, I'm mastering my mortar over here."

To train for infantry tactics, we broke our platoon into two different versions: a mortar setup, with gun teams, an FDC, and forward observers; and another version built around three traditional infantry squads. They were similar, but in the infantry squad version, my squad lost Kelly and the observers. Instead, Tuttle was the squad leader, while Cochran and Skewes were the team leaders. We had a random collection of other Marines from the gunline to fill out our teams. Some guys, like McVaugh, a speedy smartass from Amish country, were stellar Marines, while others were considered problem children. Tuttle christened us "PBR Streetgang," after the riverboat in *Apocalypse Now*.

All of us boots, the new Marines, split the sergeants and corporals into two groups: those who had seen combat and those who hadn't. We all still respected their ranks; to disrespect one sergeant was to disrespect them all, and a great way to end up on everyone's shit list. But beyond only respecting the rank, there was an idea that the leaders who had been there, been under fire, had something special, something extra. They were cooler, more esteemed. We all wanted to be in their squads and fireteams.

A sergeant who hadn't seen combat might explain something to us, only to have a corporal, who had been in Ramadi, say, "Well, when I was in Iraq . . ." That was the decisive move—pulling out their hard-won knowledge—and it meant everything in our unit.

Tuttle had been in the initial invasion of Iraq, Skewes had fought in the early days of Fallujah, and Cochran had been in Phantom Fury, the epic battle of Fallujah, as well as a tour through the Korengal River Valley in Afghanistan. They were battle-hardened men, and they had the most experience of any squad in the platoon. I was thrilled to be one of their Marines, and I tried to soak up as much as I could from them.

———

Soon after Cochran and Tuttle came to the platoon, we set off for Virginia to do cold-weather training. The Marines with Humvee driving licenses convoyed up a day ahead of us. The rest of us followed on buses. It was strange to ride a bus for hours with my rifle between my knees and my body armor resting on my thighs. We watched action movies the whole way.

When we got to Virginia, it was cold and pouring rain. We filed off the buses and stood there, shivering and soaking wet. There was an issue with unlocking our squad bays, so a large tent was set up for us. We slept on the grass under the tent while the water poured in and puddled around us.

The next morning, we found a squad bay and set up our gear: junior Marines on one side, platoon leadership on the other. Our training for the month was split in two. For the first two weeks, we practiced patrolling and squad tactics, and in the last two weeks, we did a mortar shoot. I was excited to flex my new skills in the FDC, but first, we got a crash course in patrolling.

Skewes took Kelly and I out to practice. As usual, we competed to be the fastest, the loudest, the best. We patrolled around the bivouac area, mostly cinder block squad bays, and reacted to imaginary enemies that Skewes called out. We patrolled around in a loose diamond shape and walked down the muddy roads until Skewes would cry out, "Contact right!"

"Contact right!" we would echo, as we dove for nearby cover or, lacking that, belly-flopped into the mud. From there, we would buddy rush across the terrain, *I'm-up-he-sees-me-I'm-down*, until we closed with our notional enemy.

Skewes loved sound effects. When we were buddy rushing, we had to yell, "Bang, bang! Bang! Bang, bang, bang!" to simulate firing. Maybe it was to enhance the confusion. Maybe it was to recreate the noise of a rifle. Maybe he liked watching a bunch of grown men pointing rifles at trees and yelling nonsense.

The platoon split up and ventured into the woods. Each half found a secluded knoll where we set up a patrol base. We established security, sectors of fire and watch schedules. After that was set up, we pushed out patrols. Kelly, Skewes, and I walked through the frost-tinted forest, dry leaves crunching underfoot, bare branches overhead. We roamed over the rolling Virginia hills, looking for other patrols, setting up ambushes and traps. It was fun, like a game of 'Capture the flag', but with guns.

We practiced short halts and crossing danger areas, flanking maneuvers and land navigation. We learned how to adjust our night vision goggles and use the infrared lasers on our rifles. At night, Kelly and I switched on and off on radio duty. I lay in my sleeping bag and watched the stars with the radio handset tucked next to my ear. It was great being a regular rifleman for a change.

After that, we did our first mortar shoot with Kelly and me in the FDC. We sat in the back of a high-back Humvee with our plotting boards, while the sergeants and platoon leadership chatted. Gleason and Martinez, a short Texan with an attitude, were our forward observers and they called in fire missions from a tall tower overlooking the range. Cochran had a special computer to check Kelly and my work. While the rest of the platoon dug bunkers in the sand and stood outside all night in their flak jackets, Kelly and I ate raspberry swirl cake in the warm Humvee. Being in the FDC wasn't my ideal job, but when the company commander and first sergeant came through, they met Kelly and me. We weren't leaders, but we were in a position of privilege.

On the last day of our shoot, we accidentally lit the forest on fire with rounds of white phosphorus. We packed our gear under a haze of smoke and urgency, and set out, marching down the road, the flames creeping up behind us.

———

When we got back from Virginia, we reorganized our squad. Tuttle pulled me aside and let me know that they had selected me to be the third team leader. I was still a PFC, but I was going to have a corporal's job. I was ecstatic. Skewes, Cochran, and Tuttle promised to show me the ropes and teach me everything I would need to know.

They gave me Marine Corps manuals with titles like 'Warfighting' and 'Tactics,' and handbooks they picked up at various schools. Three Marines—McVaugh, Abbott, and Schneider, a black superstar tennis player from Massachusetts—reported to me now. I was a leader. I wasn't Alexander, marching across the Dardanelles, but I was a leader.

To build team cohesion, and to try and be a cool team leader, I took my fireteam to a biker bar about an hour from Camp Lejeune. McVaugh said they didn't card people, so it was perfect for us. We played pool and drank pitchers of beer as middle-aged guys with faded tattoos and black leather jackets filled the bar. Schneider got drunk and danced over to the jukebox, where he switched off the Metallica that was playing and put on some Lil Wayne. As Weezy started to rap about licking it like a lollipop, twenty-some bikers turned and noticed us for the first time. McVaugh made eye contact with me and grabbed Abbott, as I grabbed Schneider and headed for the door before anyone decided to ask how old we were.

Soon after that, Szwebjka pulled me aside. I had been promoted to lance corporal a week before. Not an important rank, but I wasn't a private anymore. Szwebjka said the battalion was part of a new initiative to push intelligence-gathering and analysis down to the company level. They were pulling two Marines from every platoon and sending them to a two-week course on intelligence analysis. Carnahan and I had been selected as the 81s platoon reps for the new Company Level Intelligence Cell, or CLIC. I thanked Szwebjka for the opportunity and went to talk to Tuttle.

"Mo-th-er fucker, taking my Marine away from me," was Tuttle's angry response.

However annoyed Tuttle was, I was pumped. This was another feather in my cap. I was a team leader, and now I was part of a new intelligence unit. Instead of washing dishes with Frank and hunkering down alone in a library, I was leading Marines and being selected for special assignments. Never in my life had things gone so well for me.

Our CLIC leader was Sergeant Bay. Bay was a tall, bald, freckled machine gunner, who was the sunniest Marine I ever met. He was always smiling.

CLIC school was located in the part of the base where the generals and colonels worked. A lance and a few corporals walking around that building was an anomaly. On the flag pole out front, there was a flag with stars on it, to symbolize the highest-ranking officer there. Typically, there was a three-star flag. Everywhere I went, majors and colonels gave me the stink eye. Clearly, I didn't belong.

It turned into a game of rank recognition. As I walked down the plush, silent hallways, I would see a very senior enlisted man headed my way. His thick, black rank insignia was visible from twenty yards away. But it was impossible to tell what his exact rank was from a distance, so as I closed the gap—sometimes I had to guess.

"Good morning, Sergeant Major?" I would offer.

"Do I look like a fucking sergeant major?" the Marine would growl back.

I thought he did, but what did I know? "Ah no, Master Sergeant?" I would try.

"Where the fuck did you go to boot camp?" Generally, by that time, I got close enough to see their entire rank.

"Parris Island, Master Gunnery Sergeant."

"Jesus, they don't make them like they used to."

"No, Master Guns," I answered, as I hurried up to find the classroom.

At CLIC school, we learned how to conduct intelligence gathering, how to report our analysis, and most importantly, how to use the biometric screener—a handheld computer that could do fingerprint and iris scans to identify people. All across Iraq, Americans were using biometrics to catalog detained and arrested insurgents. It had a panopticon feeling to it, scanning someone's eyeball and pulling them up in a database, but it worked.

After a two-week break, I went back to the platoon. We spent the rest
of the summer training in mock buildings and cities. There were two
separate urban combat training areas, one that was full of real homes
and apartment buildings that had a Russian or Warsaw Pact feel to it,
and another made out of shipping containers that had a vaguely
Middle Eastern vibe. We ran mounted patrols and night raids in the
fake towns with smoke grenades and lasers. Sometimes we used
blanks, rushing through doorways firing our rifles like cap guns.
Other times, we used sim rounds, which are like paintballs, but
gunpowder projected. Instead of leaving welts, they broke your skin.
One time we trained with tanks, clearing rooms, and buildings alongside the huge lumbering vehicles. There was always artillery
rumbling and booming in the distance. Sometimes the blasts caught
Cochran off guard, and he would practically jump out of his skin.
When we would laugh, he'd shake his head and tell us that was going
to be us someday.

Stacked outside of a door, my team bunched up in a tight line.
Everyone had their left hand on the person in front of them, while
the point man stood a foot back from the open door. The last wisps of
a smoke grenade blew around us. I squinted my eyes through the
sweat pouring down my face and kneed Abbott in the back of the
thigh, signaling that I was ready. He passed it down the line, and
when it got to McVaugh at the front, he confidently and smoothly
strode forward into the building. He hit the door quickly but in
control, checking the corners as he peeled to the left. Schneider was
right behind him, then Abbott, and then me. We flowed like water
through the first room, shouting "Right side clear! Left side clear!" as
we scanned the room. Another team was hiding somewhere in the
building, waiting to ambush us.

I was tired and my back was covered in heat rash, but the adrenaline overpowered all that. And something else kicked in, a new

feeling I hadn't felt before. McVaugh and Abbott looked to me for orders, and with head nods and glances and telepathy, I let them know what I was thinking. The team stacked up behind Schnieder as we got ready to hit the staircase, and I identified this new sensation. With a team of highly skilled infantry Marines at my direction, I felt powerful. We rushed up the stairs, Schnieder taking out the Marine that was guarding the overlook. As we got ready to kick in the last door, we all knew the rest of the other team was holed up in there. If this was real, we would toss a grenade in first, but for now, it was pretend. Either way, I grinned as I watched Abbott kick in the door, and we rushed in. No more washing dishes, no more hiding in the library. Now I was a fireteam leader. I was a US Marine. I wasn't Alexander, but I was starting to feel like the man I had dreamed of becoming.

At night, I still stood firewatch. Even though I was a team leader, I thought it was important to share the load and lead by example. Sometimes, as I stood watch, staring out at the empty night sky, Cochran or Skewes or Tuttle would yell in their sleep. I'd watch them kicking in their sleeping bag, fighting against some unseen terror. It was a reminder that they knew what they were talking about because they had been there.

PBR Streetgang was a great squad, and I was proud of my team. Tuttle was my hero, and I followed him around like a puppy. Skewes and Cochran helped me out, both in the FDC and in patrolling. My Marines were skilled and didn't give me too much shit for being the same rank as them.

That summer, we kicked in doors and patrolled down fake streets and sang 99 *Bottles of Beer on the Wall* on long rides back to the barracks. After field ops, Tuttle bought us all Gatorade while we sat on the barracks' washing machines and cleaned our gear.

———

In July, our whole battalion packed up and headed west. We were going to 29 Palms, a Marine Corps base in the Mojave Desert. 29 Palms hosted a massive training exercise for units deploying overseas. The base had enormous ranges, allowing full company operations with heavy weapons and close air support. It also had a fake city, where hundreds of actors dressed in Iraqi clothing and spoke Arabic. A city replete with Hollywood-style IEDs and a plethora of scenarios designed to simulate combat in Iraq.

We flew across the country and took a bus to Camp Wilson, an outpost in the desert. Camp Wilson had dozens of metal Quonset huts that baked in the summer sun. The average high was over one hundred degrees.

For the first few days, we acclimatized to the heat. As hot as it was, it was also great to be out of the extreme humidity of Lejeune. Tuttle had PBR Streetgang running twice a day. We'd lace up our boots, grab our flak jackets, and run up and down the sandy hills of Camp Wilson. It was strange to come back from a long run completely dry, white salt dusting our shirts and faces.

After a few days acclimating, we packed up and headed into the desert. We pitched camp in rock-strewn fields, and set up the mortars to fire in support of the rifle companies. While they slogged through trenches and up and down hills, we sat in the shade. Kelly and I sat in the FDC and did even less. The two of us had come a long way. We were precise with our plotting boards and steady with our commands to the gunline, but it didn't feel like we were grunts.

After a few weeks of shooting mortars, we returned to Camp Wilson. There was news. The 81s platoon was being split in half. Half of us were going to be the battalion leadership's bodyguards in Iraq, while the other half would stay with Weapons Company as mounted infantry. Confusion reigned for days as squad leaders jockeyed for position, and for Marines. PBR Streetgang was broken apart. Every squad was.

Skewes, Kelly, Dolph, and Blackwood went to the newly formed personal security detail, while I stayed with the original platoon. Since I was a CLIC rep, I had to stay.

After we got the news, I grabbed my rifle and walked out of our Quonset hut. My feet slipped and sank in the sand as I trudged off to the edge of the camp. I found an empty picnic table where I sat down and lit a cigarette. PBR Streetgang was gone, my team was gone, and most of my friends were in a new platoon. I lay back on the picnic table and stared at the stars while I tried to figure out if there was a silver lining.

For our last week at 29 Palms, we went to the fake Iraqi city. It was incredible. Cars and tractors drove around, while dozens of people walked the streets. There were weddings and car bombings and restaurants.

While the rest of the platoon conducted patrols and IED sweeps and vehicle checkpoints, I carried around the biometrics scanner. The other teams and squads would raid buildings, while I waited outside to scan people's fingerprints. I had gone from being a front-line leader to the guy in the back with a fancy computer.

6

AUGUST 2008

Early in 333 BCE, Alexander and Darius, the Persian king, were playing a game of cat and mouse as they each tried to gain the element of surprise. Darius had assembled a large army and managed to sneak around Alexander's encampment, forcing Alexander to march out to confront Darius.

They met at the Battle of Issus, near the border of Turkey and Syria. Ancient sources say Darius had an army of two hundred fifty thousand or more, compared to Alexander's forty thousand, but modern scholars estimate it was a fifth of that. In the end, it was a catastrophic defeat for the Persians. At least half of their army was killed or wounded, and Darius narrowly escaped capture.

I flew home to Pennsylvania on my twenty-second birthday. Looking out the window of the plane, I tried to think of how far I had come. I was a different person, but I didn't feel like it. Before I enlisted, I assumed that becoming a Marine would change me in visible and invisible ways. I thought I'd be ripped and muscular, maybe taller with a stronger jawline. Or something like that.

But on the plane ride home, on the cusp of heading off to war, all I could think about was my poor mom. That time in church, at Parris Island, kept popping into my mind. The vision of my mom crying at my funeral. I was happy to be heading home, but I felt like an asshole. How could this trip home not be, in some ways, a goodbye? How could everyone I hung out with not feel that this might be it? How could I look my parents in the eye, knowing what I was putting them through? I tried not to think about it.

It was great when I first got home. Sleeping in my old bed and eating a home-cooked meal were fine, but they weren't my favorite things. I hadn't realized how much I missed comfortable furniture. Lounging on the couch watching TV was paradise. After months of sitting and sleeping on sand, dirt, rocks, hard wooden barracks chairs, canvas cots, and thin mattresses, a soft couch was an unimaginable luxury. It was wonderful spending time with my parents and siblings. As far as I could tell, everything was normal. There were no strained glances, no lingering hugs. At least not yet. It was like I was home for any old reason.

But every conversation reminded me that I was lying to my family. Here they were, thinking that I was headed to an office somewhere, getting ready to read intelligence reports. Instead, I was going to grab my rifle and ride around in Humvees, out on the front lines.

While I was home, I tried to see as many friends as I possibly could. My days and nights were tightly scheduled. I had to go to this house for dinner, to this bar to see this person, to see so and so at work, and on and on. It came from two places. I wanted to see all my friends and didn't want to leave anyone out. But I also wanted to let them know I was shipping out. So they would know that this might be goodbye.

. . .

The week went by faster than I expected. Suddenly, I had to head out the next day. That night, I stayed home with my family and watched a movie. I could see my mom stealing worried glances at me, but she never said anything. My flight was early the next morning.

The airport in my hometown was small, barely an airport. There were two gates, which really meant two doors on either side of a room. You walked out onto the tarmac to board the planes.

I checked my bag and printed out my ticket at the counter, still wearing my issued backpack, the greens and browns contrasting with my navy Penn State shirt. My parents walked over to the security area with me.

"We're still a little early," my dad said, glancing at his watch. I nodded and looked at the carpet. My mom had her arms wrapped around herself. She was still in her pajamas and glasses.

"I'll email and call as often as I can," I said.

"We know," my dad said. He tried to smile. My mom's lips were pressed tightly together. We stood in silence for a moment.

"How long is your layover?" my dad asked.

"An hour or so. Not too bad," I replied.

Everyone was silent again. No one wanted to make any small talk. I could see my mom's eyes welling up.

The TSA agent manning the metal detector came over to us.

"I'm sorry to interrupt, but I saw your backpack," she said. She smiled weakly at my mom. "I have a son in the guard; I know how it is. Let me scan your backpack and I'll let you stay here until they're boarding."

"Oh, thank you," my mom said, and started to cry. I handed the TSA agent my backpack and walked over to my mom. I hugged her as she cried a little into my chest. My dad came over and hugged us both.

We stood there for a while, no one saying anything. My mom's crying slowly stopped. She sniffed and looked up at me.

"I love you so much. Please, please be careful over there," she said.

I nodded. I didn't cry, but I could feel the tears in the back of my eyes. "I will. I love you, Mom."

The TSA agent called over to us. "I'm sorry but they're starting to board now."

My dad reached out a hand. I clasped it, and he pulled me into a hug.

"Be safe and give us a call when you can."

"Will do. Love you, Dad."

"I love you, too."

With that, I walked through security and headed towards the gate. Before I turned the corner, I turned around and waved. They both waved back at me, and my mom started to cry again.

———

After we got back from leave, we packed our bags and got ready to head out. The night before we left, the barracks were bubbling over with emotion. Some Marines were ecstatic, machine gunners rolling around blasting hip-hop, chest-thumping and high-fiving. Others were terrified, as they covered their cell phones with their hand, shielding their loved ones from the depravity of the barracks. Most everyone got hammered.

I was somewhere in between. I packed my gear and had it laid out ready to go, but I stayed sober. It felt like a bad omen to head off to war with a hangover.

There's a tradition in the grunts. For your first deployment, you shave your head. Not razor shaved, down to the skin, but a buzz cut with a zero guard. Like a recruit. No one *told* us to do it, but it was strongly suggested.

I lined up in the bathroom with everyone else. It was festive, friends hanging out, drinking beer, and laughing at how we looked with no hair. Two guys drunkenly shaved off their eyebrows. I watched the people in the room and smiled. Come whatever may, these were my friends, and I was proud to be standing with them.

. . .

The next morning, we packed our gear in Conex boxes. When all our big guns and seabags were stowed away, we rode buses to nearby Marine Air Station Cherry Point. I watched out the window, the humidity streaking the glass. I felt cool for now, but I could feel something around the corner; excitement or terror, I wasn't sure.

We boarded a large commercial airplane with our backpacks and weapons. It was strange to be on an airplane holding a rifle. The flight attendants asked us to place our rifles under our feet. It felt sacrilegious to put my feet on my rifle, but we did it anyway.

As we took off, everyone cheered. This was it—no turning back now. We were headed to Iraq.

We flew to Bangor, Maine, where we disembarked to see a tunnel of old vets waving us off to war. It was encouraging to see them out there, with their pins and unit hats. We smiled and waved back at them, but it felt ominous that there weren't any vets under fifty. I called my parents on a payphone and chain-smoked in the cool night air while we waited for the plane to refuel.

From there, we flew to Germany, and on to Kuwait. Kuwait was boiling hot, even at night, and during the day, the sand radiated heat like a blast furnace. It was a desolate landscape of old military equipment and barbed wire out in the desert.

Most of the boots, myself included, assumed this was the last stop for civilization. We bought cartons of cigarettes and candy and bootleg DVDs, trying to prepare for a life without access to these necessities. I ate at a chain burger restaurant and was disappointed that it had to be my last hamburger.

From Kuwait, we flew to Al-Taqaddum airfield in a squat, gray military transport plane, with a cavernous interior. We sat, wedged in tight rows of seats with our body armor on, and our backpacks slung across our chests. I could barely move; we were packed in so tight. There was a large American flag in the front of the plane. When we touched down, a chill ran down my neck. I had spent a year training

—a year pushing and striving to get here. *This is it*, I thought. *We're in Iraq*.

Commonly called 'TQ,' it was a former Iraqi air base that had been commandeered by the Americans. West of Fallujah, it was in between the Euphrates River and Lake Habbaniyah. I knew we were in a safe area, but as we disembarked, I still felt skittish. Looking at my friends, I realized I wasn't the only one who felt that way.

Everything was dusty brown, and there were palm trees scattered around the squat, drab buildings. It felt empty.

We were placed in some transient housing tents for a day or two. The platoon leadership gathered everyone around to distribute ammo. We sat on our cots and loaded our magazines with care. Everyone was aware that we might fire these rounds at someone. People joked around, but the mood was serious. We were getting ready to head outside the wire.

That night, we got the order to head out to Camp Ramadi. There was a long convoy of Humvees and armored seven-ton trucks. The seven-tons had open tops and benches running down the middle, so that its occupants could face out and fire. Standing there in full protective gear, I could feel my breath quicken. We were going to convoy from TQ to Camp Ramadi; what if we hit an IED? How would I react? What if I messed up?

I did my best to shake the nagging thoughts away and be a leader. *Act cool; act like you've done this before*. But when I checked out the guys who had done this before, they didn't reassure me. Cochran and Tuttle were grim-jawed and twitchy. *Not a great sign*, I thought.

The Marine who was leading the convoy came and briefed our group.

"This should be an easy drive. We're going to take Route Michigan from TQ to Ramadi. It's a pretty straight shot. If anything happens, my Marines will take care of it. We will tell you when to put a magazine in your rifle. Do not chamber a round, though. I repeat— do *not* chamber a round. Does everyone understand me?"

A sharp collection of "Rahhs", "Errs," and "Kills" came out of the formation.

"Good. Now get everyone loaded up on the seven-tons."

We climbed up the small ladder, and took our seats on the benches. I wasn't nervous anymore—I was scared. I had my training, but I was struggling to remember it. Heading out into one of the most dangerous cities in the world felt like a bad idea. Any bravado I had felt in the past was completely gone.

The convoy started rolling. We left the familiarity of the transient camp, and headed into the night. We passed endless waves of sand and lines of concertina wire. Nervousness swept the back of my truck. It wasn't clear where we were. We passed guard towers and fortifications. I glanced around wildly, trying to see any insurgents peeking out from behind the palm trees. No one was saying anything.

"Fuck it," a lieutenant from admin said. He pulled out a magazine, slapped it into his rifle, and racked a round. He propped his rifle on the edge of the truck and started scanning for targets in the night.

I was confused. No one else had even pulled out a magazine, let alone loaded their rifle. I made eye contact with Cocagne. He spit a long string of tobacco juice, pointed at the lieutenant, and gave a jerk-off motion. He was right—the convoy leaders would tell us what to do. I was spooked by my lack of awareness, but not as badly as that lieutenant.

Soon enough, we came to a rolling stop. The vehicle commander opened his passenger side door and shouted back to us. "Go ahead and insert a magazine, but don't chamber any rounds!" he yelled. "The last thing we need is for a truck full of trigger-happy new guys smoking some civilians."

Cocagne smiled and bobbed his head as he pulled out a magazine and slid it into his rifle. I did the same. This was it. We were heading outside the wire.

We rolled onto a highway. Street lamps illuminated the road and an interchange. Except for the lack of traffic lights, it could have been a dusty highway in California or Arizona. From my vantage point, all I could see was a ridge running along the south side of the road. Then we started rolling through a town.

I scanned around, my eyes bugging out, my heart pounding. *Shit, look at that*, I thought, as we passed a crumbled wall. Buildings were painted with bullet holes. Burned-out cars were pushed off to the side of the road. Some wild shit had happened here. My hands started to go numb with adrenaline.

I watched as we sped through the town, where houses and shops appeared menacing under the streetlights. Most of the buildings had tan walls with metal gates out front. My eyes flitted around, looking for anyone with a rifle, a cell phone, an RPG. I didn't see anyone, but the stillness and utter emptiness of the town was frightening. There was trash everywhere. Foot deep drifts of wrappers and bottles lined the streets. Cups and pieces of fabric blew away from the speeding convoy. Even if I wanted to hunt for an IED, I had no idea how I would spot one in all the trash.

The town started to peter out, giving way to more spread-out homes and compounds. Farm fields began to appear, and multiply. Long rows of irrigation trenches framed the tilled soil. I was still nervous, but empty fields at night didn't seem so scary. I tried to relax and realized that I had been white-knuckling my rifle. I relaxed my fingers, one hand at a time. I took a deep breath and checked out the other Marines. Everyone was intently staring at the surrounding fields. No one was sleeping.

The farms started giving way to buildings again. I tensed back up, tightening my grip on my rifle. There were signs of Americans: Hesco barriers, concertina wire, and sandbagged buildings. It would have felt reassuring if those buildings weren't splotched with bullet holes.

The convoy slowed a touch as we entered a city. *Ramadi*, I assumed. It was huge with tall buildings bunched up close to the road while broad cross streets gave flashing glimpses into distant neighborhoods. Everything was scarred. It didn't seem like there was a single building that hadn't been shot up. My terror mixed with awe. The city kept going and going with blocks and blocks of tall minarets and expansive compounds. Parked cars and metal fences surrounded the homes, while palm trees and streetlights lined the road. Trash was everywhere.

We blew through Ramadi, the floodlights on the sides of the

trucks illuminating everything around us. There were no other cars on the road. We slowed down at a traffic circle and headed across a metal bridge. I saw a guard tower up ahead. We'd made it. The convoy pulled in between some towers, and started snaking through the defenses.

The convoy made its way up a dirt road. When the truck stopped, the vehicle commander yelled for us to unload our rifles. I popped the magazine out of my rifle and put it back in a pouch on my flak jacket. I noticed my sleeves were wet; I was soaked in sweat.

We drove into the base and pulled into a gravel parking lot where we dismounted. Our platoon formed up, and we were directed to some barracks. Everyone was giddy with the aftereffects of the adrenaline rush.

"Welcome to Ramadi, boy-ee," someone in the platoon yelled out.

"Shut up, pussy," came a response from the darkness.

We filed into our barracks. Everything was sandy and broken. I tried to imagine Marines storming this building to set up a headquarters years ago. Our platoon sergeant told us to get some sleep, but I lay awake in my rack. A year ago, I was a recruit on Parris Island. Now I was a full-fledged Marine on a combat deployment.

————

I couldn't sleep, so I got up to smoke a cigarette. I put my boots on, slung my rifle, and walked out to a wooden bench in front of our barracks. There was a skinny lance corporal with a mustache smoking.

"Hey, man, can I grab a light?" I asked. He pulled out a lighter and offered it to me.

"You a new guy?"

"Yeah, just got in tonight." I sat down, lit my cigarette, and handed the lighter back to him.

He nodded. "I figured. Your cammies are awfully clean."

I inspected my clothes and his. His clothes were stained and had little tears everywhere. We smoked in silence.

"You know what I'm looking forward to most?" he asked.

"What's that?"

"My wife does this thing, where she puts a vibrator in her pussy and then I fuck her in the ass and I can feel the vibrator on my dick. It's amazing."

I stared at him.

"You ever try that?" he asked.

"Uhh, nah, man. I haven't."

"When you get home, you should do that. It's the best thing in the world." He pushed his cigarette into an ammo box filled with sand and stood up. "Nice meeting you," he said, as he walked away.

"Yeah, thanks for the light," I answered. I stared off into the night as I finished my cigarette, all thoughts of Iraq and combat and fear pushed from my mind.

———

The next morning, we had to attend some briefs to update us on what had been going on in Ramadi. Our platoon sat on metal chairs in a room with a low ceiling. Maps covered the walls: satellite maps, topographical maps, and heat maps, maps with red pins, maps with firing fans, and plastic maps with black marker lines. I tried to find something I recognized from my intel classes, but was interrupted when the battalion gunner burst into the room.

"Good morning, Marines!" he thundered.

"Good morning, sir," we echoed back. The gunner was the unit's weapons expert. He loved guns, all guns. Missiles, rockets, grenades, mortars—you name it. He probably loved the smell of napalm in the morning.

"How was your ride in last night? Good?" he asked, and kept talking. "I tell you what, my ride had me shaking like a leaf in fall. Last time I was in Ramadi, every garbage truck was packed full of explosives. When I saw one the other day, you couldn'ta got a needle up my sphincter with a sledgehammer." Chuckles came from the corporals and sergeants gathered at the back of the room.

"They know what I'm talkin' 'bout," the gunner said with a smile. "And I imagine many of you will too." I shifted in my seat.

"That's what I'm here to get you up to speed on. What's been happening around here." He said that the city was calm. There were sporadic attacks, but that it was nothing compared to the intense fighting of two or three years before. There were still IEDs, but many of the locals were flagging down convoys and letting them know where they were located. I scribbled down notes and worried I would get complacent on my first day.

One thing the gunner emphasized was a new form of IED that had been found in Ramadi and Fallujah. Insurgents strapped bombs to magnets, which they would toss onto Humvees. The magnets held them in place until the convoy stopped and people got out, and that's when the insurgents would detonate the bombs. It was smart, striking when our defenses were down and we were safe inside the wire. I put several stars next to those notes.

Later that day, we finally split from our remaining battalion security members. The 81s platoon was about half the size it used to be. I hung out with Kelly and Dolph in their barracks in Camp Ramadi. They jury-rigged ponchos to create small individual rooms around their bunk beds. There was a television and an Xbox.

"Fuck mortars, I'mma be a jack of all trades, master of *Call of Duty* by the time we leave this bitch," said Atchison, one of the drivers in the other platoon.

I said "See you later" to the guys, and went back to the emptier 81s hooch.

———

The rest of us left that night, another convoy of seven-tons and Humvees, blasting down the same Ramadi roads. We drove to a large warehouse on the east side of the city and pulled up to Forward Operating Base Karama. Inside, through the serpentine channels of walls and barbed wire, we checked out our new home. It wasn't much. A series of Hesco walls and towers, rows of port-a-johns, and a gigantic burn pit for trash. The pit was smoldering, with yellow flames and black smoke drifting out. There was a solitary palm tree near the front gate.

Inside the warehouse, it was dark; there were only two doors and no windows. In the darkness, you could see row after row of wooden shacks. Every shack had a pair of bunk beds with plastic mattresses. Most of the beds had ponchos strung up to provide a little privacy in the tiny rooms. My room was next to a large open-air gym. It was a hodgepodge of exercise bikes, free weights, and a towering cable stack. As soon as Marines get comfortable, they find a way to work out.

I was assigned to a shack with Longman and Haley. The plywood door had a water bottle pulley system to ensure that the door stayed closed. There was a bare bulb with a switch for light.

Welcome home, I thought excitedly. It was everything I wanted it to be.

The platoon leadership gathered us up and split us into three squads. Every day one squad would stand post, another would go on patrol, and the last one would be on quick reaction force duty. They were a standby unit in case a patrol got into trouble. They needed to be able to grab their gear and head out within a minute of getting the call. They were quite literally the cavalry.

My squad was led by Gleason, now a sergeant. The other two vehicle commanders were Sealy and Cochran. Sealy was a veteran of the invasion of Iraq, and the hairiest man I've ever seen. The hair on his head flowed perfectly down the front of his body to his feet, like a black-haired Bigfoot. I was in Cochran's truck, a guy in the back with no special duties. Our driver was a tall Marine on loan from a machine gunner platoon. And our gunner was a guy named Marshall. Marshall was the company armorer. He had been in the army in the nineties, got out, and had gone to gunsmithing school. After watching footage of Marines in Fallujah, he decided to reenlist. He was a hulking guy, who easily benched three hundred pounds.

We were squad three, and we had some skilled Marines in our squad. Cocagne and Stapleton, a wiry North Carolinian with a pointed face that earned him the nickname Desert Weasel, were in other trucks, and Cochran and Gleason were considered some of the best leaders in the platoon. I felt confident. This was why I had picked the Marines—I wanted to be with the best.

7

OCTOBER 2008

Moving down the Mediterranean coast, Alexander needed to clear the Persian defenses from the shore, to prevent his army from becoming trapped. He ran into difficulty clearing the island fortress of Tyre in southern Lebanon, whose walls were built right on the beaches. Unable to directly attack the island, Alexander laid siege to the island for seven months, while his engineers built a causeway out to the island.

The Macedonians built siege towers that stood over 150 feet tall, and launched an attack on the city. Alexander himself scaled the towers to lead the attack over the walls. When the battle was finished, Alexander sold tens of thousands of Tyrians into slavery.

The day after we arrived at Karama, we were on the react team. We spent the morning doing some chores in the warehouse: sweeping, taking out the trash, unloading supplies. Even when we were on standby, there was work to be done. In the early evening, we got the call.

"React, react, react!" went through the warehouse.

I dropped my broom and ran to my room. Slipping on my flak jacket, I grabbed my rifle and ran back out to the waiting Humvees. Some of the trucks were already started, and the air smelled of diesel smoke. As I fastened my armor and clipped my helmet on, I asked Cochran what was happening.

"There's a Fox Company patrol base under fire. They're saying AKs and possibly a rocket-propelled grenade." He glanced at a notebook. "It's Patrol Base Nassar; we're closest."

Cocagne yelled, "Aww, yeah bitches." He turned around and faced the Marines that were gathering by the warehouse entrance watching us. "Guess who's getting their combat action ribbon first," he said, as he flipped them off with both hands.

Most of them laughed, and someone yelled, "Fuck you, Cocagne." Cocagne grinned and put his helmet on.

I pulled my gloves on and took a deep breath. It was happening; we were about to roll into our first firefight. I felt excited, but professional.

Gleason was about to brief us on the situation. He strode out of the operations center and walked over to us. As he looked down at a notebook, his flak jacket straps were swinging out beside him.

Without looking up, he asked, "Is everyone here?"

"We're good to go," Cochran answered calmly. We all huddled around Gleason. The nervous energy was contagious; almost everyone was grinning. Gleason put his notebook on the hood of a Humvee and started strapping his flak jacket.

"Okay, Patrol Base Nassar is under heavy fire from their southeast. In the patrol base is a squad from Fox Company and about a dozen Iraqi police. Last year, this place was nearly leveled by a suicide bomber, so watch out." I felt the first twinges of fear mixing into my excitement.

Gleason read off the street intersections for Nassar and the Fox Company radio frequencies. That way, we could coordinate with them once we got close. He finished his brief with a simple "Alright, any questions? No? Good, load up." Nothing dramatic. Pure professionalism. I walked to our Humvee—we were the last in line—and hopped in the back seat. Cochran sat in front of me, and Marshall climbed up into the turret.

As I sat in my cramped seat, I could feel the adrenaline pumping. My breathing quickened, and my hands got cold. I started to sing a song in my head for courage.

We did some quick radio checks, and set off. As we were rolling through the gate, the call came from the front vehicle to halt. The company commander wanted to come along. This was a strange interruption. We were rolling out to help another group of Marines who were getting shot at. I stared out the window at the brown sand and tried to relax a little. *Gotta keep a clear head*, I thought.

I saw our company commander, Captain Shaw, jog past our truck on his way to the front vehicle, but after a minute, we still hadn't moved.

"What is going on?" asked Marshall.

"It looks like they're playing goddamn musical chairs up there," Cochran said.

I started bouncing my legs. Sitting still when you're full of adrenaline is an awful, helpless feeling. We needed to get moving. What the hell was taking so long?

The door to my left opened up, and Erickson, a chubby, blonde guy from New York, sat down next to me.

"Who is that?" Cochran asked.

"It's Erickson, Sergeant," he answered. "Captain Shaw kicked me out of my seat and this is the only open one left."

"Christ on a cracker," Cochran said. "Well, get in and let's go."

We started moving again, snaking our way through the concertina-wire serpentine. Once we hit the highway, we turned left and started blasting through the suburbs. I watched out the window, hand on the pistol grip of my rifle, thumb resting on the safety. People and cars and buildings flew past in a blur, as I looked for anyone who might toss a magnetic IED onto our Humvee.

I kept thinking about what I should do when we got to Nassar. *Use the doors as cover, stay off the walls, and get ready to clear some rooms.* All of the training exercises were right there. I knew what to do, but I was getting scared.

"Hey," Erickson yelled above the roar of the engine, "what's that beeping sound?"

I took my eyes away from the window. He was right—there was a beeping noise. I had been in dozens of Humvees and had never heard any of them beep. Cochran started twisting in his seat looking around.

"Holy shit," Erickson said. "Is that a fucking bomb?"

My blood froze. Had someone tossed an IED onto the truck? Was that a timer?

"No," Cochran grunted, as he reached down in between his and the driver's seats. "It's not—"

Boom! There was a sudden blast, and dust and sand filled the Humvee. I couldn't see anything, and all I could hear was a high-pitched ringing in my ears.

Oh my god, I thought, *we just got blown up.*

My hands, my entire arms were shaking. I couldn't see or hear or feel anything. I pulled my hands up to my face. They were still there. And I didn't see any blood. I reached down and patted my legs. I could feel them. At least I was in one piece.

Oh, shit! We're about to be ambushed, I thought. I waved the air by the window trying to assess the situation. I could see people looking at the Humvee. We were standing still on the road, not moving at all.

The driver must be dead, I thought. The first rule of getting hit by an IED is to keep driving. You do everything you can to keep moving so that you're not stuck in the kill zone. For our truck to be sitting dead in the road meant the driver was out.

Looking back inside the truck, I didn't see any fire, but the air was still thick with dust. I could barely see Erickson through the haze. He was slumped, lying against the door, not moving.

I figured the IED must have hit the other side of the truck, and I couldn't help but feel lucky at the moment. I unbuckled my seatbelt so I could reach over to Erickson and see what had happened to him. Through the ringing in my ears, I could faintly hear someone yelling.

"What the fuck was that? What the fuck hit my legs? Jesus, is anyone alive down there?" Marshall was screaming from the turret. I checked his legs. They were fine, and I tried to yell up to him, "I'm okay!" but my voice came out high-pitched and squeaky.

Get a hold of yourself, I thought. *This isn't the time to freak out.* I took a deep breath and yelled again. "It's Martin. I'm alright!" But my voice still cracked and squeaked.

"Why did we stop? What the fuck is going on?" yelled Marshall.

Through the swirling dust in the Humvee, I could see Cochran punching the windshield. He was alive, at least. I tried reaching over to Erickson when he started to sit up.

Oh, thank god, I thought. I watched as Cochran leaned back towards Marshall.

"It's okay!" he yelled. His voice was high-pitched like mine. "I pulled the fire extinguisher." I heard the words, but it didn't make sense. Had we hit an IED, and so he pulled the fire extinguisher?

"What?" Marshall yelled down.

"I was trying to stop the beeping, and I accidentally set off the fire extinguisher," Cochran answered. I noticed we had started moving again. The dust was gradually being blown out of the open turret.

It was slowly sinking in. We hadn't hit an IED. We were all okay. The helium fire extinguisher is designed to blast all the air out of the Humvee, putting out the fire. That was what had happened. The explosion, the dust, and our squeaky voices—it was the fire extinguisher.

We were cruising down the highway now, trying to catch up with the convoy. I started giggling. I looked at Erickson, and he started laughing too. His eyes were wide, with white showing all around his eyes. The whole Humvee was laughing. I laughed so hard my stomach hurt and my eyes teared up.

In the span of a minute or two, I had gone from thinking we were blown up, that Erickson and the driver were probably dead, to finding out everyone was fine. And we were still headed to a firefight.

It was insane. I laughed and gazed out the window, watching for anyone with a rifle, and laughed some more.

We drove on towards Nassar and staged a few blocks away to coordinate our link-up. We dismounted from the Humvees, and set up a small perimeter. I couldn't hear any more gunfire. The place was in ruins, though. None of the palm trees had tops, and there were crumbled buildings everywhere. Gleason had undersold the damage that the suicide bomber had done the year before.

Gleason talked to the squad from Fox Company on the radio for a while. Apparently, one of the Iraqi police at Nassar had slept with another Iraqi policeman's sister and dishonored the latter's family. So, that policeman gathered his friends and some guns, and they started shooting up the patrol base in retaliation. Eventually, the police commanders were brought in, and they calmed the situation down.

We got back in the Humvees, and headed back to Karama. After the adrenaline of our first mission, and the fire extinguisher going off, my arms and legs felt like logs. I was exhausted. We drove back in silence. I stared out my window, as the sun set on Ramadi. People were closing up their shops. Small groups of men sat on their haunches and smoked cigarettes. Most of them ignored us.

———

By the time we got back, it was our turn to stand post. We ran to the small chow hall, really a wooden shack with a few industrial refrigerators and a long plywood table. I opened a fridge and pulled out a bag of bagels. They were cinnamon raisin. Deeper in the fridge, I saw dozens of bags of bagels, all cinnamon raisin. There were hundreds of cinnamon raisin bagels and several logs of pre-sliced roast beef. That was it. I tossed some roast beef on my bagel and walked out to meet up for the post change-over. I never took my flak off.

We had five guard posts: one manning a doorway by the gym that led to the Iraqi police station next door, one overlooking the main entrance to our base, one along the north wall, and two along the south wall. They all had their pros and cons. The southwest tower was downwind of the burn pit, and you sucked down fumes all shift. The southeast tower was infested with a biblical plague of flies. The port-a-johns were emptied into the ground right outside that tower. Fly strips covered the ceiling, but they filled up with flies so quickly they became writhing black ropes. At one point, the tower record for the number of flies killed with a single swipe of a fly swatter was over fifty. If you stood post in the south towers, you usually brought your gas mask along. The north tower and main gate tower didn't require a gas mask, but they were frequently subjected to random inspections from the company and platoon leadership, to make sure you were awake. The guard post next to the gym was the best. You didn't have to wear a flak jacket. But it was a solitary post, with no buddy to talk to.

As we formed up to change over the guard, Zaehringer, a tall, blonde corporal from the machine gunner platoon, started berating us.

"Y'all 81s are pieces of shit. You were supposed to be here twenty minutes ago to replace my guys. And Jesus! You're fucking eating a bagel right now?"

I didn't say anything, but I took a bite of my sandwich and chewed it slowly as I glared at him. Cochran strolled up, checking his watch.

"Corporal Zaehringer, sorry we're late. We just came back from a react, and I told them to get something to eat." It was because of things like that that everyone loved Cochran. He protected us, deflected the constant shit rolling downhill on to us. I was glad he was my vehicle commander.

Zaehringer folded his arms. "Alright. Well, let's do this." Cochran gave us a quick briefing, assigned us our towers, and we set off. I drew the main entrance with Haley. We swapped out the other Marines there. They ribbed us about being late, and Haley told them to suck a bag of dicks.

We sat down in the metal folding chairs and inspected our gear. Flares—check. Flags—check. Radio—check. Machine gun—locked and loaded. With that, we settled in to spend the next few hours together.

We talked about the react mission and the deployment so far, and promptly ran out of things to talk about. We sat in silence for a while. I checked out the area. Our neighbors were out working in a small vegetable patch. Some cars drove past on the highway. Haley started muttering to himself and pushing a flashlight around like it was a toy car. I checked my watch. Fifteen minutes had passed.

8

NOVEMBER 2008

In 332 BCE, Alexander had his eyes set on conquering Egypt. The ancient kingdom had been controlled by the Persians for hundreds of years, and it was an important source of food and treasure. To get to Egypt, Alexander had to conquer Gaza. It took two months, and cost Alexander a grievous shoulder wound, but Gaza too fell.

When he and his army entered Egypt, they were greeted as liberators. An oracle declared that Alexander was the god Amun, and afterward Alexander declared himself the son of Zeus-Ammon. While in Egypt, Alexander founded the city of Alexandria, which would later become the capital of Cleopatra's Ptolemaic dynasty.

A few weeks into our time at Karama, Gleason found me in the gym.

"Hey, Martin, got some news." I stood up from the bench and walked over. "You're getting pulled from the squad. They need you to do your intel thing." I was shocked. Why would they need me? I could still do that in the platoon.

"I... uhh... Why?" I stammered.

Gleason glanced over his shoulder and leaned in towards me. "Don't tell anyone yet; Sergeant Bay's wife has cancer. He needs to go home to take care of her and his daughters."

"Damn." I let out a sigh. I felt bad for Bay's family, but I was pissed. The intel stuff was supposed to help me advance, but so far it had only gotten me pulled away from my friends, and now it was taking me away from my platoon.

"So what do I do?" I asked Gleason.

"Nothing for the moment. I'll tell Carnahan to come find you." He turned and walked off. I had lost my fireteam, and now I had lost the chance to be in a regular infantry squad. My vision of myself as a warrior was slipping through my fingers. When Gleason went around the corner, I grabbed my cover and threw it across the open warehouse floor.

"Maaar-aaar-ten!" Carnahan said, as he stuck his head in my hooch. "What's up, buddy? Mind if I come in?"

I sat up from my rack, tossing a paperback onto my sleeping bag. "I hear I'm joining you," I said, as I stood up.

"Mmm-hmm," he said through pursed lips. "Come with me; I'll show you what's going on." We walked over to the Operations Center. I hadn't been inside before; it was reserved for the leadership and the company staff.

As we walked in, I soaked in the room. There was an old metal desk near the door, with some folding chairs next to a bank of radios. At the far side of the small room was a wall covered with maps of Ramadi, a bank of charging walkie-talkies, and several computers with wires running everywhere. Sergeant Porter, a machine gun squad leader, was sitting at the desk. He was short, but muscle-bound, with large chunky tattoos covering his arms. He had a buzzed head of silver hair.

"Martin is going to be joining us," Carnahan drawled. "He's takin' Bay's spot on the day shift." He turned to me. "Oh yeah, you'll be in here from 08:00 to 20:00, and I'll take the night shift. That way I can prepare the reports for Battalion." I said alright.

He showed me all the tools I'd need. The laptops we used, the logins, and passwords I would need. He got me up to speed on what they had been collecting and investigating. It wasn't much. We hadn't been there long, and there wasn't an equivalent team in the unit we replaced, so we were starting from scratch. My first order of business was going to meet all the local leaders in the area: sheiks, police chiefs, and community leaders.

Bay ducked into the room.

"Oh hey, Martin, I was looking for you," he said. He was carrying a biometric scanner. He set it on a table along with a small digital camera. "I'm sorry you had to get pulled in here with these animals," he said, as he cocked his head towards Porter. Porter spread his arms and shrugged his shoulders in mock offense.

"No problem, Sergeant," I said. I didn't say anything about why he was leaving; it didn't feel appropriate. I knew Bay from our intel classes, but that was it.

"Here's my biometrics system. The charger is over there next to the laptops, and here's my camera. Don't lose it; it's still signed out to me."

"I won't."

"You'll have fun doing this. You get to travel all over the city, and meet interesting people like Colonel Ahmed."

Porter laughed. "That Ahmed, he's something else."

"I still need to pack, but do you have any questions?" Bay asked me.

"I don't think so," I answered.

"Alright. Well, good luck. If you have any problems, just see Carnahan here. He's your new team leader. Welcome to the head-quarters platoon." With that, he turned around and ducked out the door.

. . .

The next day, I officially started my intel duties. I got up, ate a cinnamon raisin bagel for breakfast, smoked a cigarette, and joined my old squad on a patrol to meet one of the police chiefs.

We headed west, across the city. I was sitting in the "extra" spot, the spot for visitors, for people who might not be trusted to handle themselves if something happened. The spot for people who weren't in the squad.

We pulled into a police compound called Camp Hero. The police stationed here covered the western part of the city. I climbed out of my seat and tried to find Shaw. As I walked towards his Humvee, Cocagne yelled down to me from his turret.

"Hey, Martin, you need a hand with that notebook? I don't want you to hurt yourself." He and Marshall laughed from their turrets. I flipped them the bird and walked over to Shaw. He stared at me and cocked his head to the side like he was waiting for me to say something. Then he remembered who I was.

"Ah right, this is a good meeting for you. Colonel Ahmed is the best police commander in the city. You'll see."

"Yes, sir. Thanks for bringing me along," I said, but he started walking away while I was talking. I wasn't Martin the team leader; I wasn't Martin the member of a squad. I was a Marine without a home.

I followed Shaw and our interpreter, Big Dave, inside a concrete building. Big Dave was at least three hundred pounds and walked with a limp from when an Iranian paratrooper shot up his legs during the Iran-Iraq war. We went down a white-tiled hallway towards a young policeman standing guard outside of a wooden door. As we approached, he pulled the door open and waved us inside.

It was a mostly unremarkable room. There were mismatched couches and chairs around three sides of the room. There was a circular table off to the side and a small tube TV with rabbit ears. All unremarkable, but the back wall was wild.

Behind a large wooden desk, the entire wall was covered with war trophies. There were military plaques, with unit insignias representing battalions and regiments. There were photos of high-ranking

US military personnel posing with a thick Iraqi man, his bushy Saddam style mustache visible the whole way across the room. And in the center of all that, there were axes and swords and knives. *Ceremonial battle axes, what the hell*, I thought.

As I was checking it out, a man burst in through a side door. He wasn't wearing a police uniform, but tan contractor pants and a tan, long-sleeve shirt. He wore a thick belt that was stuffed full of red shotgun shells. Colonel Ahmed had arrived.

"Salaam, salaam!" he boomed and strode over to Shaw. They shook hands, each of them holding both of the other's hands. They murmured to each other and air-kissed each other's cheeks. Ahmed strode over to his desk and gestured at the couches. Big Dave chimed in, "He says please sit." We did. Ahmed pulled out a cigarette and lit it, so I did too. I had my notebook sitting on my lap, ready to go.

Ahmed held his cigarette by the filter with his thumb and first two fingers. Instead of holding it in between his fingers like Americans, he held it pointing straight up, like a little smokestack. He asked who I was. Shaw told him I would be taking notes to help piece things together. Ahmed nodded his head.

Alexander was welcomed as a god in Egypt; I was welcomed to Camp Hero as the official scribe.

They started bullshitting, talking about the weather, how their families were doing. I smoked my cigarette and thought about lighting another. It was tedious. I couldn't believe that I had to leave my squad for this.

After thirty minutes or so, the side door opened, and two policemen carried in some trays of food. There was a platter with a roast chicken and fresh vegetables, and a plate of Khubz, the Iraqi flatbread. There were sauces and spices in little dishes. It smelled amazing. One of the policemen left, and returned with an armful of sodas. The condensation dripped down the sides of the bottles and on his sleeves. Big Dave smiled at me.

Ahmed stood and ushered us over to the table. I swung my rifle around, so that it was slung on my back, pocketed my notebook, and walked over. After living on bagels and roast beef, this was heaven.

I watched Ahmed as he reached out and grabbed some bread, still talking with Shaw. They were talking about movies. What a bunch of goons. As the lowest member of the totem pole, I waited at the table until Shaw and Ahmed had started eating before I grabbed a piece of bread, tore a strip off, and helped myself.

Iraqis make incredible pickles. Americans pickle cucumbers, but Iraqis pickle everything: carrots, okra, potatoes, cauliflower. Often, they use purple vinegar, giving all the vegetables a muted lavender color.

Using the bread, I tore off some chicken breast and scooped up some pickles. I glanced up and saw Ahmed watching me. Shaw was using his fingers, grabbing food off the platter and placing it into a whole piece of bread and rolling it up, like a burrito. One of the policemen that brought the food out came back with a small tureen. It was filled with a creamy, green mixture. He set it down by Ahmed, turned, and left the room again.

Ahmed tore off a chunk of bread and used it to pinch up some of the greens. He gave an exaggerated groan of pleasure and pushed the tureen towards us. I could see small yellowish cubes mixed in with the greens.

"Is that *saag paneer?*" I asked Big Dave. Ahmed heard me, and he started speaking excitedly to Dave.

"He says yes; how do you know this?" Dave asked me.

I told him I had a friend in America whose parents were Indian. I grew up eating at their house. Ahmed beamed.

He launched into a story about his days in exile. Gesturing broadly with his hands and stroking his mustache as he remembered, he told us about moving to Hindustan when he was exiled by Saddam. He fell in love with the food and hired some immigrants to make it for him sometimes. It sounded like he loved India.

He encouraged us to eat more of the *saag paneer.* Shaw politely tried it, but stuck to eating chicken.

After we were finished eating, we moved back to the couches. Ahmed and I lit cigarettes. I offered him a Marlboro, but he waved me away and said it was too strong. One of the policemen cleared the table, while another brought us *chai*, tiny shot glasses filled halfway up with sugar, and a tall, metal teapot. He poured the dark brown tea over the sugar and offered each of us a glass. It was thick and sweet. I set my glass next to the ashtray to cool.

Ahmed leaned back in his chair and placed his hands behind his head. "So, what have you come to see me about today?" he asked through Dave.

Shaw leaned forward and started telling Ahmed about some men who had been picked up by a different police station. He wanted to know if Ahmed and his guys could pick them up and handle transportation to Baghdad.

Ahmed held a hand up, palm out, then brought it in, and placed it on his chest. "Of course," he said. "You know you can trust me to take care of this."

And that was it. I hadn't written a single line of notes down, but we were done. An hour of hanging out and eating, for a one-minute request. A request that Big Dave could have called in on a cell phone! The food was great, but Jesus, this was what the officers did? I was disappointed.

As we strolled back outside, I watched my old squad get ready to go. They were eating Pop-Tarts and drinking from warm water bottles. Marshall had sweat stains on his sleeves. It was hot, and they had been standing watch around a building for an hour. As I walked past Cocagne, he didn't even make any sarcastic comments.

I walked back to my spot with Big Dave. We climbed in and sat down, my position as an outsider firmly established.

———

A few days later, I was sitting in the operations center, working on the intel laptop, reading up on new reporting, when Szwebjka strolled in.

"Ah Martin, just who I was looking for," he said.

"What can I do for you, sir?"

He leaned against the corner of the metal desk. "I need you to scan a prisoner next door. Dave got a call that they were holding a high-value individual."

I closed my laptop and grabbed my rifle. "No problem, sir," I said, as I walked over to the back wall and unplugged the biometrics system.

We headed towards the guard post next to the gym. Two Marines and Big Dave were waiting for us. I ran to my hooch and grabbed my flak jacket.

We went out the side door and headed over to the Karama police station. In between their compound and ours were rows and rows of razor wire, forming a narrow path. As we walked up, policemen were sitting in the back of pickup trucks and standing around talking. Some were busy, but most of them were hanging out. They had AKs on short slings. Szwebjka had Dave yell at a policeman, who was carrying his rifle by the pistol grip. The guy stopped, stared at us for a moment, and kept walking. The Iraqi police didn't answer to us.

We went up a short staircase into their headquarters. It was an opulent building, or it used to be. Lots of white marble, tall ceilings, and carved pillars. In the center of the room was a cavernous spiral staircase heading down into the basement. It looked like a pit. A police officer was waiting for us. He and Szwebjka talked for a moment, and we headed down.

As I walked down the staircase, I could see a door made of rebar, like a jail cell. There were sacks of rice and yellow buckets at the bottom of the steps. Everything was wet. A hose was lazily curled up off to the side of the landing.

A police officer sat up from a plastic lawn chair, pulled out some keys, and opened the rebar door for us. It was dark as we entered; I couldn't see more than a few feet into the basement. The officer that escorted us down hit a light switch.

Fluorescent lights started to come on, one at a time. *Flash, flash, flash.* They were slowly illuminating the dark basement in their blue glare. A hallway was appearing. There was a jail cell to the left. I could see men, lounging about, looking out at us. *Flash.* The lights kept going. I could start to make out the end of the hallway. *Flash.* A jail cell was taking shape. *Flash*. I could see people inside moving around. *Flash, flash*. The men inside the cell were scurrying away from the light. I glanced back at the cell on the left. Those men seemed fine, more curious than afraid. *Flash*. All the lights were on. The men at the far end were a pile of shaking terror, as the officer who turned on the lights walked towards them.

I could feel the hair standing up on the back of my neck. This place smelled like piss and blood and fear. The floor was wet, small puddles pooling under our feet.

The officer walked to the far cell and started yelling at the men inside. They cowered, but didn't say anything. The officer called back to the policeman who opened the door for us. He jogged down and opened the cell. The men all jumped and pushed further into the corner. The two policemen went into the cell and grabbed a man dressed in black pants and no shirt. They dragged him out of the cell, locked it back up, and brought him over to us.

The two Marines that came with us lifted their rifles slightly. I opened up my kit and fired it up. While it was loading, I stared at the man. He was thin, with a shaved head, sitting on his knees. I could see his feet over his shoulders. Long red and purple stripes criss-crossed the soles of his feet. He held up his hands to protect his face. One of the policemen kicked him and yelled in Arabic. The man put his hands down.

I showed him my thumb, put it on the fingerprint scanner, and motioned for him to do so as well. He glanced around, at the other Marines with their raised rifles, at me, at the other cell. The policeman yelled again. The man put his thumb on the scanner. A spinning wheel turned on the screen as the computer scanned its databases. It registered a match. He had a dossier, a long one. Big Dave's tip was right—this guy was Al-Qaeda.

The police dragged him back to his cell. When he was locked up again, they let us out of the basement. As I walked up the stairs, the stench started to clear. We climbed the stairs, back into the daylight, and headed back home.

9

DECEMBER 2008

After Egypt surrendered to Alexander, Darius tried to negotiate for peace. He offered Alexander all Persian lands to the west of the Euphrates, almost two million pounds of silver, and the title of co-ruler of the Persian empire.

One of Alexander's friends and officers, Parmenion, is supposed to have said, "I would accept, if I were Alexander."

"I would, too," replied Alexander, "were I Parmenion." Instead, Alexander sent a counter offer to Darius, that he should unconditionally surrender to Alexander, or meet him on the battlefield.

It was shocking how quickly I fell away from my friends in the platoon. I spent most of my days locked away in the operations center, reading and writing reports, answering radio checks, and making coffee. Even Carnahan and I only saw each other for a few minutes each day when we changed shifts. I had worked so hard to be a grunt, to earn my station amongst warriors. But when I finally deployed, I got put in the office, making coffee.

The platoon spent all of its time standing post and running patrols, and I started to go days without seeing any of my friends. I was in a warehouse full of people I knew, but I was lonely. Other than some small talk with Porter or Zaehringer in the office, I frequently didn't talk to anyone all day.

When I wasn't researching or writing, I sat in meetings. Meetings with Colonel Ahmed. Meetings with tribal sheiks. Meetings with government officials. They were always the same. We'd smoke cigarettes and eat lavish lunches. After we ate, we'd work for five, ten, maybe thirty minutes, and call it a day. Then I would head back out to the convoy, stuffed full of *dolmas* or potatoes or falafel, while my friends guarded us under the blazing sun.

When I did talk to Cocagne or Stapleton, they said the platoon was struggling. They were burning both ends of the candle, trying to maintain the operations tempo. Ramadi used to be patrolled by multiple battalions. Now a single company ran all the patrols. They were exhausted, and bored.

I fell asleep in a meeting at the Ramadi city council. There was a long discussion over potential economic stimulus programs. One council member wanted the Ramadi hotel to be rebuilt; it had been destroyed by the Marines years earlier. The council member really wanted the money and jobs for his district. Everyone did. So, they argued about building hotels or dams or factories, and I found myself sliding down in my seat, my chin dipping into my flak jacket as I nodded off. I woke up when my cigarette burned my fingers.

Ramadi was peaceful. The Anbar Awakening that had swept through the province in 2007 had started in Ramadi. The tribes had had enough of civil war and started working to maintain their own order. It worked. That model spread throughout the country. By the end of 2008, Iraq was still war-torn, but it was healing.

————

On Christmas Eve, Stapleton found me in the gym. To pass the time, I had taken up rowing. I would row ten miles just to kill a few hours.

"Hey, man, Merry Christmas," he said, as he squatted down next to me.

I pulled out my headphones. "Yo, Merry Christmas."

"I've got a surprise for you. Come to my room." I unhooked my feet, and followed him to his hooch. Cocagne and Marshall were already sitting on footlockers in there.

"Oh hey, pogue, how's the office?" Cocagne asked. I grinned and told him to tell his mom I said hello.

"Stapleton, what the fuck are we doing here? I need to call my wife," Marshall said. With a flourish, Stapleton went to his rack and dramatically grabbed the corners of his blanket.

"As you may know, I was poking around Camp Ramadi today."

"I don't give a shit what you do," Marshall said.

"Now, now," chided Stapleton, "I might not have any presents for you with that kind of attitude."

Marshall laughed. "Oh, look at Kris Kringle over here! Excuse me, sir."

Stapleton scanned the room, measuring our silence.

"As I was saying," he stared at Marshall, "I was snooping on Camp Ramadi, and found some refrigerators." He paused for dramatic effect.

"Stapleton, I'm going to kill you," Cocagne said.

"You guys suck," Stapleton whined. "I found some coolers and acquired these!" He ripped the sheet back to reveal a few cans of eggnog and a couple of mangos.

"Oh, hell yeah," Marshall said. He stood up and grabbed a mango. "Real fucking fruit."

"Good job, buddy," Cocagne said.

We gathered around Stapleton's bounty. It was an odd combination, but it made me drool.

We all went back to our rooms to pitch in. I had some Little Debbie cookies my parents had sent me that I had forgotten about.

Marshall had some Christmas cookies from his wife. Cocagne had a few tins of sardines.

We didn't have a can opener, so we used a bayonet and a helmet to open the sardines and eggnog. Cocagne patiently tapped the butt of his bayonet with his helmet until the metal was pierced, moved on to the next piece of tin, and did it again. It was slow, but it worked.

We sat on the concrete floor and leaned against footlockers and the walls as we drank eggnog and ate. I rolled the piney mango around my tongue and swished the thick eggnog around my mouth. I passed on the sardines. We talked about what we would do when we got home. Lots of drinking, lots of sex, and lots of sleeping were the goals.

I sipped from my canteen cup as I soaked in the conversation. These guys were my friends, my brothers. It felt good to be included in the squad again.

On Christmas day, life went on as usual. There aren't any breaks on deployments. Patrols went out, people stood post, and I wrote reports and made coffee. Everyone was festive, though. Porter wore a floppy Santa hat around until the first sergeant told him to take it off. Even if it was just another day, it was fun to see some holiday spirit. One of the 81s Marines, Galentine, a red head from Tennessee, was particularly festive. He stood by the front entrance to the warehouse and gave everyone that passed by a cigarette.

I emailed my family to say that I'd call home the next day. There were a lot of guys with wives and kids. I was single. They needed to call home on Christmas.

Sometimes, it felt intrusive to be in the lounge when guys called home. They hunched over the phones, cupping the receiver to their mouth. Whispered affections coming from the corner. It was worse when they fought with their significant others, yelling about bills or children or money, the frustration of being thousands of miles away and unable to help. More than a few guys cried after calling home.

· · ·

The day after Christmas, I got off my shift and went to the lounge to call home. It was about noon in Pennsylvania. I called home and wished my parents and siblings a merry Christmas. They got on multiple lines so they could recount unwrapping the presents. I told them about eating mangos and drinking eggnog, while they told me about seeing Joe Paterno and his family at mass on Christmas Eve. It was great to call home and have everyone so happy. So many of our phone calls had a tense undercurrent of concern and fear. This time it was light and happy. I smiled a lot.

In the background, I could hear gunfire from somewhere in the city. It wasn't uncommon for celebratory fire to pop off at random times. I didn't think much of it, at first. When the firing started to quicken, I put my hand over the mouthpiece of the phone and glanced around the lounge. Everyone had noticed. There was a lot of gunfire. This wasn't normal.

I turned back to the phone. My mom asked what that noise was. I lied and told her some guys were watching the movie, *Apocalypse Now*. Really a lie on top of a series of lies. I'm not sure she bought it. A machine gunner came bursting into the lounge.

"React! React! React!" he yelled, and ran back out. Something was going on, and I needed to get to the operations center.

I abruptly told my family that my time was up, that there was a line for the phone. I said I loved them, wished them a merry Christmas, and hung up.

Grabbing my rifle, I ran to the operations center. It was packed. Half of the squad leaders were in there, already suited up in flak jackets. Carnahan was briefing them on what we knew.

"There was a jailbreak at Forsan police station," he said. Forsan was in southern Ramadi. They had a jail like Camp Hero and Karama. One cell full of common criminals, and another cell of Al-Qaeda-affiliated insurgents. It wasn't clear who was leading the breakout, but we assumed the worst. A platoon of machine gunners lived close by.

"They already pushed out a squad to help to contain the outbreak. They're setting up a cordon as we speak."

"Tell them not to enter," Shaw said. "I don't want my Marines getting killed by some trigger-happy police because they don't know what's going on."

"Roger, sir. I'll pass it along," Carnahan said, as he picked up the radio and called it in.

"Who's on react?" Shaw asked.

"I am, sir," Zaehringer said, as he moved to the front of the group.

"Get on the trucks. We're going to go help them out."

"Yes, sir," Zaehringer said, as he walked out the door, and yelled to his squad to mount up.

"Martin, get the biometrics system ready. We might have to ID a lot of people to determine who escaped and who was captured," Shaw said, as he headed out.

"Aye, sir," I said, and booted up my kit.

Our deployment had been so slow that tonight's firefight was the most exciting thing that had happened in months. If you couldn't be out there, listening to the play-by-play over the radio was the next best thing. Even though it was late, I started brewing a pot of coffee. I had a feeling it was going to be a long night.

I went back to my hooch, grabbed my gear, carried it back, and staged it in a corner. I was ready to roll out if they needed me at Forsan. I hoped they needed me.

We gathered around the radios. Things sounded like they were under control. The machine gun squad had the cordon in place, and Zaehringer's squad was on its way to them. We could still hear gunfire from the police station, but it was impossible to tell who was shooting at who. At least prisoners were no longer pouring out the front door.

A voice came over the radio; they were calling in an enemy killed in action. A Marine from the machine gun squad was in a Humvee turret, watching the wall of the jail. He saw an insurgent poke his head up and peek around. When the insurgent saw the Marine cordon, he lifted an AK and started to aim at the dismounted Marines. The machine gunner whipped his gun up and let off a burst that cut the top of the insurgent's head off. We all cheered.

I went outside and pulled out a cigarette. Sucking down cold air and smoke, I stared up at the moon still piecing together what Shaw meant by needing to identify people. The police would know who was who if they caught them. They would only need the biometrics if they couldn't see their face, if they didn't have a face. I took a deep drag and went to find some latex gloves.

I spent the next several hours listening to the radio. Once the firing ended, the Marines on the scene entered Forsan and surveyed the damage. The police had piled up the dead like logs. Someone in Zachringer's squad did some impromptu intel-gathering and took pictures. The bodies were laid out on a blue tarp. Most of them were naked. They had black holes where they were shot, and they were all covered with smears of blood.

The pictures from inside the jail were horrific, too. According to the police, someone in the non-insurgent jail cell had been freaking out, and some Al-Qaeda guys convinced the guard to let him join them in their cell to pray. But when the guard opened their cell door, the Al-Qaeda members rushed him, grabbed his rifle, set everyone else free, and made their way to the police armory. Once there, they killed the guard on duty and took all the weapons.

There were photos of the hallways where the police and Al-Qaeda battled. It looked like the set of a horror movie. Blood streaked the walls, and the floor was covered in black, coagulated pools.

In the chow hall the next morning, I saw my old roommate Shen. He was eating a bagel and staring at the wall. I sat down next to him.

"Hey, man, how was it last night?" I asked.

He glanced at me out of the corner of his eye, and shook his head. "On the way back," he said, "Doc pointed out I have something on my boot. It was brains. I stepped in someone's brains."

I stared at him for a moment, and let out a slow whistle. "Damn dude. That's wild."

He nodded and picked up his bagel. "I have to go post," he said, his back to me as he walked out. I watched him go, wondering how it would have been to be there. Part of me was glad I didn't have to see the horrors, but another part of me wished I did. Not to see the gore or kill anyone. I wanted to stand near the fire, on the edge of violence. I wanted to know if I could do it, if I could handle it.

———

Our time in Ramadi blurred together after New Year's. The routine, combined with a lack of violence, settled everyone into a lull. I'd get up, row for an hour or so, stand my shift, and read before going to sleep. Sometimes I'd head out with a squad to Camp Ramadi or a police station or city council meeting, but even those meetings became more and more rote.

Meanwhile, Kelly had been meritoriously promoted to corporal for being a vehicle commander. I was sick with envy and entitlement, thinking that it should have been me.

One cold winter afternoon, I was at Camp Hero with a machine gun squad. I needed to scan some guys the police had picked up. We suspected they were associated with an IED smuggling ring.

I sat on my haunches outside the jail, my rifle slung across my back. The light was weak, and the swirls of a sandstorm were blowing in. Everything was hazy with moon dust. One of the guards came out.

"You can't see them right now. Come back in a few days," Big Dave translated.

"We're here now. We're not coming back later," I told the guard.

Dave and the guard argued back and forth, before the guard glanced around and whispered in Dave's ear.

Dave nodded gravely. "He says you can't do that," he said pointing to my kit, "right now. Can't do this." Dave used two fingers to spread his eyelids open. I got it. They beat the prisoners, and their eyes were swollen shut. Roger.

I told the lieutenant who came with us. He was a decent guy, a Naval Academy grad. Not the kind of officer you imagine in a grunt platoon, but he was kind and cared about his Marines. He was equal parts incredulous and angry about the prisoners.

I wasn't surprised. I had been to the Karama police station too many times to think that it wasn't business as usual. He tried arguing with the police leadership, but they were adamant. "Come back later."

When we got back to Karama, I made a note of it in my report and sent it up. We went back a few days later to scan the prisoners.

———

Soon we started shuttling the company back to TQ. This time I sat in a seven-ton and watched the scenery roll by. Iraq was peaceful. I didn't worry. When I saw the Euphrates sparkling through the trees, I thought about Alexander and his time in this part of the world. I had followed in his footsteps to Mesopotamia and left as an office worker.

While we were in TQ, people did everything they could to while away the time. We played chess and cards. We went on two-hour runs through the old Iraqi airplane hangars. We disassembled, cleaned, and reassembled our rifles, only to do it again a few hours later.

When you're so close to going home, to seeing your family, to having a beer, every minute crawls by. It was like the last week of school, when the sun is shining and you'd cut off your arm to be outside. The sense of anticipation was hard to deal with, as was being with the same people for every minute of every day. Tempers flared. People got in shouting and shoving matches. Everyone was ready to get home.

After a few days, we piled into another cavernous, gray cargo plane, ready to leave for Kuwait. Once again, we smashed ourselves in the jump seats, body armor preventing most of us from actually sitting down. Another American flag was suspended from the ceiling. I leaned back in my seat as we built up speed heading down the runway. When the wheels lifted off, everyone cheered.

"Congratulations, Marines, you just left Iraq," the pilot said over the loudspeaker. We cheered some more. We'd made it; we were headed home.

When we got to Kuwait, we were told we were only going to spend a night there. Weapons Company would be the first group to head back to Lejeune. Typically, Marines, myself included, revel in getting the hard jobs, the shitty jobs, but this time I couldn't have cared less. I wanted out of my uniform and a cold beer in my hand. That night, I went and got another burger from the chain restaurant. It was better than I remembered.

Landing in Cherry Point was anticlimactic. When we touched down, everyone cheered and clapped, but then the usual airplane waiting games began: waiting to taxi to the terminal, docking at the terminal, every single person standing up, knowing that they still had to wait to get off the plane. Watching with frustration as it took eons for the plane to empty out. And finally, deliciously, walking off the plane into the airport.

We had to unload all our bags and pack them up into an eighteen-wheeler. Every lance corporal's sense of decorum was long gone. Seabags and backpacks were tossed into the truck with fierce abandon. The squad leaders stood to the side, fidgeting as they waited for us to finish.

When we finished, we piled on buses and headed to Lejeune. I watched out the windows on the ride. I had spent months imagining this day, but everything seemed bland. There wasn't any music, no celebrations, or fireworks. I was annoyed that the world continued without us.

We drove past tire shops, tattoo parlors, and strip clubs. Everything looked the same. It felt unfair that people's lives kept going while we sat in towers covered in flies, breathing in smoke from the burn pit.

. . .

When we pulled up by the barracks, there was a crowd waiting for us. But they had to wait a little longer. First, we went to the armory to drop off our rifles and night vision goggles. It was a frantic dash, slapping everything in place. Guys started yelling for people to hurry up. Most of them had a wife or girlfriend waiting a few hundred yards away.

Once everything was turned in, we marched over. I watched the crowd as we walked up: young mothers with children, middle-aged parents, younger siblings, white-haired grandparents, black people and white people, Asians and Latinos, people from California and Ohio, Texas, and Alaska. It wasn't a lot of people, but America was waiting for us. My family wasn't there, but it felt reassuring to see people excited for us to be home.

"Company... halt!" the first sergeant called out. We pulled up and stopped. "Left, face." We pivoted in unison, facing him. It was probably the first time since boot camp I felt confident marching. I was bad at it, but it felt like we were putting on a show.

"Weapons Company, dismissed!" he yelled, and we scattered. Guys sprinted off to their families. I watched a Marine scoop his wife off her feet and twirl her around. Joy and relief filled the air. I smiled a lot as I shook my buddies' parents' hands.

I was grateful not to hear "Thank you for your service." Every one of these family members served their country, too, and they knew it. They had spent seven months paying bills, sending care packages, and taking care of kids, supporting us in all the ways they could. Unrecognized patriots.

I grabbed my bags from the pile. As I strolled into the barracks, it felt the same. New room, but the same building and hallway. Cases of beer materialized. I grabbed five cans and stuffed them into my cargo pockets.

While a lot of the company left that night, off at home or in hotels, the barracks turned into a rocking party. We shotgunned beers and told stories. The play-by-play of the Forsan prison break. Stories about having to clean up after a suicide bombing at the beginning of the deployment, how they put body parts in piles to try and determine how many people had been killed. One guy had found a penis. We talked about the Iraqi police and sheep, trash-strewn streets and falafel, standing post and patrols, and fire extinguishers.

The stories were cathartic. It let us know that we weren't crazy, that having strange feelings about seeing gore and violence, even secondhand, was normal. It brought us back together and started to heal the rivalries that had festered during the deployment.

Shen lent me his phone and I called home. I was hammered. My mom was ecstatic that I was back.

We drank until we blacked out and smoked cigarette after cigarette, trying to blot out Iraq. I wanted to forget the deployment. I wanted to forget that I spent all my time there in an office. I wanted to forget that I had gone to war and never seen combat.

10

APRIL 2009

In 331 BCE, Alexander set out from Egypt and headed into northern Iraq, seeking to avoid spending the summer in the desert heat. By October, they had made their way back down the Tigris River and met with Darius' forces near Mosul at Gaugamela. Darius' army far outnumbered Alexander's, and included two hundred armored chariots and fifteen war elephants from India.

Alexander began the battle by driving his infantry into the center of the Persian lines, while drifting his cavalry to the right, hoping to create an opening for him and his Companion Cavalry to crash into. The Persian chariots charged the Macedonian infantry, but the infantry opened ranks and let the chariots ride through the gaps. This helped create the opening in the Persian line that Alexander was looking for.

In a repeat of his actions at Issus, Alexander led the charge into the breach and reached the rear of the Persian forces. While Alexander hunted Darius through the Persian camp, Darius fled and his army collapsed.

Darius escaped to the mountains of western Iran, but his army was destroyed. The Macedonians sustained only a few hundred casualties, while the Persians suffered tens of thousands.

Things drifted into a routine when we got back. We got up, did roll call, went for a run, and stood by in the barracks all day. I played a lot of video games. Finally, ten to twelve hours after we started the workday, we were dismissed, having accomplished exactly nothing. We cleaned the barracks and our rifles. We did some gun drills with mortars, but not very often.

Most of our leaders were getting out of the Marines. Tuttle, Skewes, Gleason, and Carnahan were all short timing and were checked out of the day-to-day. I was conflicted about seeing them go. They were my mentors, and I looked up to them like older brothers, but their leaving also created space for the rest of us to take on more responsibility. The officers were getting moved around, too. Platoon commanders were becoming company executive officers, and company commanders were being promoted to major. We had no mission. We floated through life, moving only through inertia. Things went on like that for weeks, and then months.

The forward observers were reorganized. Martinez took over the team, and Blackwood was selected for one of the coveted positions. I suspected Martinez's selection criterion was mostly based on who he thought was cool enough to be an observer.

Dolph and Longman were both placed in charge of a mortar team. Neither one of them had the kind of mentorship or support that Kelly and I had had. They were both in the trenches and succeeded out of sheer hard work and determination. Cocagne was also placed in charge of a mortar team, but I suspected that was more because the other Marines were all a little afraid of him.

I was back in the FDC and back to being a team leader. As a senior lance corporal, being a team leader wasn't as impressive; it was good, but not great. Since Kelly was a corporal now, he didn't hang out with us much anymore. Sometimes, I watched him during morning roll call, standing off to the side with the other corporals and sergeants. My stomach curdled with jealousy, and a little bit of betrayal. We were still friends, and it hurt to be excluded only because of the rank on my collar.

———

Spring faded into summer, and I got orders to Mortar Leaders' Course. It was fun being away from the malaise of the platoon. We trained hard, trained smart, and went home. I'd get back to my barracks room after a full day and see the rest of the guys still in uniform, waiting to be dismissed.

While I was away, we got a new platoon commander, and a handful of new sergeants came to the platoon. One of them, a short, dark-haired guy named Ricci had a tattoo of a rat on his arm. Apparently the first time he went to Iraq, he had spent a lot of time crawling through tunnels, looking for high-value targets and weapons of mass destruction. He embraced the idea of being a tunnel rat, like the storied units in Vietnam.

We also got some new Marines fresh out of the School of Infantry. All of us senior lance corporals descended upon them with a fury. We ran them until they puked and made them clean until three in the morning. We were the vicious fleet Marines that I had heard about when I was a boot. We were Iraq veterans and mean as hell, except we'd never seen any combat.

When the boots found out that we hadn't seen combat on our deployment, they mentally put us into that 'other' category. The same way I'd done when I was a boot, they had sorted the platoon leadership into two groups. In an organization that venerates violence, me and my peers were the lessers.

One of the boots, a six-foot-five Marine from Ohio named Gross, approached me one afternoon. "Excuse me, Lance Corporal," he said, his hands behind his back. "I was wondering where I could get information about the Marine Corps basketball team."

I made a face. "Basketball team? I don't know what you're talking about."

"My recruiter said that once I got to my unit, I could try out for the Marine Corps basketball team."

I eyeballed him, trying to tell if he was messing with me. He had a tattoo of a flaming basketball on his forearm, and his face was earnest. I sighed. "Gross, I think your recruiter lied to you. I don't think there is a basketball team. And even if there is, you're a grunt; you're not going to have time to be on a team."

He nodded his head and slowly turned away. Everyone's recruiter stretches the truth a little, but I really felt for Gross.

As fall approached, I finished up at Mortar Leaders' Course and went back to the platoon. The rumor was that our next deployment would be with the Navy. We would float around on an aircraft carrier, bar-hopping in the Mediterranean. It sounded fun. Some of the older guys had done it before. They told us stories about getting in fights in Spain and sailing through the Suez Canal. But I didn't care how much fun Greece was; I still wanted to fight.

The war in Iraq was more or less over, but the war in Afghanistan was picking up. That was where I wanted to go. I needed to know if I had what it takes, but I was losing hope that I'd ever be the man that I had wanted to be.

In early December, there was news that President Obama was giving a speech at West Point. The rumor buzzing around the battalion was that it was going to be about Afghanistan. Some of us crowded in Stapleton and Rodriguez's room to watch. As mischievous as Stapleton could be, Rodriguez was a kind Floridian that was all smiles. I brought a six-pack and dragged a chair down the hall from my room. As we settled in to watch, we argued about Obama.

I leaned back in my chair as Obama came out and faced the cadets, a sea of gray uniforms. He started out talking about 9/11, and the invasion of Afghanistan. I glanced at Rodriguez. He arched an eyebrow at me. Obama continued. He talked about Iraq and the drawdown currently underway. I thought about the unit that replaced us. After a while, he got to the point.

"And as commander in chief, I have determined that it is in our vital national interest to send an additional thirty thousand US troops to Afghanistan," Obama said.

Stapleton had been barely paying attention when he shot up and threw his arms over his head. "We're going to Afghanistan, boys!" he yelled and tore out of the room. I could hear him in the hallway banging on doors and yelling at people. "Put your boots on! We're going to Afghanistan!"

Rodriguez leaned forward in his seat. "You think we'll go?"

I shrugged and took a swig of beer. "Who knows," I said. "We probably won't, and we'll get out having never seen combat." Rodriguez nodded.

"Either way, it's lame that he went to West Point. None of them are going to do this. They still have to graduate, get to a unit, train…" He was ticking off fingers to show how much time it would take before any of those in the audience were deployed. He was right. We turned the speech off and put on a movie.

The next morning, the news was rippling down the hallways even before roll call. Change of plans—we were going. We were heading to Afghanistan.

———

December rolled on without any new information. We went home for the holidays, and came back to a new decade: 2010. No one knew for sure, but the lance corporal underground said we were deploying sometime in the summer. Meanwhile, everyone on Lejeune knew that two battalions had already left for the dangerous Helmand Province in Southern Afghanistan. They were going to be the tip of the spear. It was rumored that another unit and we would follow in their footsteps.

As January began, nothing happened. We still sat in our rooms and played PlayStation. Even our morning runs were being scaled back. The winter wind whipped in off the bay, and outside of a few motivated squad leaders, every team was getting fat and lazy. I went on long runs in the cold, to spite myself and vent my frustration.

On Mondays, Kelly and I would take our new Marines to the armory to clean rifles. We would bring along our flak jackets to do burpees and run through magazine reloading drills, to simulate adrenaline and fear. Outside of that, and teaching them about the FDC, there wasn't any training going on. It was fun working with Kelly again. I put aside my jealousy that he had been promoted, and he stopped acting too important to hang out with someone of lesser rank. We were too good of friends for some petty work squabbles.

One morning, the sun oozing a watery blue light over the barracks, Kelly and I had enough. We sketched out a plan and called a platoon meeting right before lunch. I had a copy of the *Marine Corps Times* slipped in my cargo pocket. We knew how to scare the platoon into shape.

As the platoon formed up, Kelly stepped out in front of everyone. "Hey, guys, let's do a quick drill."

Groans came up from the platoon. It was lunchtime.

"Hey, shut the fuck up. Corporal Kelly is talking." I stepped up to his side, crossing my arms.

"We're going to break into sections and do some quick clearing. You don't need rifles or flak jackets. Just pretend you're holding your rifle," Kelly commanded.

"Classic 81s, notional rifles," someone said from the back of the formation. Kelly ignored it. I could feel myself getting angry, heat creeping up the back of my neck.

"Section one, form up over there," Kelly pointed to an open area between the barracks, "and start patrolling towards us."

They walked over in a jumbled mass as they sorted out into fireteams. Three vague fireteams appeared. They were bunched up and lackadaisical. Instead of a trained squad with proper dispersion, they looked like beginners.

"Contact, upper deck!" Kelly yelled as he pointed at a balcony of a neighboring barracks. The squad ran towards it in a mass, no taking cover and no notional covering fire. They bunched up at the stairwell and ran up it in a long line. It was awful. The Marines in the other section were shaking their heads. Even the boots knew it was bad.

"Alright first section, come back down." Kelly waited until they came back. "Well, how did that look?"

"Like ass!" someone yelled out.

"Awful."

"Like a squad of boots."

First section seemed shocked. They thought they had done better than that.

"Alright second section, go form up. Same deal," Kelly told them.

They jogged out, and started patrolling. Their dispersion was a little better. They took it more seriously at least, but it was still a pitiful performance. Kelly called the platoon back together. Some people were laughing, while others were grab-assing. I saw someone check their phone. Now I was pissed.

"Who here thinks that shit would fly in Afghanistan?" I asked. Everyone stopped and straightened up. "No, seriously. You think that was good enough to survive in Afghanistan?" There were some weak murmurs of "No" rising from the crowd.

"That was fucking terrible," I said. "You think you're grunts? That was the worst shit I've ever seen." I stared hard at the platoon. No one was looking at their phone anymore.

"We're going, guys. We're going to Afghanistan sooner than you think. Marines are getting ready to kick in some doors right now. We're next." I felt my face contort into an angry sneer. I reached into my pocket and pulled out the newspaper. "You guys know what this is?"

"*Marine Times?*" someone answered.

"Yeah, the *Marine Corps Times*. You know what this is?" I turned to a page with several rows of faces and held it up. "You see this? These are the people that died there last week. And they were all better trained than you." I turned the newspaper so everyone could see it. About fifteen faces started out of the page.

"This is real. I'll be damned if I'm on this page, and I'll be damned if you are too. No more fucking video games all day. It's time to start training. Rah?"

Forty scared faces cheered back at Kelly and me, "Rahh!"

"Lance Corporal Martin and I are building a training plan. We're going to do this, but you guys need to get your heads out of your asses," Kelly said.

"Aye, Corporal," they answered.

"Good. Now go get lunch. We'll let you know what comes next." They broke the formation and headed off, unusually quiet.

Our new platoon commander helped Kelly and me out. He gave us his training manuals and sketched out the basics of unit training. Individual skills first: weapons handling, general military knowledge, and tactics. Small team tactics next, followed by squad and platoon tactics. It was unusual for a corporal and lance corporal to set up the training, but our senior leadership was still in flux. People moving around drove our momentum into the ground. Kelly and I set out to fix that.

We worked into the night and through the weekend, designing training templates. We assigned other squad and team leaders topics to research and present. We met with the machine gunners to provide classes on how to use and assemble their guns. We scheduled mortar drills and patrolling exercises, room-clearing demonstrations and patrol base operations. We plunged the platoon in satellite-patrolling theory and practice. We buddy rushed across the barracks' lawn again and again and again.

As we trained, the platoon changed. The boots started meshing with their teams. Guys leaned out as we started running more. The winter lethargy started to dissipate. When we went to the field, people complained less. We were getting tougher. We were getting back into the swing of being grunts.

———

In the spring, Dolph and I finally got promoted to corporal. We had a company formation in front of the barracks. Our new first sergeant called Dolph and me to the front of the formation where we marched out and faced him.

He began, "To all who see these presents, greetings..." as every promotion warrant begins. I stood at attention and made sure not to lock my knees. You can't be passing out when you're getting promoted.

I had Skewes pin my new chevrons on. He came jogging out of the formation, stood in front of me, pulled my old chevrons off, and tossed them in the grass. I opened my palm, and he pulled out the brand-new corporal's chevrons: two stripes up with crossed rifles underneath. He pushed the pins through my left collar, and then my right. With a grin and the thick part of his palms, he slapped me over my new rank insignia, pushing the pins down into the flesh by my collarbones. "Snakebites," they're called. He clapped me on the shoulder and jogged off.

Dolph didn't have anyone pin him. He never had a mentor like Kelly and I did. He had a string of difficult and bad team leaders. Dolph was a self-made Marine, and he didn't need anyone to pin him.

Later that afternoon, Tuttle, Skewes, and Cochran found Dolph and me.

"Hey, Corporal Dolph, Corporal Martin, congrats again," Skewes said, as he shook our hands. "We'll take you guys out for a beer tonight. Come meet us at eight." I worked with these guys every day, and it felt different to be included. Nothing had changed since yesterday, except the piece of metal that I wore on my collar, but it made a difference.

. . .

"You guys ready to get your blood stripes?" Atchison asked. Dolph and I looked at each other. In Marine dress blues, commissioned and noncommissioned officers have a red stripe that runs down their trouser legs. It's called the "blood stripe" in remembrance of the leaders that were killed leading the battle of Chapultepec. Lances and privates don't have one. There's a tradition that, when a Marine gets promoted to corporal, the other sergeants and corporals gather around and knee the new corporal in the sides of their legs. If you've ever been "dead legged," imagine that, but over and over again. Whenever news organizations report on military hazing, "blood striping" always gets included.

"I don't want to, but it's tradition," Dolph said as he opened a plastic bottle of whiskey. He poured some in a plastic cup, topped it off with cola, and handed it to me.

"Yeah, I hear that," I said, as Dolph started to pour another cup.

"You guys are nuts," Atchison said. He pushed a wad of tobacco around in his lip. I shrugged. Blood striping was a tradition; what could I do about it?

Dolph and I had a few drinks while we got ready. Then we had a few more. By the time we climbed into a cab, we were lit. We stumbled into the bar to find everyone waiting for us at a high-top table. Cochran, Tuttle, Skewes, Zaehringer, and a few others were there. Dolph and I pulled up some stools.

"Jesus, you guys started early," Skewes said.

"You only get pinned corporal once," I said, opening up a menu upside down.

We sat around and bullshitted. We argued about football and tried to not talk about work. I had never talked about things outside of work with these guys. It was strange to spend so much time with people and not really know anything about them. Zaehringer started talking about his recent engagement; he seemed like a decent guy.

I thought back to him berating my squad when we first got to Ramadi. I had to begrudgingly respect it now. He was only looking out for his guys, making sure they didn't have to stand one more minute of post than they had to.

After a few beers, Dolph stood up from his stool. "I can't take it anymore. Are you guys going to kick the shit out of us or what?" He looked around the table. Zaehringer glanced at Skewes and Cochran, and burst out laughing.

"What are you talking about? We're not going to jump you."

"What?" Dolph seemed confused. He glanced at me. I couldn't believe he was bringing it up. "You're not going to blood stripe us?"

"No, dude. That shit sucks," Zaehringer said.

"Yeah, fuck that," Cochran echoed.

Dolph raised his arms up and dropped them to his sides. "Well, shit, now I feel like I have to get it."

"Dolph, are you asking us to haze you?" Skewes asked.

"Well, yeah, I guess so." Dolph stared at the table. Tuttle and Skewes made eye contact, shrugged, stood, and walked over to Dolph.

"Hey, man, if you want it," Tuttle said. Zaehringer hopped up, too. They escorted Dolph out the bar door and around a corner, out of sight.

Cochran leaned across the table to me. "You don't want to join him?"

I looked at Cochran, his eyes round and magnified behind his glasses. "Nah, I'm good," I said.

Cochran nodded.

We sipped our beers and waited for Dolph to get back. It was classic Dolph, earning absolutely everything he had the hard way. They carried him back in after a few minutes. He was smiling, but he needed help walking.

"Ya sons of bitches, ya got me," he said. His head rolled to the side as Skewes and Zaehringer carried him back to the table. Part of me wished I had joined him, joined in the tradition. But a bigger part of me was glad I could walk on my own two feet.

11

JULY 2010

With Darius defeated, Alexander rode to the ancient city of Babylon, near Baghdad. He was greeted as a king, and declared himself the King of Babylon, and included it as one of his official titles. In a generous move, he allowed many of the Persian bureaucrats to continue running the area. This allowed him to continue moving east and chase Darius without having to reorganize, but it was upsetting to many of his Macedonian troops.

Meanwhile, Darius was trying to raise another army. Working with his relative, Bessus, he attempted to rally enough men to keep Alexander from advancing further.

We flew out of Cherry Point again. As I sat on the plane, I thought about the timing. Three years ago to the day, I arrived on Parris Island. I had one year left on my contract. In that year, I had an entire seven-month deployment to Marjah, a tiny town in the Helmand River Valley and the most dangerous city in Afghanistan. The next year was going to feel longer than the previous three years put together.

It was like a boulder was sitting in front of me. The rest of my life was behind the boulder, but I couldn't see it. Maybe it went on and on into the distance. Maybe it ended on the other side. My future seemed impermanent. A Schrodinger's future—it existed and didn't exist at the same time. The only thing that was for sure was Afghanistan.

We landed in Bangor, Maine, again. Same deal as last time, World War II and Korea vets greeted us as we deplaned. I called my parents from a payphone and smoked cigarettes. It had a pleasant symmetry to it. Then we hopped back on the plane and set off for Kyrgyzstan.

Manas Air Force base in Kyrgyzstan was a caricature of the USSR. There were old Soviet buildings with Cyrillic lettering. You could see mountains in the distance, their snow caps hovering like clouds. Birch and poplar trees were everywhere. It was charming, like a beat-up ski resort in the Rockies.

We got off the plane and took a bus to our transient barracks. On the way, we passed small guard huts and fences. If Kuwait felt like a former war zone, Kyrgyzstan was lovely. All the people in uniform seemed out of place.

Our temporary barracks were huge, with triple-story bunk beds. We were going to be there for a few days. As soon as our gear was set up and squared away, we established a watch schedule, and set off to explore. There was a gym, a small movie theater in a trailer, and a pizza place. Small shops sold traditional Kyrgyz trinkets for souvenirs. But, most importantly, there was a bar.

Manas was a permanent station for the air force jockeys that worked there. So there was a bar with a selection of mostly European beers and drinks. We watched with envy as the airmen strolled in and ordered drinks on the patio, tossing corn hole bags, and sipping Russian lagers. We were banned from having anything to drink.

. . .

I went to the chow hall with McVaugh. Dolph and Kelly had gone over early on the advance party to help set things up for the company, while Blackwood had been attached to a rifle company to direct their mortar fire. McVaugh and I ate steak with mac and cheese for dinner. Might as well get it while we could.

After dinner, I smoked a cigarette and watched a pair of Marines walk up to the chow hall. They were filthy. Their cammies were torn, and you could see their legs through massive holes. Their hair was long, and they didn't say anything. I finished my cigarette and figured I'd find out who they were eventually; I assumed they had to be the Marines rotating out of Marjah.

The next day, there were more Marines in tattered cammies. They chain-smoked in silence outside of their barracks. They looked awful. They were gaunt, with gray and yellow skin. Their eyes were sunken.

I checked myself out in the reflection of a window. My cammies were spotless, and I was chubby from drinking too much on predeployment leave. I looked round and happy. I wondered how long it would be before I looked like the guys cycling back home, and what kind of person I would be when I looked like them.

Sealy, the tall, hairy Marine, approached one of the new Marines at a smoke pit.

"Hey, man, can I bum a light?" Sealy said, a cigarette clamped in between his teeth. The Marine was sitting on a bench, his rifle slung between his legs. He glanced up at Sealy with a blank stare.

Sealy flicked his thumb like he was sparking a light. The guy rummaged in his pocket, pulled out a yellow lighter, and handed it to Sealy. Sealy lit his cigarette, took a drag, and handed the lighter back.

"Thanks, man." They stood in silence for a while.

"So, you excited to head home?" Sealy asked the guy. He didn't move. He just stared at the smoke rising from his cigarette.

Sealy stuck his free hand in his pocket and walked around. He sat on an adjacent bench.

"I was in the initial push, back in '03," he informed the guy. The

Marine made eye contact with Sealy. His eyes were dark and filled with fire. Sealy stared vacantly back. Neither one of them said anything.

The Marine broke eye contact, flicked his cigarette in the general area of the trash, and walked away. His right hand firmly on the pistol grip of his rifle.

We left for Afghanistan the next day.

————

We flew on a cargo plane to Kandahar, over Tajikistan and Uzbekistan, but there weren't any windows to watch. Everyone slept, their heads bobbing in the turbulence. We landed at a massive base. Kandahar is the second-largest city in Afghanistan, at about half a million people, it is similar in size to Ramadi.

Kandahar takes its name from *Iskandar*, the Pashto pronunciation of Alexander. The old part of Kandahar was founded by Alexander the Great during his conquests. I was still chasing after him.

We filed into a small airport waiting room. Most of the company crammed in and tried to sleep on the cold linoleum floors, tan camo legs sprawled out with rifles poking out like black arms. Cochran and I stayed awake and watched a movie on TV.

Cochran didn't seem nervous, but he wasn't calm. Any time there was a noise outside—the wind, a baggage truck—he jerked a little. I bounced my foot and tried to watch the movie.

After a few hours, we got the call—our ride was ready.

We put on our flak jackets, shouldered our packs, and set out for a smaller cargo plane. We squeezed into our jump seats and took off for Camp Dwyer in northern Helmand Province.

Camp Dwyer was a wasteland in a desert. The wind blew hot and dry, while reddish-brown sand swirled around us. The camp was a few rows of tents, Hesco barriers, and concrete walls. Heavily fortified guard towers stood above us. All the comforts of Camp Ramadi—a luxurious chow hall, multiple gyms—all of that was gone. This was an expeditionary base. We slept on green canvas cots and listened to the wind howl at night.

The new guys—they weren't boots anymore, not after we landed in Kandahar—were getting spooked. Our platoon didn't have a clear mission. In the morning, we would be told that we were going to be a helo-based SWAT team, flying missions all over Marjah. In the evening, we'd hear that we were going to be driving huge armored trucks called MRAPs. They didn't use Humvees here; the IEDs were too powerful. The next day we'd hear something else. The lack of direction freaked some of the guys out.

I did my best to keep people calm. I read books on my rack and played chess with Cochran. Whenever someone asked about a rumor, I'd tell them not to believe it. But it was hard to be that close to danger and not know what our mission was. I felt for the new guys. Going to Ramadi was scary; this was worse.

———

After a few days, word came down. We were splitting into our mortar teams, kind of. Two mortars with four Marines would be attached to each of the three rifle companies. The rest of the platoon would have their own battle space to the west of Marjah. An FDC member would go with each of the gun pairs. Kelly was headed to Fox, and Cochran was going to Golf. Dolph, Stapleton, McVaugh, and Cocagne were all staying with the platoon. I was going to Echo Company with Ricci, Galentine, and Gross. Once again, I was separated from my friends. My group was the misfit crew: Gross was too tall, Ricci was too short, Galentine had his bright red hair, and I had the thickest glasses known to man. We were the opposite of intimidating.

That said, Echo was considered the best company in the battalion. I took it as a sign of respect that I was attached to them. Additionally, they were the only company in the city itself. Fox was out to the north, and Golf was to the east. To the south of Echo was a different unit.

A few hours later, we got the call to pack up.

In the dark, we shouldered our packs and formed up in a line behind the helicopter. There was a bright moon, and our shadows stretched away from our feet as we walked. Sand and little rocks whipped around from the rotor wash. Everyone pulled their goggles down to protect their eyes. We boarded the helo in a single file, sitting in jump seats along the wall.

Directly across from me was a door gunner. He was dressed in a jumpsuit and harness that attached him to the side door. He had a massive .50 caliber machine gun mounted on a complicated swivel that let him lean far out the door. There was another one at the back of the helo on the loading ramp.

With a lurch, we lifted off into the night. I could see moonlit fields pass as we flew through the night. Occasionally, mud-brick houses flashed by the open side door, but it was mostly fields, black under the night sky.

I watched the gunner standing in the door as he scanned far and near, gently sweeping his machine gun side to side. He did a double-take and I took a sharp breath, as he leaned the machine gun out of the helo, sighting in on something. I was expecting him to open up. But he said something over his headset and pulled back inside. My eyes sparkled with excitement, and I was intoxicated by the adrenaline and cold air.

I was in a helicopter flying to the front lines! A machine gunner was hanging out the door hunting for the Taliban! It felt like I was flying into Vietnam, on a moonlight chopper ride to the battlefield. I adjusted my grip on my rifle and hoped I was ready.

We landed with a jolt. People were startled awake, the red light inside the helo shining on their surprised faces. We stood up and walked off, into Camp Hansen.

If Dwyer was Spartan, Hansen was austere. It wasn't much more than a few walls and tents. There was a small parking area for a couple of MRAPs and a few rows of Conex boxes that had been turned into buildings. Green sandbags were stacked up everywhere.

Our platoon was led to an open area covered by camouflage netting. It was shockingly humid. Even though it was late at night, I was sweating everywhere. So much for a dry heat. We piled up our gear and tried to sleep under the netting. Dust whirled in from the helos idling nearby.

In the morning, we separated into our teams. Ricci, Gross, Galentine, and I gathered together with our packs. Our seabags would be brought out later, whenever they arrived. I said goodbye to some guys.

"Have fun with those pussies in Echo," Cocagne said. I smiled and clasped his hand. His face turned grim, "But seriously, watch yourself out there."

"You too, buddy," I said.

The four of us loaded in some MRAPs and headed south, towards Echo Company. As we left Hansen, that familiar fear came rushing back. I kept my eyes glued to the window, watching for anything suspicious, my rifle between my legs, thumb on the safety.

We slowly drove down a dirt road with canals on either side of us. Long mud-brick walls bordered the canals. Inside the truck, radio wires and the gunner's harness swayed as we moved. I only turned away from the window to chug water. Even in the morning, it had to be at least eighty degrees. I wiped the sweat off my face with my sleeve.

After a short drive, we abruptly stopped and I could feel the panic rising inside me. *What happened?* I didn't hear any firing, and I strained to see what was up ahead of us. All I could see was a plume of dust from the MRAPs up ahead.

"Hey, guys, grab your gear. We're here," the vehicle commander called out. "This is Aries II."

I turned the handle and pushed the heavy door open. The sun was bright, and the heat was immediate. As my eyes adjusted, I could see a wall running along a path and a canal to my left, green fields and a wider canal to my right. I walked down the steps, thumb on the safety, and scrutinized the area.

We were at a T-shaped intersection. There was a ramshackle tower at the intersection of the roads, while two mortars sat in small sandbag bunkers off to the side. I saw a tall Marine waving at me. He was next to a pair of MRAPs parked in front of a tan mud building. There were only some sandbags and a string or two of concertina wire separating him from the busy street. He was wearing a T-shirt and pants, no armor. I grabbed my pack off the back of the truck and headed over. The other guys fell in next to me as the trucks took off to the south, thick plumes of dust trailing them.

"Hey, you must be the guys from Weapons Company," he said. "I'm Sergeant Mott." He held out his hand.

I took off my glove and shook it. "That's us. I'm Corporal Martin, your FDC guy, and these are Sergeant Ricci, Corporal Galentine, and Lance Corporal Gross." I turned to point at each of them. Ricci and Galentine stepped up to shake Mott's hand. Gross was looking around, both hands on his rifle.

"Alright. Things are a little tight right now. Some of the guys from the previous unit are still here, so we don't have enough cots for everyone. Put your stuff down over here and we'll sort it out later."

We walked over to the "entrance" of the patrol base. It was a metal stake that held the end of a loop of concertina wire. Mott gingerly lifted it up and let us inside. Behind the MRAPs was an open building. Looking inside, I could see three rooms. One was stacked full of cases of water and MREs, and the other two rooms had green cots. There was an American flag hanging up in the back of the one on the right. We set our packs down in the storage room.

Mott pulled his flak on over his shirt, and popped his helmet on, the straps dangling. "Let me give you a tour."

Aries II was situated in a perfect grid. The main road ran north–south, and another road ran to the west. Running parallel to the north–south road were two canals. The building we were in was on the west side of the main road. Further to the west was another parked MRAP.

We walked out to the middle of the intersection. A few beat-up cars were parked a ways from the tower. Afghan police were searching the cars and patting down the people inside.

"So we have four guard posts," Mott said. "We've got the tower here. It looks west down Route Joanne over there. And we have the north and south trucks." He pointed up and down the road to two MRAPs, the gunners hidden by makeshift camouflage baskets over the turret. "This is Route Elephant; it's the main artery of the city. We get a lot of traffic driving through here." He waved dismissively at the cars driving through.

"We also have a post on that building over there." He pointed across the canal. There was a squat mud building with concertina wire surrounding it. Green cots with sleeping bags were visible from the road.

"Do people sleep outside over there?" I asked.

"Yeah. That's where the other half of the squad lives."

I tried to take it all in. There was barely any protection. Some sandbags and a few strings of concertina wire were all that separated sleeping Marines from a busy intersection. This was beyond expeditionary—we were on the front line.

I tightened my grip on my rifle and watched the stream of cars pour past. If any of these were suicide bombers, we wouldn't last long.

Mott led us to the other building. We went behind the tower and crossed a rickety wooden bridge over the canal. The bridge was only wide enough for one person to cross at a time.

As we approached the other hooch, a dirt road headed east from the building, while a mud wall ran alongside. To the north and east were open fields. Directly to the south of the building was a small tree-lined field. I could feel the sweat rolling down my back as we walked up.

"Hey, guys. Come meet the mortarmen from Weapons Company,"

Mott yelled. A head poked out of the darkness. I recognized him immediately.

"Hey, holy shit, it's Blackwood!" I said.

"Well, I'll be," Blackwood came strolling out, twitching his mustache. He was naked from the waist up. "What's up, guys?" He smiled and put his hands on his hips. I was thrilled to have someone I knew at this patrol base. That he was one of the best grunts from our platoon was even better.

"Jesus, Blackwood, put your flak on," Mott chided him.

Blackwood rolled his eyes. "I'll be right back," he said as he ambled back into the building. "Hey, y'all, the new guys are here," he called to the other Marines in the building.

A couple of guys from Echo came out.

Mott introduced them. "This is Hannibal," he pointed to a lean, athletic black guy, "and Berg," he added pointing to a white guy with a mohawk and circle tattoos running around his entire arm, giving it a striped appearance. We shook hands.

"The rest of the guys are standing post. You'll meet them soon enough," Mott said.

"Hey, Sergeant, can you show me the mortar setup?" I asked.

"Oh yeah, sure." We walked back across the narrow footbridge to the tower.

"You know I'm pretty good on a plotting board myself," Mott said.

I gave him a vague, "Mmmm."

Under the tower, there were two Marines and a few Afghan police and soldiers.

"Hello, hello," Mott said, as he strolled into the sandbag bunker under the tower. "These are the 81s guys that just got in. This is..." he paused and stared at me blankly.

"Corporal Martin," I said, as I reached out a hand. I pointed to Ricci, Gross, and Galentine. They were over in the other hooch talking to Blackwood.

"Nice to meet ya," a muscular guy with light eyes said. He had a thick wad of tobacco in his lip. "I'm Sergeant Compton." He spread his arms out. "Welcome to our little home." He chuckled and spat on the dirt floor.

"Sup," a Marine from the old unit gave me a head nod from the corner of the bunker.

Inside the bunker, the walls were lined with cans of mortar shells: high explosive rounds, illumination or "illum" rounds, phosphorus. I raised my eyebrows.

"So you guys run the FDC out of here?" I asked.

The Marine in the corner shook his head. "Nah, we use the operations center in that first MRAP over there." He pointed to the truck next to where I dropped my pack. "We use the computer, but we've got plotting boards if you need 'em."

I nodded and said thanks. "You guys do a lot of shooting?" I asked.

"Yeah, here and there." He paused and adjusted his glasses. "Wait, are you talking about mortars?"

"Uh, I was."

"Oh yeah, we shoot some illum. Occasionally we fire some high explosive, but not all that often." He pointed to the inside edge of the bunker. "We do a lot more traditional shooting."

I followed where he was pointing. On the inside support beam, a row of machine gun rounds had been pounded into the wood. There were ten or twelve of them. Their brass sparkled against the wood.

"What's that?" I asked.

"One for each Taliban," the Marine replied. I couldn't see his eyes behind his dirty glasses, but his face was expressionless.

I stared at him for a moment, to make sure I understood what he was saying.

"Hey, Martin, what's going on, man?" Blackwood strolled into the bunker. He pulled out a cigarette and lit it. Only a mortarman wouldn't worry about smoking in a room packed full of high explosive rounds.

"Just getting the tour," I said. "We landed at Hansen last night. I didn't know it'd be so fucking humid here." Everyone nodded. It was mid-morning and creeping towards ninety degrees.

"Yeah, when you're standing post out in the trucks," the Marine in the corner pointed at an MRAP, "be sure to bring a whole case of water; you'll need it."

Compton spat a long string of brown spit into the dirt. "Blackwood, tell him about our trip out here."

Blackwood smiled and crossed his arms before taking a drag. "Man, we hiked out here from another patrol base. We were staggered out, crossing this road, one at a time. When it's my turn, I get up, look around, and jog across. When I set back down for security— kaboom!" He lifted his arms miming an explosion, cigarette clamped between his teeth. "The Afghan solider that crossed after me stepped on a fuckin' IED. Ripped his jaw clean off of his face, bleeding fuckin' everywhere. He died right there." Blackwood took another drag. "Shit was unreal."

"Whoa," I said. Mott solemnly nodded. His eyes were glum and downcast.

Compton stood and slapped the dust off his pants. "Well, Corporal Martin, how about you and your boys stand some post? No better way to learn the ropes." He winked at me.

"Yeah, sure. I'll go get everyone," I said, as I turned to walk back out of the bunker.

"Oh, one more thing." Compton stopped me. "It woulda been better if we'd brought jungle cammies; it's so damn green out here. But turn your helmet cover inside out. It's not much, but the green will help."

"Roger," I said, as I walked out into the baking sun and headed to find the other guys.

We spent the next eight hours standing post, from ten in the morning until six at night. The heat roared down from the sky and sizzled off the brown dirt, while humid waves poured out from the grass and fields. I sweat through my blouse sleeves and pant legs; even my boots were soaked through. As I sweat, dirt stuck to me. I was already losing some of that clean, new-guy look.

Sucking down bottle after bottle of water, I stood underneath the tower with some Afghan police. I didn't know any Pashto and they didn't know any English, but we managed to talk through hand motions and pointing.

I'd point at my rifle and say, "Rifle, rifle."

A tall policeman with a graying beard would say, "Ahhh, rye-full," showing off his missing teeth. Then he'd point at his AK and say, "Kalash-nek-off." I would nod my head and repeat it back to him.

Between the heat and being tossed into guard duty so quickly, it was an exhausting shift. By the time we finished, I collapsed into a wet puddle inside the MRAP they used as an operations center. Mott was inside smoking a cigarette. I lit one up, too.

He went over a plan to build three squads, one headed by Compton, one by Blackwood, and one by Ricci. I would be with Ricci. Mott would run the patrol base. In total, we had sixteen Marines and a corpsman, three squads of five to stand post. When we went on patrols, we would have to borrow some Marines that weren't standing post. It was clear how thin we were stretched.

12

AUGUST 2010

Having destroyed Darius' army, Alexander began to push into the center of the Persian empire. He and his army entered the capital, Susa, in 330 BCE. The city surrendered to Alexander and opened up the royal Persian treasury, which contained 2,850,000 pounds of gold, worth over five billion dollars today.

From there, most of the army marched on famous Persian Royal Roads to the spiritual capital, Persepolis. Meanwhile, Alexander took a smaller force and beat a Persian army contingent that had been occupying the strategic Persian Gates. From there, he raced back to meet his army at Persepolis.

After our shift was over, I went into the storage room and made a makeshift cot out of MRE cases. The mud walls radiated heat; it was hotter inside than outside. Stripping down to my shorts, I lay on my improvised cot and watched cars driving past. They were less than forty feet away, but I was too tired to care. I rolled on my side and fell asleep.

A few hours later I woke up, scratching at my chest and arms. I had bug bites everywhere. Grabbing my glasses, I saw fleas jumping off the wall and onto me.

Jesus fucking Christ, I thought as I ripped open my pack and grabbed my bug spray. The fleas were everywhere. I sprayed my whole body, and put my sweaty cammies back on, the wet, gritty cloth rubbing my limbs.

"Fuck this," I said, as I lit up a cigarette and strolled over to the operations center MRAP to see who was around.

Compton was sitting in there reading a book, bathed in red light.

"Hey, man, I got attacked by fleas," I said. "Mind if I hang out for a while?" He smiled, spit into a water bottle, and waved me in. I sat in the jump seat next to him. My cigarette left dark trails in the red light.

"So what's it been like out here?" I asked.

"Oh man, last night was wild!" He held up his hands in excitement. He seemed like a cool guy.

"Yeah? What happened?"

"We spotted a person digging a hole in Joanne from the tower. Probably putting in an IED." He paused to spit. "Anyway, the guys from the other unit called us around. They're like 'Yo check this out'." Compton excitedly waved his hands as a grin spread across his face. "This guy grabs the machine gun, brings it over to the bunker under the tower, and slaps on a thermal sight."

"Pas-thirteen?"

"Nah, we got the new ones out here."

"Cool."

"Oh yeah. So he slaps on the sight and feeds a belt in, and I'm standing there with my night vision trying to see this fucker, but I can barely make him out in the distance. Just this green dot moving around, you know?" He spit again. "And then he—" Suddenly the mortar radio crackled to life.

"Notional Boom, Notional Boom, this Typhoon Three," the caller was whispering into the radio. I picked up the black handset and keyed the button.

"Go for Notional Boom One."

"Standby for... Standby call for fire."

"Roger. Standing by." I turned to Compton. "Yell over the other hooch and get the mortarmen up."

"Got it," he said, as he grabbed his rifle and hopped out the back of the MRAP. "Fire mission! Fire mission! Fire mission!" he screamed, as he ran into the night.

I pulled up my plotting board and started copying down Typhoon Three's call for fire. They had some suspicious movement outside their patrol base and wanted a few illum rounds to check it out.

Pulling out the mortar computer, I spun up the mission. When I had the data, I popped my head out of the emergency hatch. Both guns had small teams ready to go. Most of the Marines were in shorts, boots, and armor, their bare arms and legs visible in the dark.

I called out the gun data in mortarman's song. "Three-two-five-seven." Flat-flat-up-down. They repeated the numbers back to me. When they were ready, I called out. "Gun one, half load!"

"Hanging on one!" Galentine called back.

"Gun one, fire!"

Boom! The night was broken in half by the immense blast. Everything was temporarily illuminated by the flash, before plunging back into darkness. The flash burned into my vision.

"Typhoon Three, rounds out."

"Tango," came the response. I counted the seconds on my watch. Right on cue, I could see the illum round open up in the sky. It started its lazy descent, floating gracefully from its parachute. That was it, my first night, and I was already coordinating fires. I grinned and lit another cigarette.

"Notional Boom, that's a good placement. Can we get a continuous illum, same location? Over."

"Roger that. Standby for continuous illum."

I did some quick math on the corner of a plotting board, checking the time of flight with the remaining burn time on the round. I had a few seconds to spare.

"Gun two, half load!"

"Hangin' on two!" came a voice I didn't know. Must be one of the mortarmen from Echo.

I counted down the seconds on my watch. Four, three, two, one... "Gun two, fire!" There was an ear-shattering blast again. I turned to watch the round pop. It popped right before the first one extinguished. Perfect.

We continued firing for a few minutes. Typhoon Three called back and thanked us. They didn't see anything suspicious.

"End of mission!" I called to the gunline.

"End of mission," they echoed.

"Hey, nice work, guys! They said it was perfect." A tired "Kill" came out of the darkness.

Compton came back to the MRAP a few minutes later. "That was great!" he said. "Man, those things are loud. I'm used to little ole 60s." I grinned. My hearing was so shot I didn't think they were that loud anymore. We settled back into our seats, buzzing a little on adrenaline. No one said anything for a minute.

"Hey, so you didn't finish that story," I said.

"What story?"

"Last night? You guys were watching the guy digging in the road?"

"Oh yeah, well, we took a shot at him with the machine gun, but missed. That was it for a while, but a couple of hours later, there he was, right back at it," he said, and spit.

"So what'd you do?"

"We called in air. Had an A-10 on station."

"No shit?" A-10s are planes that were designed to fight tanks.

"No shit, man," he smiled. "It was cool. We called him, and used the laser to guide him on target. Came tearing in, that chain gun just cookin' down the street." Compton flew his hand around like a plane. "But he pulled it right at the end, totally missed." He spit, and said, "Ended up hitting a cow. Cut the thing practically in half," he shook his head disappointedly.

The next morning, I woke up disoriented. It was already hot, and the street was bustling. A donkey cart was going by, an old man dressed in brown and white clucking the donkey along. My chest and arms were still itchy. I made a mental note to send my parents a letter asking for bug spray and flea collars. Rummaging through the storage room, I grabbed an MRE for breakfast.

Sitting on a stack of empty sandbags, digging through the plastic bag, I heard gunfire crackling to our south. It was close. Throwing my food aside, I grabbed my flak jacket, tossed it on, and slapped on my helmet. I ran the edge of an MRAP and listened. It didn't sound that close from over here and I couldn't hear anyone else firing. I yelled to the Marines nearby. "What's going on? Where's it coming from?"

"Don't worry about it," Mott said from inside the MRAP. He sounded bored. I turned around.

One of the Echo guys was sitting on his cot ogling me. "Chill out, bro," he said. "That's the contractors." I blinked. Contractors? What was going on? Why wasn't he freaked out? There was a firefight down the street, and this guy didn't move a muscle.

Mott stuck his head out the back of the MRAP. He was holding a canteen cup full of coffee. "Some local contractors are paving the road, and they get shot at every day by the Taliban." I stared at him. "It's a way down the road, at least a mile. Nothing we can do about it." He looked me over. "Take your shit off; you're acting like a boot." He pulled his head back and disappeared into the MRAP.

"Yeah, boot," the other Marine said, as he lay back down. Sheepishly, I took my flak jacket off and sat back down on the sandbags. I had heard distant gunfire in Iraq, but this was close. It seemed absurd to not be a little freaked.

Can't let that happen again, I thought. I needed to cool my shit if I wanted to get any respect out here.

. . .

My squad spent the rest of the morning and afternoon standing post in the heat. Once again, the police and I swapped a few more words and names. Raheem was the man with the graying beard. He liked talking to me, learning new words, and I appreciated having him around for company. Raheem was a genial guy, but it was clear he wasn't in charge; a younger man with a mustache was the leader. The leader sat on a folding camp chair and smoked hash all day. His eyes were always bloodshot.

All day long, the police searched dozens and dozens of cars. Route Elephant was busy. Most of the cars were beat-up sedans, but there were several tractors carrying sacks of grain or cotton. In Iraq, they would have pulled all the sacks off and searched everything, but we didn't have enough manpower here. We could barely stand post and push out patrols. And the Afghan police were too stoned to do that. So we patted down the drivers and sent them on their way.

I stood under the tower and watched the traffic roll past. Ancient dump trucks and jingle trucks full of cotton rumbled past us, *tut-tutting* and *sput-sputtering* along. Motorcycles with three people on them, and children pushing wheelbarrows full of yellow water jugs watched us out of the corner of their eyes. Sheepherders corralled twenty, thirty, fifty sheep down the road, small clouds of dust rising behind them. It was spectacular, exciting, and dangerous. I stood under the tower with Raheem and tried to soak it all in. It was all brand new for me, but it was just another day for the people of Marjah.

———

The next day, we got a call from a neighboring patrol base. They found an IED on Route Donkey, about a kilometer east of Elephant. Echo Mobile was headed our way with an ordnance disposal team that would disarm the IED. Echo Mobile was the company's mounted squad that drove people and supplies around our area of operations.

Ricci and I quickly assembled a squad and assigned roles. He would be the squad leader and I his assistant. Berg would walk point, the man out in front, while Hannibal would guard the rear. We snagged a few other guys as well: a smiley North Carolinian named Brown who took the grenade launcher, and Demorrow, a squat Marine, who was strong enough to carry the machine gun.

When Echo Mobile showed up an hour or two later, we were ready to head out. Almost everyone was giddy—my squad, the Echo Mobile guys—only the ordnance guys weren't. We headed out into the lush afternoon, the cotton plants and corn stalks concealing us.

Berg and I were upfront, guiding everyone. We would push from compound to compound, stopping in someone's front yard to check the map. Every time I turned around, Marines were bunching up behind us, small groups of three or four standing together.

I'd wave them back. "Get some dispersion!" and they'd stumble around trying to open up a little.

When I would radio in checkpoints to Ricci, he seemed like he was having trouble following along on the map. He had a lot of questions about where we were and which way we were headed. I caught Berg listening to the radio traffic, but he didn't say anything.

We patrolled past mud brick homes, fields, and irrigation canals. I was sweaty and excited. For years, I had trained, dreamed, to lead a patrol in a combat zone. The smell of burning trash, sweet grass, and sewage from the canals melded together under the humid sun. I had never felt so alive. The combination of fear and excitement was heady. There was that undercurrent of power too, the same way I felt when I first held a loaded rifle, or directed my fireteam back in training—the sense that I was dangerous, that I was controlling something powerful. Looking back at Brown with his grenade launcher, I guess I was.

Berg and I skirted a small trail, called a ratline, until we hit Route Donkey. The squad we were meeting up with was somewhere close. So was the IED we were looking for. Cautiously, we took a knee at the intersection. He faced north, and I faced south. I triple-checked the ground before I knelt at the edge of the road.

Across the street, in some bushes, I saw someone waving at us. I waved back.

A tall, thin Marine stood and scanned the area before yelling over to us. "Hey, y'all got the bomb team?"

"Yeah, where's that IED?" I yelled back across at him.

"Oh, you're good; it's down the street aways. We're all holed up in the school over here. Come on in," he said, as he motioned us in. I turned around and passed the information back.

Our squad crossed the dirt road and piled into the courtyard of the building. Another squad from Echo was already inside. Everyone was soaked in sweat.

"Hey, welcome to the party!" someone yelled, as we walked in. I grinned from ear to ear. We all sat down in the dirt and leaned against the walls of the courtyard. The Echo guys all knew each other and started talking shit. Some guys pulled out disposable cameras and started taking selfies and group pictures. A rocket launcher was passed around for people to pose with. Twenty or so dirty, sweaty Marines gathering around machine guns and grenade launchers, getting high on life in a combat zone.

"Hey! Hey, everyone! Open your mouth and cover your ears!" someone from outside the courtyard yelled. I clapped my hands over my ears right before the bomb team blew up the IED. A towering column of smoke and dust rose into the air. We all cheered.

When we got back to Aries II, Ricci, Mott, and I got together. Despite Ricci's higher rank, we decided that I would take over the squad. Ricci had recently gotten back to the operating forces after a stint working on Parris Island. While I had spent the last three years training, he had been helping out behind the scenes. I thought it was commendable of Ricci to recognize that he was a little rusty and pass the command to me.

That night, I lay on my cot and smoked a cigarette to keep the fleas away. Now that I was a squad leader, Marines would be depending on me to get them out of here.

I thought about Alexander fighting in this area two thousand years before, and what he would do. I thought about Tuttle and

Skewes too, and all that they had taught me. My imagined mentor and my real mentors—I wanted to live up to their examples.

Alexander led every charge from the front, so I decided I would, too, and vowed to walk point on every patrol. Typically, a squad leader is in the middle of the patrol, but I didn't want to ask my Marines to do anything, or go anywhere, that I wouldn't. From Tuttle, I took the importance of intelligent planning; he always worked to outsmart the opposition. And Skewes instilled aggression in me; when it was time to fight, we would hit them as hard and as fast as possible.

I made a mental note to let Berg and Hannibal know they would be my team leaders. Hannibal was a private and Berg was a lance corporal, so technically I should have put Ricci in charge of a fireteam since he was a sergeant. But I didn't care about that. Berg and Hannibal were skilled at patrolling and using the radio. More importantly, they commanded respect from the other guys from Echo and were brave as hell. They would be perfect for what I wanted to do.

————

A few days later, I was standing under the tower with sweat pouring down my back when Echo Mobile rolled up. They dropped off fuel, food, water, mail, and gossip. We were completely cut off from any outside news. Unless we heard it on the radio, we didn't have a clue what was happening. There was no Internet, no phones, nothing. Echo Mobile was our primary source of news.

Whenever they dropped off mail, there was a rush to see who had gotten a letter or package. Some guys got mail right away, they clearly coordinated to have extra supplies sent over. I didn't, and neither did Berg or Hannibal, but the rest of my guys all got something from home.

Once the mail was passed out, we formed a line to unload cases of water, MREs, and ammo. I grabbed a box from a Marine on the back of a seven-ton, and passed it down the line. It felt safe having a bunch of armored trucks with machine guns in the intersection, like reinforcements had arrived. As we passed the boxes along, Sergeant Demmingware, the bald, muscled leader of Echo Mobile, chatted with Compton.

"Did you guys hear about Carbajal?" Demmingware asked.

"Corporal Carbajal? Nah, what happened?"

"Very first patrol, got zipped in the armpit, sucking chest wound."

"Holy shit. Is he okay?" Compton asked, as he crossed his arms over his chest.

"Listen to this," Demmingware said, leaning in. "This motherfucker sees something and points at it. *Crack*—takes a round right in the side. He acts like it's nothing, directs the squad to move on them, and treats himself. And while they're pushing through, he calls his own medevac! By the time they clear the objective, he's like 'Later, guys' and walks onto the chopper by himself." Demmingware grinned and shook his head. "Fucking badass, man."

"Jesus, what a wildman. You hear anything about him recovering?" Compton asked.

"Nah, nothing yet. Last we heard, he should be alright."

"Was he the first guy in Echo to get hit?"

"Yeah. A couple of close calls judging by the radio traffic, though."

"Yeah, I hear that." Compton turned to our bucket brigade. "Y'all almost done? The guys gotta keep moving."

We finished unloading, and Echo Mobile rumbled away to the west, down Route Joanne, to Typhoons Three and Five, two other Echo patrol bases down the road from us. And just like that, we were alone again.

———

We settled into a routine. Post shifts were changed to six hours, and every third day a shift would be eight hours, to keep our routine changing. Couldn't let the Taliban know our schedule. When we weren't standing post, we had a patrol shift and a sleep shift. The eighteen-hour cycle took over everything. Some days we got twelve hours to sleep; some days we stood post for twelve hours. Post and the heat and the fleas were inescapable.

One morning I woke up, and Compton's squad was buzzing. I lay in my cot and watched them high-fiving and smiling. They had been out on patrol that morning and got into a firefight. I got dressed and watched them eat breakfast and drink coffee. They were full of smiles and laughter. I found Compton in the MRAP.

"Hey, man!" I said. "Glad you made it back." I punched his shoulder.

He smiled broadly and thumped a tin of Skoal with his index finger. "Thanks, man. It was wild!" he drawled. He opened the tin and took out a huge pinch of tobacco. I wanted to start peppering him with questions, but figured I shouldn't push it.

Mott was leaning against the MRAP door, a steaming canteen cup of coffee in his hand. "I'm just glad you guys made it back," Mott said gravely. His eyes were brimming with concern. He had been in Afghanistan before, but he never talked about it.

"Yeah, man, we're good. They're good guys, knew what to do." Compton leaned his head out and glanced around. "Some of 'em needed a li'l kick in the ass, but I think they were just surprised." I nodded. I bet it was surprising.

Compton spat in a water bottle. "Craziest thing, man, we were in a cotton field. You know how knotted that all is?"

"Yeah, it sucks," I said.

"I know, right? Well, we're walking along the edge of this cotton field, and *bang*," he clapped his hands together, "we start taking fire from the north across the field." I glanced at Mott. He was staring at the ground as he listened.

"Behind us was that wall on the compound up there, so we didn't have any real cover. So I took a knee and started scanning, and man," he paused to spit, "I'm looking across the field and the cotton balls are getting cut off like this." He held up his index fingers and looked into my eyes. "*Zip*," he said and dropped a finger into his fist. "*Zip*," and he dropped another finger. "It was wild."

I turned away as he continued the story, pointing out on the map where they were, how they maneuvered, things they'll do differently next time. It was helpful information, and it was exciting knowing that there were Taliban in the area, but I could feel the envy curdling in my belly. I wanted to fight, to be the squad that gets in firefights, beats back the Taliban, and comes home for a triumphant breakfast. I wanted to stand tall in a field of fire. I wanted it, and I was jealous that Compton did it first.

13

SEPTEMBER 2010

When Alexander and his army got to Persepolis in 330 BCE, they looted the city for days. His men were war-weary and wanted to exact revenge for the last four years of fighting and the repeated Persian incursions into Greece.

At one point during the two months the Macedonians stayed there, the palace to Xerxes burned down. It's unclear whether it was deliberately set as revenge for Xerxes' burning of the Athenian Acropolis 150 years earlier, or if it was a drunken party that had gotten out of hand. By this point, Alexander's drinking was becoming a problem that would continue to haunt the rest of his expedition.

"Echo Main, Echo Main, this is Badger. Over."

"Badger, this is Echo Main."

"Hey, Echo Main, we're talking some sporadic fire from the northeast. It's mostly small arms fire. Over."

"Roger, Badger. Do you have a direction and distance? Over."

"Standby to copy."

"Standing by."

I was sitting in the MRAP with Blackwood. We could hear the crackle of gunfire from Badger, an observation post a few kilometers to our north. It was a small outpost on Elephant, full of Afghan police and a handful of Marines.

"Echo Main, Badger."

"Go for Echo Main."

"Hey, that fire is picking up. I've got that direction and distance here. Shit."

The radio went silent. We could hear the staccato firing pick up. It was more than sporadic fire now.

"Echo Main, this is Badger. Over!" the Marine was shouting into the handset.

"This is Echo Main."

"Roger. We're getting hammered here. The police are saying there are RPGs across the street." I glanced at Blackwood. He lit a cigarette.

"Copy that, Badger. We're looking into getting some air assets transferred to you. Do you have a direction and distance for us?"

"It's across the fucking street!" It was getting hard to hear the Marine on the radio; the firing was too loud.

"Solid copy, Badger. We'll let you know when you have air on station."

"Roger. Badger out."

I bummed a cigarette from Blackwood. We smoked in silence and listened to the firing.

"Hey, COC, this is north post," Demorrow came over the walkie-talkie. COC was the call sign for the guys sitting in the MRAP all day.

"Go ahead, north post."

"What's all that firing?"

"Badger's getting hit hard."

"Damn. Tango, north out."

The gunfire rose and fell in waves. Blackwood and I lit fresh cigarettes with the embers of our last ones.

"Echo Main, this is Badger!" I could hear shouting in the background, along with the gunfire.

"Badger, Main."

"Standby for casevac nine-line." I closed my eyes, rubbed my forehead, and listened to the guys at Badger call in a helicopter to evacuate a Marine that had been shot.

———

To make things easier, Compton, Blackwood, and I divided up our area. Compton took the north and east, Blackwood took the west, and I took the south. Every north–south road was named after an animal. We were on Route Elephant, to our east was Donkey, and to our west was Fox. There were only two roads in northern Marjah without a patrol base on them: Fox and Donkey. The Taliban had freedom of movement on the roads around us. To help shut that down, we decided that our patrols needed to touch on the surrounding roads every day. It wasn't much, but it was something.

It was better having a set area to operate in. I started to meet people in my area. There was a boy with autism right down the road from us. He always came out and said hello. In the bazaar or "*souk*" to our south, there were dozens of children. We would bring candy down and give it to the kids. Little girls in red and gold clothes hid shyly behind their fathers. Boys in tan and beige wore skull caps, similar to yarmulkes. Smiling old men smoked cigarettes, and one very old woman would always hold my hand.

We would wave and say hello. "*Sengay! Salam!*" Pashtuns are famous for their hospitality.

We patrolled through cotton fields, cornfields, and marijuana fields, over canals, across small trees turned into bridges, over tires stuck in the mud, and down through the muck. We skirted tall mud walls and short waist-high courtyard walls, under poplar trees and across dusty ratlines. But we didn't patrol down the roads; there were too many IEDs. Better to change the route every time—Tuttle taught me that.

. . .

A compound a kilometer or so directly south of us had a tall building, maybe fifteen feet high. On the outside of the house, under a broad tree, we came across a small cook fire. Chickens were clucking around a small pile of sticks next to the fire. On the wall were charcoal drawings of stick figures. Helicopters with stickmen inside. Lines of stick figures with guns. An airplane. Dead people.

The drawings were rough, and based on their height, I guessed a seven- or eight-year-old had drawn them. When I was that age, I drew forests, animals, and my family. These kids drew planes, guns, and dead people.

The patrol kept going. We had places to be, but we nicknamed it "the helicopter house". I never saw any kids playing there.

We found a suspicious burlap bag on a path. There was something inside, but it was impossible to tell what it was from the folds in the fabric. Maybe it was an IED, or maybe it was just a bag. I tried inspecting it through my rifle scope, but it didn't help. None of the locals had any idea what it was, either.

I called Compton in the MRAP to ask how long it would take to get the explosive ordnance team out to investigate.

"They're saying at least four hours," was Compton's reply. I rubbed my sweaty face with my left hand. It was almost a hundred degrees, and we didn't have the water to wait and watch this thing for four hours.

As I was trying to think of a way to get a water resupply, I heard Hannibal say, "Oh fuck this," and he walked up to the burlap sack. "I ain't waiting four damn hours." With that, he wound his leg back and kicked the pile of fabric.

I cringed and waited for a blast, but nothing happened. When I glanced back up, Hannibal was picking up the sack and shaking it.

"See? Nothing in it. Just a dumb bag on the ground," he said, as he tossed it off to the side of the trail. "Let's get out of here. It's too hot out."

―――――

My birthday is in late August. We had been in country for a few weeks, and outside of Compton's squad, none of us had been in a firefight. We could hear battles raging all around us, and heard regular casualty evac requests on the radio. It seemed like there was a war everywhere except for Aries II.

But I had a plan. I drew up the patrol and sat down with the squad. It was early, before 5:00 a.m. They gathered around, bleary-eyed, canteen cups of coffee in hand.

"Y'all know what today is?" I asked. No one said anything. Demorrow raised his hand. I nodded at him.

"The day we cancel our patrol and sleep instead?" he asked, with a crooked grin.

"Sorry, Demorrow, not today. Today's my birthday."

"Oh shit, happy birthday," Berg said enthusiastically.

"Uh, thanks, man." I was surprised by his excitement. "Here's the thing. I haven't gotten any mail yet this deployment, so I didn't get any presents." I glanced away from Berg and Hannibal. I knew they hadn't gotten any mail either, but they never said anything about it.

"But I do want something for my birthday." I made eye contact with everyone in the squad, and smiled. "I want to ambush some goddamn Taliban."

"Oo-rah!" Ricci yelled, pumping his short arms in the air.

"Oh hell, yes," Hannibal said.

It had been a tough few weeks. Everyone was tired, covered in flea bites, and sick of constantly sweating. I was glad to see Marines getting excited about going on patrol instead of bitching and moaning.

Their enthusiasm rubbed off on me. I wanted to get into a firefight for a change too. The past three years were full of songs about blood making the grass grow, people yelling "kill," shooting, fighting, and training. We were all frustrated that we were here and nothing was happening.

Everyone was fired up as they suited up for the patrol. Waves of seductive power washed over me as I took the scene in: the squad's hard eyes looking back at me, the collection of rifles and rockets and grenades piled around, the barbed wire and sandbag fortifications. Four years ago, I had been a dishwasher and a failing college student. Now I was leading a squad of US Marines.

I spread the map out on the ground.

"We're going to set up an ambush in this cornfield here," I pointed at a spot on the map. "The contractors have been getting hit from a little south of here. So when the Taliban show up, we'll roll out of the cornfield guns blazing." I detailed our positions, making sure everyone knew where the machine gun would be. After that, we finished suiting up and rolled out.

Using the trees and tall fields of cotton as cover, we patrolled south, and slunk into the cornfield shortly before the sun came up. I crouched down and duckwalked through the rows, making sure everyone was in place. After making sure Berg and Hannibal knew to check on their guys periodically, I took my spot. I was seven or eight rows deep into the corn. Deep enough that I could make out people on the other side, but not well. Then the waiting began.

The first hour was exhilarating. I rubbed my thumb on the safety, scanning people's faces to try and divine if they saw anyone unusual in the morning traffic. But everything seemed normal. I watched a man pick his nose and flick his booger away. I saw a woman in her black burqa walking with her children. I saw donkey carts, motorcycles, and wheelbarrows go past. It seemed like a typical day.

The second hour, I started to get distracted and my mind began to wander. Random thoughts and daydreams took over my line of sight. To shake myself out of it, I duckwalked down the line, checking on everyone. They were awake, but the sense of boredom was extreme. I caught Gross making a mud castle, piling dirt up, and shaping it into tiers. I reminded them that the Taliban usually hit in the mornings, so they needed to stay frosty.

By the fourth hour, the sun was unbearable. The heat radiated out of the corn. The water running between the rows felt like bathwater, and my canteens were running out. The Taliban hit the contractors almost every day, but it seemed like we had picked one of their off days. Either that or they knew we were there. It was impossible to say.

I passed the word down to Berg and Hannibal, "Get ready to go. We're heading home." If we weren't going to ambush the Taliban today, we could at least do a little show of force.

Once the squad was ready, my team and I burst through the corn simultaneously. The effect was immediate. Traffic stopped and people stared. A kid ran behind his mom. They had no idea we were in the cornfield.

That's right, I thought. *Let them pass the word. We're everywhere.* We set up security, and the rest of the squad came trudging out of the corn. As we headed home, I felt like we had accomplished something. Even if we didn't succeed in the primary mission, certainly the Taliban would get the message that we were around, waiting for them.

The next morning, I was shaving when I heard the contractors getting attacked. The south post said it was coming from where we set up the day before. The Taliban weren't fazed at all.

———

Life started to settle into a rhythm at Aries II. We got up, patrolled, stood post, and went to sleep, in that order. It wasn't great, but it worked well enough.

I learned all the Echo guys' names, and they learned everyone's from my little crew. Generally, everyone got along. Ricci was a little standoffish, but he was like that with everyone. I hung out with Compton or Blackwood in the MRAP anytime I wasn't sleeping or patrolling. There wasn't anything else to do.

The rest of the Marines and Doc tended to hangout on the other side of the canal, in the other building, mostly to stay away from us squad leaders and Mott. Over there they played poker on stacked ammo boxes and cooked local chickens over propane cookers they bought at the *souk*.

Compton's right-hand man, a thick, mustachioed guy named Weeks, always had home-cooked food on hand. He cooked chicken and okra, and fancy rice dishes with food he bought from the locals. He'd offer you a chicken leg in his smooth Southern accent and was a great chef given his lack of supplies.

Plant was Compton's machine gunner. He had a buzzed head and enough constant humming energy that he seemed like the Energizer bunny. Plant was small for a machine gunner, but he exuded love for the heavy black gun.

Berg was always working out. He'd take off his shirt, displaying his dozens of tattoos, run his fingers through his mohawk, and crank out pull-ups from a homemade pull-up bar.

Hannibal always seemed to be hanging out. Everyone liked Hannibal; he was loud, funny, and personable. He talked to me a lot about his daughter back home.

A few days later, I was trying to sleep through the afternoon. A rotating schedule is brutal when your sleep shift falls during the hottest part of the day. I would lie in a puddle on my cot with flea collars on my wrists and ankles, and try to sleep. Waking up in the ninety-degree weather felt like waking up with a fever: sweaty, thirsty, and disoriented.

That afternoon, I woke up to gunfire. The steady *chunk-chunk-chunk-chunk* of machine gun fire and the intermittent *crack-crack* of rifles. It sounded like it was right outside. As I sat up in my cot, my pulse skyrocketed. I couldn't tell what was happening. I put my glasses on and saw Mott run past, rifle up looking west down Route Joanne.

Shit. I tossed on my flak and shoved my feet into my boots not stopping to tie them. I grabbed my helmet and ran out of the hooch over to Mott.

"What's going on?" I yelled.

He kept his eyes down the street, his jaw muscles working up and down. "Compton's guys got in it. Not sure what's happening."

I ran back to our concertina wire gate and peered down the street. I couldn't see anything. I waved up at the tower post.

"Hey! I'm going to run to the west truck. Don't fucking shoot me!" The Marine in the tower waved me on from behind his machine gun. I took off sprinting down the street, past our hooch, past the wire, and up to the empty MRAP. I slammed into the back and wrenched the door open. It was full of old trash from when it was a post. I kicked the pop tart wrappers and magazines aside as I climbed up to the turret. Cautiously, with my rifle poking out, I scanned around.

Some of Compton's guys were in a dusty ditch on the side of the road. Plant was behind the machine gun, rocking and rolling. I followed his tracers with my eyes. The stream of red was pouring into the corner of a building about a hundred yards to their south. Even with my higher position, I couldn't see much. There were too many trees. I put my rifle scope up to my eye and scanned, but I couldn't ID any targets. Standing in the turret, I swept my rifle back and forth, watching, hoping I'd see a Taliban gunner.

The fire started to slow down. Plant tossed a new ammo belt on the machine gun in the lull. As I continued to scan around, I wished I'd brought a walkie-talkie so I could coordinate with them. As the firing slowed and ended, they started to push south. I watched as their teams bounded through the fields. There wasn't much cover, save for a shallow canal running between the fields. The squad quickly moved out of sight. I climbed down from the turret and headed back to the operations MRAP.

When I opened the door, Blackwood laughed at me. "Oh, hey there, killer."

I glanced down at myself. I was in green shorts and a T-shirt, untied boots, and my flak jacket. The adrenaline was starting to wear off, and I started cracking up. It reminded me of the fire extinguisher in Iraq. I couldn't stop laughing.

"Are Compton's guys okay?" I asked through the laughter.

"Yeah, they're good. Sweeping the area now," Blackwood answered. I sat down in all my ridiculousness and listened to the squad coordinating their search.

"Fuckin' Compton, hogging all the action," Blackwood said. I hadn't even thought about it, but he was right. Two firefights for Compton's squad; none for Blackwood and me. That made me stop laughing. I thought about coming home from Iraq without having seen combat, and started to worry that would happen again.

"I'm going back to bed," I said. As I walked back to my rack, I saw Mott standing by the concertina wire staring intently down Route Joanne. His jaw muscles were still working.

———

I knelt at the edge of a mud wall and scanned the area through my night vision goggles. Relaxing my grip, I glanced around, looking for the signal. The Taliban almost never attacked at night, and ambushing patrols at night was unheard of. We had night vision; we could see everything they couldn't. We even had lasers mounted to our rifles that only we could see, lasers that we could use to direct helicopters and drones onto targets in the darkness. So the Taliban went to bed at night.

Across the field and on the other side of Route Fox, I saw the signal: three quick flashes of infrared light. I flashed twice, and when one flash came back, I turned and signaled to my guys.

"They're here," I said in a loud whisper. "Let's go." With that, I stood up and started walking across the field towards the patrol from nearby Typhoon Five. They had brought a pair of Female Engagement Team (FET) members, for us to pick up.

All the women in Marjah wore head-to-toe burqas with their faces covered. Only a thin slit let them see, and other than that they were completely covered. Men from different households were forbidden from speaking to women, so there was a whole fifty percent of the population we were unable to engage with. The FETs could go into homes and see if the women needed anything, and try to win some hearts and minds that I, as a man, couldn't. It was a great idea.

When I met up with the other squad leader from Typhoon Five, he had a pair of female Marines with him: two brunette corporals, standing comfortably next to the squad leader with all their gear. They introduced themselves. The shorter one was Cantu, and the taller one was Tracey. I brought them back to my squad, and we set off into the night, back to Aries II.

We had no phones, no Internet, no news. Our entire world shrunk down to Aries II. There were no parents, no spouses, no bills, no errands to run. It was simple. We stood post, we patrolled, and we slept. Our life revolved around what we could see, what we could hear on the radio, and what people in convoys told us. Echo Mobile let us know what was going on at the patrol bases. Random patrols that stopped through brought news from the far corners of Marjah, but no further. There was never any news from outside a twenty-mile radius. That was our world: Elephant and Joanne, with trips out to Fox or Donkey. We heard rumors. Some locals told us that the Taliban had kidnapped a man and dragged him to death behind their motorcycles out in the desert.

Sometimes we got some insight from the radio. A patrol called in an IED, and they needed the bomb team to dismantle it. Other patrols got into firefights. We usually heard about those because the mortar radio sprang into action. We'd spin it up and wait. Even if they didn't ask for help, I would write down their location and where the fire was coming from to get ready. That way help would be there, should they ask. Flying steel and shrapnel and high explosives were always just a call away in Marjah.

Sometimes we'd hear the casualty evac calls. If it was a civilian, an Afghan soldier, or a Taliban fighter, they made a note of it. If it was an American, they used their battletag. A battletag is your initials, your blood type, and the last four of your social security number. We'd listen to the far-off gunfire, the explosions, the ebb and flow of a gun battle, rising and falling with the tempo of the fight. Then it would come, sometimes in the middle, sometimes after it was over—the nine-line, that request to save one of our brothers' lives. We would cram in the MRAP and listen for the battletag. "JCB? Who's that?" someone asked. Based on where the fire was coming from, we could narrow down the possibilities. "The east? Isn't that first platoon? JCB? Has to be Bishop. Shit." Sometimes we knew instantly who it was. Sometimes no one knew. Maybe it was an attachment? Maybe it was someone no one ever really noticed. We'd try and divine meaning from the urgency of the call. An urgent evac was what we wanted; it meant they were breathing. A routine evac was the worst. It meant they were dead, come pick him up when you can. Save someone else first if there's a backlog.

We had been in Marjah for over a month, but outside of Compton's two firefights, nothing much had happened at Aries II. Then, out of nowhere, Blackwood's squad got into a short, intense firefight. They were near the intersection of Joanne and Fox, an area with a handful of shops that the Taliban was known to hang out at.

After they got back and debriefed, I asked Blackwood how it was and what happened. He chuckled and lit another cigarette before looking around to make sure we were alone.

"I took both of the FETs for this patrol," he said with a grin, "and when we got to the market I told everyone there, 'Look, since the Taliban won't come out and fight us, we brought some women from America to fight them.' Then we just hung out for a little while, and headed home. We got hit maybe ten minutes later." He took a deep drag on his cigarette and leaned back in his seat. Blackwood the

Brave, going out and taunting the Taliban until they would come out and fight him.

Every night, or morning, or afternoon, before I went to bed, I pulled out a pack of baby wipes and wiped down my face, armpits, and groin. I washed my hands and tried to scrub the dirt off my neck. It wasn't much, but it was something. It was impossible to keep clean. Moondust blew in the wind, we waded through mud and canals every day, and I sweat through my clothes by ten every morning.

One unusually hot day, I was in the other hooch planning a patrol with Berg. We were looking over the map trying to think of a new route to take when Jacobs walked past. Jacobs was Blackwood's number two, a bespectackled southerner who was tight with Hannibal. He was naked except for some shorts and flip-flops, a towel in one hand and his rifle in the other.

"Where the hell are you going?" I asked.

He stopped and cocked his head to the side. "Uh, to the canal?" he said.

"The canal?"

"Yeah, I'm going to take a bath."

"Oh."

"Is there a problem?" he asked.

I shook my head. "Nah, you're good, man. Just don't let a convoy see you," I said.

Jacobs laughed. "Fuck a convoy, I don't want Sergeant Mott to see me." He walked out of the wire, his flip-flops clapping behind him. Mott was always getting on the Marines for little things like not shaving every morning. He especially picked on Berg. I didn't care if Berg ever shaved again; he was an incredible grunt and leader, that was all that mattered to me.

But I hadn't thought of taking a bath in the canal. The water was filthy. I watched a dead dog float by one day, its legs poking up out of the water. A dead donkey was rotting in an eddy further downstream. Still, the water was cold, and at least it was moving.

Berg told me that everyone on that side of the road had been taking baths. They never told us because they thought they would get in trouble.

I gazed at the soft grass lining the banks. The water was swift and sheltered. I decided I would take a bath that night after our patrol.

We got back a little after dinner time. I debriefed the squad and told them to grab some food. I spent an appropriate amount of time hanging out in the MRAP talking to Mott before I made my move. I couldn't just walk across the street with a towel. So I put on my helmet and tucked a towel inside in my flak jacket before putting it on. I tossed a bar of soap in my cargo pocket. I told Mott I was going to the other side to borrow Berg's iPod. Mott was smoking a cigarette and watching the sun go down. He waved me off.

Heading past the tower, I crossed the small wooden bridge. Dusk was the perfect time for a bath. The air was still warm. I grabbed Chris, one of the Afghan National Army (ANA) soldiers, and told him I was going into the canal, "so don't shoot me."

He took a drag of his spliff, and said, "Cool."

I found a spot right near the bridge and started undressing. I made sure to put my gear a ways from the edge. If my rifle fell in, I would be fucked. I undressed quickly and slid into the water. It was frigid. My skin broke out in goose bumps, but the escape from the heat felt incredible. I dunked my head under the water and shook my hair like a dog. It felt amazing. I ran the bar of soap over my face and neck and squatted down in the water to rinse off. When I opened my eyes, I felt like a warrior. I was off on an adventure overseas, my rifle lying in the tall grass next to me. Afghan sheepherders were walking down the street. There were massive military vehicles and machine guns up and down the road. It finally sunk in. *This is it. I'm in a war. And on the front lines.* So what if I hadn't been in a firefight? We were roughing it in one of the most remote and dangerous areas of the globe. Expeditionary Marines. *Oo-rah. Kill, kill, kill.*

I started washing the rest of my body, my skin growing numb in the cold rushing water. But, before I got too far, I saw headlights bouncing in the distance. The locals didn't drive at night, so it must be a convoy. *Oh fuck*, I thought as I grabbed fistfuls of grass and hoisted myself out of the water.

"Convoy coming from the north!" the Marine in the tower yelled.

Shit, shit, shit, I thought as I raced to put my clothes and gear back on. My dirty clothes clung to my wet limbs and back. The trucks were getting closer, their headlights about to hit me at any second. Grabbing my flak and rifle, I ran to the other hooch, hoping that no one in the convoy saw a half-dressed Marine without his protective gear running around outside the wire.

Sliding down behind the wall of sandbags like a baseball player, I lay there and listened to the trucks rumble past. My clothes were wet and freshly plastered with moondust, which quickly turned to a light sheen of mud. I was dirtier than when I started, but I felt refreshed. Sometimes you have to dodge the enemy; sometimes you have to dodge the higher-ups.

———

One afternoon I was standing under the tower, instead of in the MRAP, during my squad's post shift. The ANA and police were slacking off in the heat. Between the weather and their Ramadan fast, they were wiped out by the afternoon. I was there to make sure they weren't letting cars go past without searching them.

Mott came out to join me. The two of us stood under the tower and watched the police work. They were all different, young and old, Pashtuns and Hazaras, Uzbeks and Tajiks—a little slice of Afghanistan in a blue uniform. Some of them didn't get high during Ramadan, which was a pleasant surprise.

In the distance, there was a short burst of fire. I turned to Mott.

"That sounded pretty close," I said.

"Yeah, it did." He squinted as he scanned to our south. "You see anything?"

"Nah," I said. "Yo, Ricci!" I yelled up to the tower. "You see anything?" I could hear him moving around on the wooden planks above us.

"Nope, but I'm lookin'," he said. I picked up my walkie-talkie to radio to the south post when the corner of the tower exploded in a shower of wood chips.

Sawdust and pieces of wood splattered across my face as I ducked down. It took a moment to sink in. *Someone is shooting at us!* Grabbing my rifle, I popped my head up over the sandbags.

Chris, the Afghan soldier, was standing to my left, on the other side of the canal. He had his machine gun at his hip and was firing on full auto as he swept his machine gun side to side. I turned to the south to try and see where the fire was coming from.

Whoomp! There was a heavy crash behind me. Spinning around, I saw Ricci lying in the street, spread out. I felt my stomach sink. *Holy shit, Ricci got shot*, I thought. But as I took a crouched step towards him, he pushed himself up and onto a knee.

"Jesus fucking Christ, are you okay?" I yelled at him. I could see people in the hooch behind him putting their gear on and running over to us. Chris was still firing away.

"Yeah, I'm good," Ricci said, as he ran up to Mott and me. He set his rifle on the sandbags and peered through his scope. After a second, he started popping off rounds. "Down there!" he yelled. "By the tall wall!"

I grabbed my walkie-talkie and radioed it down to the south post. The south post had an enormous .50 caliber in his truck, the biggest machine gun in the Marine Corps. If he saw anything, he could take care of it quickly.

"I'm not seeing anything down there," Hannibal radioed back. Ricci had stopped firing. Mott was still scanning the distance through his scope. I watched Chris dunk his smoking hot barrel into the canal, a hiss of steam rising up from the filthy water.

"Ricci, you see anything?" I asked. I was in the corner of the bunker, my rifle resting on the ledge looking out, the walkie-talkie in my left hand. My legs felt a little rubbery.

"Nah, I don't see him anymore," Ricci said, his eye fixed to his scope.

"I never saw anything," Mott chimed in. He was standing up, looking around. I glanced around, too. Everyone who wasn't on post was suited up and scanning to the south. Blackwood was on a knee near the other hooch. Plant had a machine gun propped up on some sandbags. Compton had shaving cream on his face, his head poking out of the operations MRAP. Chris and the other Afghan soldiers were standing out in the street, their hands raised as they taunted the shooter in Pashto.

I radioed to the posts. "Hey, guys, looks like our shooter is gone. Keep an eye out for anything unusual. We can always punch a patrol to check something out. Break." I unkeyed the walkie-talkie, taking a second to figure out what I wanted to say.

"Hannibal, nice work holding your fire. If you don't have an ID on a target, don't open up. Good work following the rules of engagement, everyone. COC out."

I sat down on a folding metal chair in the bunker and lit a cigarette. There it was. I was in a firefight, albeit the world's shortest firefight. I took a drag and exhaled. Everyone had done well; no one had panicked. The whole patrol base turned up to fight back. The Afghan soldiers were wild, but that was probably better than if they cowered in fear. As I smoked my cigarette, I felt content. No one had gotten hurt, and everyone had done well; what more could I ask for?

———

Ramadan ran until early September that year. We theorized that the Taliban were too hungry to attack us during their fast. That didn't seem to stop other patrols from getting hit, but it was an acceptable rationalization for us.

Occasionally, we would hear a single shot ring out, but those were impossible to place. We couldn't tell how far away it was, and if it was aimed at us. It all seemed random. At first, the Marines on post would call it in, and try to coordinate to find the shooter, but we never did. After a while, we ignored it. No impact, no idea.

One day I was in the MRAP with Mott while my squad stood post. A shot rang out. Mott and I paused mid-conversation, waiting for a post to call something in. Silence. I grabbed the walkie-talkie.

"Anyone see anything?" I asked. Four versions of "No", "Nah," and "Negative" came back. Typical. Mott and I started chatting again. He was telling me stories about being stationed in Hawaii, when one of the Afghan soldiers walked up to the open back door of the MRAP.

The front of his chest was covered in blood, running from his shoulder down to his belt. It was dark and shiny against the dull browns and greens of his uniform. Mott and I stared at him in shock.

"Um," he said. "Uhh, doctor." He pointed at his chest. Besides the blood running down him, he seemed perfectly fine. His voice was level, and he was acting like he had a question.

"Holy fuck!" Mott yelled. "Corpsman! Corpsman, up!" Mott ran to find the Medkit.

I grabbed the walkie-talkie. "Hey, if you have eyes on Doc, send him over immediately. One of the ANA got hit."

Mott came rushing back with the bulky Medkit, and snapped on some blue latex gloves. He helped the soldier take off his uniform jacket. I was shocked at how calm this guy was. He seemed sheepish that he was asking for help.

Doc Fenner, our Navy corpsman who was built like Hulk Hogan, came running in. "What's going on?" he asked.

"Gunshot wound to the chest," Mott said, as he ripped open a package of gauze. He pushed the white gauze against the soldier's chest, over the tight red hole in his brown shirt. Weeks came jogging up, and snapped on a pair of blue latex gloves as well.

"Hey, man, let's have you sit down first," Doc said. He pantomimed sitting on the MRAP steps. The soldier smiled, sat down, and clasped his hands together. If it weren't for all the blood, you would have never known this guy was hurt.

I pulled out a laminated casevac nine-line card and started filling out the information: one ANA, GSW to the chest, urgent evac.

"Doc, is it a sucking chest wound?" I asked. Had his lungs been punctured?

"Nope, no bubbles. He's one lucky dude," Doc said. He had used his scissors to cut off the ANA's shirt and was taping a wad of gauze to his chest. I could see the exit hole in the ANA's back. It seemed like a clean through and through. Lucky guy.

I called Echo Main and radioed up the casevac. We coordinated a helo landing zone across the street, to the south of the other hooch, in an open field. Mott and a few guys headed over with the Afghan solider and set up security. When the helo was inbound, they popped a smoke grenade. As the green smoke blew across the empty field, a Blackhawk helicopter came thundering over us, barely clearing the treetops. It settled down in the field, blowing the smoke and dust everywhere. Mott and the other guys helped the shirtless Afghan solider on to the helo, who gave a thumbs-up as he climbed aboard.

As the Blackhawk took off, I saw an Apache attack helicopter flying security overhead. The two helicopters raced off into the distance. All in all, from call to pick up, it took fifteen, maybe twenty minutes.

Mott came back to the MRAP and dropped his flak. He had blood on his shirt and down his arms. He tried to light a cigarette, but his hands wouldn't stop shaking. I held out my lighter for him. He took a deep drag and rubbed his forehead.

"Another day, another man's blood on my hands," he said. I rolled my eyes. He sat on a case of water and smoked his cigarette. I wondered if I got hit like that how I would take it.

14

OCTOBER 2010

Alexander continued to head east, chasing Darius across Iran, but as Alexander drew close, Bessus killed Darius and left his body in a cart. When the Macedonian army found Darius, Alexander was beside himself that he hadn't been the one to capture him.

With Darius dead, Bessus declared himself the King of Asia, and set off east, deeper into the mountains. Alexander was enraged at Bessus, but before he set off in pursuit, he sent Darius' body back to Persepolis for a royal burial.

Around this time, Alexander had begun to incorporate Persian princes and cavalry into his army. He had a vision of blending his Greek and Persian troops together, to help solidify his control over both the armies and territory. The Persians appreciated being treated with respect after being conquered, but the Greeks were suspicious and envious.

F all was coming to Marjah. The heat had started to abate, and the mornings even had a hint of a chill. Winter was a ways off, but October was better than August in southern Afghanistan. The cornfields were turning yellow, and the cotton bolls were a beautiful white against their dark green leaves.

We patrolled, stood post, and slept when we could. Sleeping during the day got easier as the flea situation got better. But my clothes got dirtier and looser. My pants were getting so baggy I had to tie my belt down to hold them up. One night, alone under the red lights in the MRAP, I inspected my hands. Yellow nicotine spots stained my fingers. I was smoking at least a pack a day now. There was always dirt under my fingernails. I scraped it out with a pocket knife every day, but it always came back, and the skin was starting to pull away from my nails.

Echo Mobile dropped off an interpreter, or "terp," for us. It had been difficult trying to engage with the locals through hand gestures and charades, but now we would be able to speak to them. Our terp was nicknamed Kobe, because he looked a little like Kobe Bryant. He had brown skin, short hair, and soft hazel eyes. When you talked to him, the first thing you noticed was how gentle he was. He was soft-spoken and moved with a slow grace.

On a beautiful fall morning, we were out patrolling along Route Donkey when we came across a wedding. I saw the groom and his family. They were dressed quite spectacularly. Instead of the drab neutral colors that most of the men wore, they were wearing whites and turquoises with gold trim. The father of the groom asked us to leave; he didn't want us to attract the Taliban. I felt a little ashamed and told him we would stay away, but we still did a loop around the wedding, just to be sure they weren't up to anything.

On our way back, we dipped to the south, straddling the edge of our area of operations. I was planning on shooting back up through the center. The farmers were out preparing recently harvested fields.

I wanted to see if they were using banned fertilizer that could be used to make IEDs. As I mentally made a list of farms to swing past, Berg came over the walkie-talkie.

"Hey, Martin, we've got some shady shit going on over here." He was whispering.

I pulled the radio out of my magazine pouch. "What's going on?"

"We're by the helicopter house and two motorcycles pulled up, maybe two hundred yards north of us. They hopped off and took cover by the *souk*. I can't tell if they have weapons." I could hear leaves rustling. It sounded like he was in a field.

"Did they see you?" I asked. This was interesting.

"Negative. What do you want us to do?"

My mind started spinning. There were a few possibilities. It could be completely normal, farmers coming in to help with the harvest. Or they could be Taliban, setting up an ambush for the contractors—it was the right time of day. Or they could be putting in an IED, or setting an ambush for us.

I lifted the walkie-talkie to my mouth. "Berg, hold tight and keep eyes on them. Make sure your guys are hidden."

"Roger that," he whispered.

"Hannibal, I need you to take your team to the ratline north of Berg. There's a tree up there; get the machine gun set up behind it."

"Copy all," Hannibal chimed in.

"I'm going to take my team down the middle. We'll use the corn-field as cover to get closer," I let them know. I picked up the other radio to call it back to Aries II. "Aries II, Aries II, this is Mobile. Over." I could hear my voice bounce as I jogged over the uneven ground.

"Hey, Mobile, we're tracking you on the black gear," Blackwood said. They were listening in on the walkie-talkies. Perfect. I could also use the south post to coordinate fires, if it came to that.

"Roger that. We'll be near buildings thirteen and fifteen in the Lima sector."

"Copy all."

I had Doc, Kobe, and Ricci with me. Keeping my voice down, I called out to them. "You guys catch that? We're going to head north, then push through that cornfield when the machine gun is in place to see if we can tell what these guys are up to." Ricci nodded and swapped out the smoke round in his grenade launcher for an explosive round.

We pushed north, trying to keep a low profile, as we skirted compounds and walls. Thankfully, some of the fields were still up, and they helped give us some concealment.

As my team hit the east side of the cornfield, we paused. I wanted Hannibal's guys set up before we pushed into the field. It would let us get close, but we wouldn't have any cover if anything happened. The machine gun would be our cover if things got crazy.

As we waited for Hannibal, I scanned the area. The fields were empty. No one was cooking outside, and the kids were all inside. The hair rose on the back of my neck.

"Hey, Martin, we're in place," Hannibal whispered. "I don't see anything going on, though."

"I lost them," Berg chimed in, "but the motorcycles are still here. Not sure what they're up to."

"Alright, stay focused, guys. We're pushing into the cornfield." I waved to the rest of my team, and we walked into the corn. It was hard to not make a lot of noise. The corn was dry and rustled with every step. At least the ground was dry, and we moved quickly.

We were about fifty yards into the field when the firing started, deep-throated AKs barking in unison. I took a knee. Glancing around, I could see Ricci, Doc, and Kobe. They were alright. The machine gun started to roar, and I could hear M-16s popping, too.

"Martin, they're shooting at the contractors!" Berg yelled into the walkie-talkie. I could hear his team firing away near him.

"Keep firing! Pin 'em down. We're going to keep moving," I yelled into the radio. I could hear my voice squeak. I hoped it sounded better on the radio than it did in my head. When I stood, I could feel my legs shake. My hands felt wooden. All of a sudden, this felt like a really bad idea. I took a step forward, and then another. I turned to my team. "Follow me!" I yelled. Despite my fear, I felt super corny. We were pushing into a firefight, and I sounded like a boot lieutenant.

I rubbed my thumb on the safety as I crouch-walked through the corn. An ear of corn a row ahead of me exploded. Sticky, wet bits of corn splattered all over my face. I dropped to a knee. My legs started to shake even more. *Keep going*, I urged myself. Skewes had taught me to be aggressive, and this was the time to pull it out.

As we pushed through the corn, I could see the rows ahead start to thin. We were getting close to the end of the field. Berg and Hannibal's teams were still cranking away. Demorrow on the machine gun was doing a hell of a job. I watched some corn stalks ahead of me get cut down, the invisible spray of bullets cutting through the field like a scythe.

I took a knee and waved for my team to join me. Beyond the corn, I could see a compound on my right, a couple of haystacks, and some trees. I turned to my left and saw Berg and his team rush up to the corner of a wall.

Berg stood tall, his backpack swinging behind him as he lifted his rifle and started firing when the wall next to him exploded in a shower of dust and chips. I watched him twitch and jerk to the side. I thought he was hit, but he immediately pulled his rifle back up and started firing again. The guy was a warrior.

To my left, Ricci started firing. "They're going for the motorcycles!" he yelled as he squeezed off a couple of rounds.

As I raised my walkie-talkie, I realized that it had never left my hand. "Hannibal, we're on the edge of the cornfield. Push up to the next compound and see if you can cut off the motorcycles."

"Say again," replied Hannibal. The machine gun was still unloading.

"Move to the next compound!" I yelled. "Cut off the motorcycles! We're in the cornfield!"

"Copy!" Hannibal yelled. The machine gun stopped firing.

"Ricci! Doc! Pick it up. Cover for Hannibal," I yelled. They started firing, a rhythmic *pop-pop-pop*.

I scanned the empty field in front of us. I couldn't see the Taliban or their motorcycles. Some of the haystacks were burning, black smoke soaring into the sky. I scanned the area with my scope. My ears were ringing, and my hands shook. Ricci reloaded and started scanning for more targets.

"Hey, we're in place," Hannibal said over the radio. "I can't see any motorcycles from up here, though."

"Yeah, we don't have anything down here," Berg added.

They were both in strong positions. And we needed to get out of the cornfield.

I called over to my team. "Get ready! We're going to push through to those haystacks. Kobe, you hang back behind us, okay?" Kobe was kneeling in the dirt; he gave me a thumbs-up.

"Berg, Hannibal, stay put. We're going to push to the haystacks." I stood in a crouch and started walking out of the corn, my rifle up and ready.

The shooting had stopped. Everything seemed quiet, but I could hear my heart pounding in my ears. I swept my eyes across the field, my rifle following along. We were completely exposed out here.

Out of the corner of my eye, I saw movement to my right. I swung my rifle over and pulled the buttstock tighter into my shoulder. A man was running towards the haystacks, white buckets in each hand. Two more men followed him, with stacks of burlap over their shoulders. They were yelling to each other.

"Ricci!" I yelled over to him. "Hold security. I'm going to take Doc and Kobe and help them put out the fire." Ricci nodded and jogged over to find some cover. I waved for Doc and Kobe to follow me.

My hands were still shaking and my legs felt wobbly, but I was excited. *We'll help these people put out the fire*, I thought. *We scared off the Taliban, and now we can win some hearts and minds helping these people.* I headed over to the men, cautiously lowering my rifle. I held out my left hand in greeting, my right hand still firmly on the grip of my rifle. They were dipping the burlap sacks into the buckets and slapping them on the fire. Smoke was mixing with steam, and the air smelled of burnt grass and cordite. There were big, black, charred patches on the haystacks.

A man saw us and started walking over to me. He wasn't just

yelling; he was screaming at me, his mouth snarled in anger, but his eyes still bulging with fear.

I turned to Kobe. "What's he saying?"

"He say, 'Why you burn my food'?"

"Food?" I asked.

"Yes, this is, hmm, like grain for bread."

The man was gesturing wildly at the burning stacks. When I took a closer look, it wasn't hay; they were stacks of wheat.

"He say, 'What I will eat this winter? You burn my food.' Something's like that," Kobe said.

My initial confusion was giving way to frustration. I thought I was about to help these people. Now it turned out we lit their food for the winter on fire.

"Ask the man what he wants us to do," I told Kobe. He asked the man. The man waved his arms across his body several times.

"He say you should leave Marjah. You are no good for him." I couldn't blame him.

"Hey, Martin, what's going?" Blackwood came in over the walkie-talkie.

"We're good," I said. "The Taliban is gone, but we lit a farmer's crops on fire. I'm trying to deal with it now. We're at the same position."

"Copy all. Out," Blackwood said.

I stared at Kobe. This wasn't the kind of thing we were trained for. I thought fast and pulled out my notebook.

"Kobe, tell him I'm going to write a letter for him. He can take it to the big base up there," I pointed towards Hansen, "and they will give him money for his crops." We did this in Iraq regularly, so I assumed we could do it here as well.

Kobe paused. "Hmm, I don't think that's a good idea, Mar-ten." I glanced up at him from the letter I was quickly writing with a green map pen.

"If he goes to the big base, the Taliban will kill him," Kobe said, very matter-of-factly. My shoulders dropped a little as I turned to the piles of wheat. The fire was under control, and several children and teenagers were out picking out the wet, blackened stalks, putting them into a pile.

"I'll write him the letter. If he wants to go, he can go, otherwise..." I trailed off.

Kobe shrugged and held his palms up. "Okay, Mar-ten."

I quickly scribbled a note letting the Marines at Hansen know who I was and what had happened. I tried to approximate how much damage had been done so they could compensate him. When I finished writing, I tore the page out of my notebook and walked up to the man with Kobe.

"I'm sorry about what happened to your food," I said. The man glared at me. "Kobe, give him your cell phone number so he can call us if he sees any Taliban. That way we won't accidentally—make sure you tell him that—*accidentally* light his food on fire." While Kobe exchanged his number with the man, I grabbed my radio. "Hannibal, Berg, get ready to move out. We'll keep the patrol going to checkpoint six." I called Blackwood on the green gear, to make sure they were in the loop, too.

As we left the field, I glanced back at the farmer and his family. They weren't crying. They didn't even seem angry. They were all working together, trying to save the wheat as best they could.

When we got back from the patrol, the guys standing post cheered for us. Compton came out of the MRAP clapping.

"Welcome to the club, boys!" he said, as he messed up my hair. I grinned. We did it. We got into a firefight, maneuvered on the enemy, and pushed them back. And none of us got hurt. It was a good day for the Marines of Aries II.

I gathered up my squad and told them to take ten minutes to grab water and some food, and meet back by the storage room for a debrief and after-action review. I pulled my cigarettes out and lit up. It was delicious.

Waves of emotion crashed into each other and over me: relief that none of my guys got hurt, euphoria that I survived, and the feeling that I was finally doing what I had longed to do. I led a squad in quick ambush. It wasn't perfect and I certainly wasn't Alexander-esque, but I was getting there.

I strolled over to the MRAP, my flak jacket still on, and sat down next to Blackwood.

"Hey, buddy, nice work out there," he said.

"Thanks, man." I took a deep drag, and blew it out the open MRAP door. "How'd I sound on the radio?"

Blackwood smiled and set his magazine down. "You want me to tell you that you sounded cool, or do you want the truth?" he laughed. I pushed him away. "Seriously, you sounded pretty freaked out, all high-pitched 'n stuff."

I nodded. "Well, guess I'll have to work on it."

"Berg and Hannibal did too. Don't sweat it, man."

I grabbed the patrol base map that stayed in the MRAP and put a little red dot on it where we made contact that day. Dot number five. Using the ember of my cigarette, I lit another one. Smoking after getting shot at was bliss.

Compton stuck his head into the MRAP. "Hey, something's going on over at the other hooch. Someone is yellin' their head off."

I jumped out of the MRAP and peered across the street. I couldn't see anything, but it sounded like Hannibal was cussing someone out. Compton, Blackwood, and I all looked at each other. Sometimes people needed to settle their differences on their own.

"They'll figure it out," Blackwood said. I agreed. Let 'em fight it out. I went back to my rack, took off my flak, and carefully arranged my sweaty gear at the foot of my cot. Heading to the storage room, I grabbed a water bottle and waited for the squad to show up.

Brown came up first. "Corporal Martin, Hannibal is lightin' into Jacobs over there," he said.

"Why? What's up?"

Brown glanced around and leaned in towards me. "He found a note on his cot," he whispered. "It said, 'Kill yourself, n*****'."

I was floored. Hannibal was the only black man in the patrol base.

He was an incredible grunt. He even volunteered to come on this deployment. Who would do something like that?

"Stay here," I told Brown as I marched over to the MRAP. I told Compton and Blackwood what was up.

"Are you fucking me?" Compton said.

"That's what Brown just told me," I said.

"My God," Blackwood said, as he rubbed his eyes.

"Well, that explains why he's so pissed," Compton said.

"What should we do?" I asked the group.

"Not a whole hell of a lot we can do."

We sat in silence and thought. Could we trade Marines with another platoon? Impossible—that's not how the Marines work. We barely had enough manpower to run the day-to-day operations; we couldn't send someone away without a replacement.

"Let's have him switch racks with someone, stay over here," Compton suggested. It was a trash solution, but I agreed.

When Hannibal made it over for the debrief, he was livid. He paced around in full gear, with a piece of loose-leaf paper balled up in his fist. I could see thick Sharpie letters on it.

"Before we debrief, I want to say one thing up front," I said. "Who wrote the note?" The Marines glanced at each other, but no one said anything. I turned to Hannibal.

"I think it was Jacobs. He's a racist motherfucker," Hannibal said. I didn't doubt Hannibal. He was probably right. I still thought it was odd, he and Jacobs hung out all the time. Why would Jacobs do that?

"Alright, we'll sort shit out with Corporal Blackwood and Jacobs. In the meantime, Hannibal, how would you feel about living on this side of the street? We can find someone to swap racks with you."

Hannibal nodded, but he didn't say anything.

"Okay, we'll get that set up. Now, if I find out any of you wrote the note, or say shit like that—" a murmur of dissent came up from the squad interrupting me.

"Shut—the fuck—up!" I yelled. I stared hard at each member of the squad, letting the silence hang. "If I find out that any of you wrote that note, or I hear any of you saying shit like that, I will beat the ever-loving fuck out of you. Do you understand?"

There were a few quiet "yes corporals" and a lot of looking at the ground. Sometimes it hurt my credibility that these guys didn't train with me before the deployment, that they didn't know me. Other times, like this, it was easier to play a wild card.

Blackwood, Compton, Mott, and I tried to get to the bottom of who wrote the note, but no one would fess up. Everyone had their suspicions, but nothing more than that. The squad helped Hannibal move his gear to my side of the street. Hannibal never mentioned it again, but god knows he must have thought about it every day.

15

OCTOBER 2010

Alexander continued to chase Bessus into Afghanistan. Setting up permanent camps as he went, he founded the cities of Herat and Kandahar, before turning and heading north up the Helmand River Valley. The army chased Bessus from southern Afghanistan, through the north into modern Tajikistan and Uzbekistan.

As they traveled, Alexander fought off some local tribes and made alliances with others. Eventually, in 329 CBE, a tribal leader captured Bessus after his men deserted him. When he was handed over to Alexander's army, Bessus was stripped naked, whipped, tortured, and executed.

With Bessus dead, Alexander was unquestionably the ruler of Persia, and he declared himself the King of Asia.

Often, sitting in the MRAP, out on patrol, or even sleeping in our cots, we'd hear a massive explosion. Sometimes they were close; other times far away. We never saw anything, and weren't hit, but everyone would pause. We'd stand there, not saying anything, waiting for the radio to crackle to life, waiting to hear who was hit, waiting to hear if everyone was okay, waiting to hear those awful words: "Standby for casevac."

Sometimes it was okay; other times it was terrible. But now and again, nothing came over the radio. The silence hung heavier and heavier until someone would call in asking if anyone had eyes on the explosion. In those rare times, no one ever did. The only explanation was that some Taliban blew himself up.

In those seconds after a boom, when I took a deep breath and waited to hear the news, it was easy to find out who my friends were. In the middle of the night, I'd jerk awake to a distant blast, and think, *Shit, is Blackwood on patrol?* Or during the day, when we were waiting for Echo Mobile to swing through, I'd hear something, and worry about Demmingware. Either way, I'd hear an explosion and I'd wait, with bated breath, hoping it wasn't one of my friends who lost a leg, an arm, a life. I'd hope it was someone I didn't care about, someone I never met that died. I put that on their family so I wouldn't have to think about it.

So those times when something blew up, and no one knew what it was, I smiled. I smiled and grinned, and I was happy there was one less Taliban running around, one less person trying to kill me and my friends. I'd smile and grin, but the happiness would catch in my throat because I'd tell myself it was a Taliban, but deep down, I knew it was some poor farmer. Someone who was paid to do it if they were lucky, or told to do it—or else—if they weren't. But I'd smile and pretend and tell myself it was a Taliban, because that's how you deal with bombs going off. I'd hope it wasn't someone I knew or someone that came with me, and I'd hope that maybe it was someone who deserved it, because, in that moment, when I was holding my breath and waiting for the radio to crackle to life, it was all I had.

Not long after the firefight in the cornfield, we were heading in from a patrol. We were a half-mile or so from Aries II when a long burst from an AK rang out. I hit the deck, and paused. I couldn't see anything, and there wasn't any more shooting.

"Anybody see anything?" I asked.

"Were they shooting at us?" Berg yelled back. I glanced at Cantu, but she shrugged. It was strange. I got on a knee and scanned around. The fields were being harvested. In some places, you could only see twenty feet ahead of you; other places, you could see for a hundred, two hundred yards. I didn't see anything suspicious. Hannibal radioed in from the next ratline.

"Hey, Corporal Martin, there's a car that just crashed in the canal up here."

I glanced at Ricci. He seemed as confused as I was. "A car crashed in the canal?" I asked.

"Yeah, it's fucked."

I got to my feet and waved the squad up. We headed west to Hannibal's position. Sure enough, there was a sedan that had crashed into the canal. The windshield was smashed, and the side windows were blown out. An Afghan policeman was flopping around in the canal, and another one was in the car. The one in the car was clearly dead; most of his head was missing. The one in the canal had water mixing with blood coming from his head, turning his face to a wet, pink mess. We helped pull him out of the water, and called Doc over.

"Holy shit, his ear is gone," Doc said. The man was completely disoriented and had trouble standing up. We were still out in the open, and someone had been shooting nearby, so we took the policeman back to our patrol base.

Doc cleaned him up, and bandaged the wound. Most of his right ear was missing. Kobe asked him what happened. He was a high-ranking Afghan policeman. He said was driving from southern Marjah to Camp Hansen when his car was shot at. He turned to look at the shooters and his ear was shot off. The driver was killed instantly and crashed the car into the canal. We were all staring at the policeman, when Blackwood started maniacally laughing.

"This motherfucker is the luckiest person I've ever met in my entire life. He turns to look at something and loses an ear instead of his head. Ho-lee shit!" He doubled over in laughter.

We didn't have anything that could move the car, or have any way to give the guy a ride to Hansen, so we told him to call somebody. He pulled out a cell phone and held it to his remaining ear.

One morning a convoy came through and stopped for a while. There were a few Marines and a ton of Afghan soldiers. The Marines wanted to hang out with some other Americans for a while, so we offered them bottled water and beef jerky and small talk. I mentioned that I was an attachment from Weapons Company.

"Weapons, huh? Sorry to hear about that guy," a thin Marine with tribal tattoos said.

"What guy?" I asked.

"That guy that bit it, German name, Z-something or other."

"Zaehringer?" I could feel the color draining from my face.

"Yeah, that's it," he paused. "Wait, you didn't know?" I opened my mouth, but nothing came out, so I shook my head.

"Ah shit, I'm sorry, man. I figured you would have known. They had the funeral on Hansen a week or two ago. Lotta people came out. Seemed like he was a good guy."

I stared into the distance. "Yeah, I guess he was," I said as I walked away. Pulling out a cigarette, I lit it and took a deep drag. I had to go tell the other guys from the 81s platoon, but I didn't know what to say.

It all seemed wrong. I knew Zaehringer, had known him for years. How could he be dead? Emotions careened through my mind: anger, sadness, rage, confusion. Zaehringer was one of the best Marines in Weapons Company; how was this possible? I thought about drinking beers with him after I got promoted.

Then I got mad. *The Taliban is killing my friends. We should pay them in kind*, I thought. So I stewed and bottled up my anger as a salve to protect myself, to protect myself from the idea that, if they could get Zaehringer, they could get me too.

––––––

We started doing more night patrols. We'd set up on Fox or Elephant or Donkey, and wait in the darkness, watching for anyone sneaking around, anyone with a shovel. Our cammies were dirty and dusty and more of the earth than not, so we could sit down on the side of the road and disappear. I'd lean against a wall and bask in the moonlight and wait.

One night, we patrolled over to Donkey an hour after sunset. I arrayed the squad to watch north and south. Demorrow on the machine gun was facing north, while Ricci with the designated marksman rifle was facing south; both had infrared scopes. It was cool at night now, and the air was refreshing. It felt like fall days in Pennsylvania, with changing leaves, football, and apple cider. I sat on the bank of a canal and waited. The moon crept up in the sky, casting shadows across me. A man came out of his house and stood five feet away from me. He reached inside his robes and started to take a leak. I sat there, motionless, watching him piss into the canal. I was so close to him I could see the lines on the backs of his knuckles. He had no idea I was there. He finished, gave himself a shake, and headed back inside, blissfully unaware of the men that surrounded him.

An hour or two later, Ricci spotted someone digging in the road, about a kilometer away. I walked over to him, the moondust deadening my footsteps in the night. I felt like a ghost, silent and invisible, a terrifying presence for everyone who lived there. Ricci handed me the scope. There he was, some guy digging a hole in the road. The infrared made the dirt coming off the end of his shovel darker than the surrounding ground.

I grabbed the radio and called Aries II. The digger was too far away for us to get to. They called Echo Main and put us in touch with another Echo patrol in the area. We compared positions and figured out an approximate location of the digger. I sat next to Ricci as he watched. The moon crept higher. It was a bright night.

The other patrol came out of the bushes and surrounded the man. Ricci said the man didn't notice them until it was too late. They were probably every bit as dirty and blended in too. Ricci said they just walked up and grabbed him. No shots fired, nothing fancy, only dirty men hiding in the bushes in the moonlight. Once they radioed to us that they had him, we packed up and headed out. I walked through a dry canal and thought about raking leaves.

———

"Hey, Martin, I have eyes on four or five guys with AKs. They're just watching the road," Berg said over the walkie-talkie.

"Where are they?" I asked.

"They're about a hundred yards south of me." Berg was off to my east. We were near the southern edge of my area, by a marijuana field. The tall stalks formed a dark green jungle for us to hide in.

"Nice work, Berg. Hannibal, are you guys set up?"

"We're on our way. Give me three minutes," Hannibal said. I could hear his gear rustling as he sped up.

"Perfect. We'll get on line with you guys. Have Brown open up with the grenade launcher when we're all in place."

I signaled to my team to push south to the ratline at the end of the pot field. We crept up, using the tall, leafy bushes as cover. I pointed two fingers to my eyes and waved to our south: *Find the targets.* Ricci and Doc scanned the area, while Kobe sat back and picked some leaves and twirled them between his fingers. I was on the rightwing of the squad, closest to Elephant, with a tall mud wall to my right. We waited for Hannibal to get set.

"Okay, we're good to go," he radioed in a minute later.

"Roger. Berg, have Brown unload that grenade launcher. Everyone else open up when you hear it."

I listened for the *shunk-shunk-shunk* of the 40mm grenades being fired. I couldn't see past the vegetation on the other side of the ratline, but I had a clear line of sight diagonally if the Taliban pushed east, away from Elephant. The canal and our southern post's .50 caliber would keep them from trying to head west across the road.

I never heard the grenade launcher fire, only the eruption of rifle fire. Ricci and Doc joined in while I scanned the field for any runners. It was perfect. Berg spotted out the Taliban setting up an ambush for the contractors, but we hit the Taliban first. I knelt in the soft soil and listened to my Marines firing. There was only the slightest tremor in my knees. This time we had the advantages, the surprise, the manpower. We were going to get them this time.

"Hannibal, go ahead and advance to the next ratline," I said over the radio. I wanted to cut off their escape to the east. If we moved quickly, we could envelop them, and pin them up against the canal. Alexander would have done the same thing.

Hannibal's team rushed ahead and pushed up about fifty yards. As soon as they were set, I sent Berg's team across. It was working. Hannibal had the machine gun rocking, suppressing the Taliban, keeping them in place so we could advance on them.

When Berg's team headed across the open ratline, we started to get pounded from my right by an enormous gun. I watched a small tree in front of me get shredded, branches falling into the street.

Ricci and Doc dove into the dirt, while I braced myself against the mud wall. I peeked out around the corner. The contractors had a pickup truck with a machine gun mounted in the bed. They were posted up at the end of the ratline, firing at us.

"Berg!" I screamed into the radio. "It's the contractors! Get the fuck down." I grabbed a flare and edged back to the corner of the wall. I prepped it and blindly fired it around the corner towards Elephant and the contractors. I didn't see it fire, but judging by the smoke coming from around the corner, the flare must have hit a tree. It was burning on the ground. *Fuck.*

I radioed to the south post. It was a guy in Compton's squad named Bergman.

"Bergman, wave those fucking contractors off before they kill us!"

"I'm trying!" he replied. "I'm waving the flags, but they haven't noticed."

"Jesus, I'm about to start throwing grenades at them if they don't stop now."

"Okay, hold on," Bergman said.

I waited and watched as another tree in front of me split in half like some invisible lightning hit it.

"Berg, you guys okay out there?" I asked. I could see them pressed into the dirt, hunkered down in a canal.

"Fuck this," Berg answered.

I glanced back across the field. If we didn't do something, the Taliban were going to get away. We needed to act.

"Ricci, get ready to move!" I yelled above the noise of the machine gun. He gave me a thumbs-up. Between Hannibal's team and the contractors, the noise was deafening. I grabbed Kobe.

"Kobe, when Ricci runs, follow him!" He nodded. His hazel eyes were brimming with fear, and his hands were shaking.

"Ricci, go!" I yelled and waved. He and Kobe set off parallel to the ratline. The soil was soft, and with every step their boots sunk into the ground, churning up deep furrows. They were moving impossibly slow.

"Doc, go!" I yelled as they were halfway across the marijuana field. Doc's massive frame rose up from the ground and set off after them, slipping and stumbling in the soil. I watched as the plants next to me started getting ripped to shreds. I threw myself to the ground. The Taliban were back up and firing at us. Berg's team couldn't suppress them anymore. We were now taking fire from the Taliban to the south and the contractors to the west. We were stuck in an L-shaped ambush. Couldn't move forward; couldn't hide.

This had to end. I pulled out a grenade and flipped it upside down, with the spoon against my left hand's fingers. I grabbed the pin, but before I could pull it, the firing to my right stopped. The machine gun went quiet.

With the grenade cradled in my hands, I got on a knee and

peeked around the corner. The contractor's truck was twenty yards away. It was a white pickup. In the back of the truck, their machine gun was pointed skywards. They were gesturing north, towards Aries II. My walkie-talkie crackled to life.

"Corporal Martin, I got them to stop," Bergman said. Relief washed over me. I put the grenade back in my pouch. We still had the Taliban to chase down.

I turned to find my team. They were set up near a small footbridge. I waved over to them, and started running. As soon as I stood up, the Taliban started firing again. The plants to my left were shaking in the hail of bullets, branches and leaves tumbled to the ground next to me.

I couldn't move my feet fast enough. Every step took forever. Then the soil churned up around my feet as I fell down.

I couldn't hear anything as I squirmed in the dirt, trying to get back up.

Move, move, move! my brain screamed as I pushed myself into a crouch. A marijuana stalk fell on top of me. I started running again and closed the distance to the footbridge. Once I got there, I slid down into the small canal. Lying on my back, I stared up at Ricci as he popped off some shots. The brass ejected out of his rifle onto the ground near my head as I lay there sucking wind.

"They're running. They're running!" Hannibal said over the radio.

"Where are they going?" I asked.

"They're headed to that compound by Berg's team."

I sat up and peered across the field. "Berg, set up a cordon on the southwest corner. Hannibal, move in on the northeast corner. We'll hit the front," I said, as I rolled onto my feet. It wasn't ideal to have all of us moving at once, but we didn't have time. The initial trap had failed, and the Taliban were moving east, away from the canal. We needed to trap them in this compound as fast as we could.

I grabbed my team, and we set off south to the next ratline. The compound was on the next one beyond that.

"Corporal Martin, there's a side door over here," Hannibal said.

"Roger," I made a mental note of it. If we could flush them out into Hannibal's waiting arms that would be perfect. I could see Berg's team bounding across an empty field. Hannibal was in place. We needed to move. I signaled to Ricci.

We sprinted to the front of the compound. It had tall metal doors painted blue. I wanted to get these motherfuckers so bad. I ran at the door and saw they were chained shut. *Shit*, I thought. I started kicking them and screaming at the top of my lungs.

"US Marines! Open the fucking door!" I felt like an idiot. No one inside knew what I was saying. I was ranting and raving with adrenaline, spitting froth and malice. I kicked the metal doors over and over while I radioed Hannibal. "The doors are locked over here. Send your team in that side door." It was a risk. We would collapse our cordon, with no eyes on that whole side of the compound. I hoped that our noise would be enough of a distraction to get Hannibal and his team inside, and then we could clear the compound. The clock in my head kept ticking down.

"Roger. We're moving," Hannibal answered. I kept pounding on the door and yelling like a lunatic.

"Shit, there's two motorcycles gunning it away from the back of the compound," Berg radioed in. My heart sank. *They were getting away!* Berg's guys were taking shots at them as they drove away. I didn't say anything. I just watched Ricci whaling on the door.

After a minute that felt like a year, I saw boots under the lip of the blue doors. Weeks unlocked the doors from the inside. He saw me standing there and knew immediately.

"Moth-er-fuck-er," he drawled. Ricci and I walked inside. I ordered a quick search of the compound. We put the family that lived there in a corner of the courtyard. It was a terrified elderly man, a few women in burqas, and some kids. The kids were crying and holding on to the women's legs. I was so angry I didn't care about them. I hunted through the rooms of their home, flashlight on in the darkness. I knew the Taliban were gone, but my anger and adrenaline kept it from sinking in.

When we finished the search empty-handed, I took Kobe to talk to the old man. He was trembling.

"He say the Taliban take their motorcycles," Kobe translated.

"I know that," I spat. "Did they know them?"

"He never see them before."

Staring at the old man, I ground my teeth together. I wanted to kick something. I wanted to hurt someone. I wanted to ruin something beautiful.

Instead, I apologized to the old man. I told him I knew it was hard to be trapped in the middle of a war. He didn't say anything, but he trembled and shook. Staring into his dark eyes, something clicked—he was afraid of me.

Good, I thought. *He should be.*

I rallied the squad: time to head home. When I called Aries II to let them know, Compton said there was a surprise waiting for us when we got back.

On the way back, we passed the marijuana field from earlier. The distance I ran, which had felt like it took half an hour to cross, was twenty feet, thirty tops. Shredded marijuana plants and broken trees lined the street. Children were picking up all our spent brass.

All that firepower, from the contractors and the Taliban, and we survived. Not just survived, we maneuvered and closed with the enemy. We were in charge of this area now. Alexander was the King of Asia, but we were the princes of our sector. I felt powerful, but I was livid that the Taliban had been so close and we had let them get away. Just making it through the deployment wasn't enough; I wanted more. I wanted to pound an empty casing into the bottom of the tower. I wanted to avenge Zaehringer. I wanted to hurt someone.

When we got back to Aries II, it was a party. While we were out running and gunning, a convoy had dropped off some early supplies for the Marine Corps' birthday, a cooler full of steaks and hamburgers. As we walked up, the smell of meat cooking overpowered the constant smell of burning garbage. It was incredible. I started drooling like a dog.

Tracey was manning a grill made out of Hesco wire, while the other Marines surrounded her, paper plates in hand and expectant looks on their faces.

I sent my guys to grab some food, while I headed to the MRAP. We would debrief later.

16

OCTOBER 2010

In Uzbekistan, near the modern border with Kazakhstan, Alexander faced an unfamiliar foe. The Saka, nomadic archers on horseback, would ride up to Alexander's army, launch their arrows, and ride away before the heavy Macedonian infantry could counter attack.

To the best of the Greeks' knowledge, only once in their history had a Greek general defeated such an army. It was Philip, Alexander's father, when he defeated the Scythians in 340 BCE. Seeking to prove his worth, Alexander formed a plan to crush the nomadic warriors at the Jaxartes River.

Using a small contingent of infantry, Alexander baited the Saka into attacking a much smaller force. Then, when they were engaged, Alexander swept in with his cavalry and archers and decimated the nomads.

Tracey and Cantu were speaking with some local women a few yards away from me, hidden by a wall. I could hear their laughter and halting speech as they tried to communicate through broken Pashto and hand signals. Besides some children and the ancient grandmother that liked to hold my hand, I hadn't spoken to a woman since I had arrived in Marjah. The local women wore head-to-toe burqas in rich shades of blue and black, and were forbidden from speaking with unrelated men. The women still had power and sway in the community; it was just behind the scenes.

Standing under a poplar tree, I watched leaves drift down from the half-empty branches. In the field in front of me, some locals were out picking cotton, their nimble brown fingers pulling the white tufts from the drying stalks. A few kids ran out of a nearby compound. They huddled together at the edge of a wall where they pointed and giggled at me. I smiled and waved at them. The kids pulled their hands up to their chins, laughed, and ran back inside. I took a deep breath and exhaled through a smile. I felt great.

"*Manana, manana*," I could hear Tracey saying. "Thank you, thank you." She and Cantu came walking around the corner of the wall, bowing slightly. They had fresh henna on their hands. A small Afghan woman in a bright turquoise burqa followed them around the corner. I turned away, scanning across the cotton field in front of me.

Even though I couldn't see them, I knew where Berg and Hannibal's teams were. I could feel their presence beyond the compound walls. I could visualize their teams patrolling, stopping, setting up security. They trusted me, and I trusted them.

I trusted Tracey and Cantu as well. When they first came to Aries II, I wasn't sure they would be able to keep up with the rest of us. They weren't infantry and didn't have the years of training that everyone else had. But they proved me wrong, keeping up on patrols and holding their own as well as anyone in firefights. It took me a while to understand that they had volunteered to come to Marjah. They were chasing Alexander, too.

Peeking over my shoulder, I watched Tracey and Cantu say their goodbyes, two Marines in dirty camo, their flak jackets covered in grenades, while their black rifles hung loose at their side. The Afghan woman in billowy blue pressed her hands to her chest before turning around and heading back inside.

"Good to go?" I asked Tracey.

"Roger," she said, as she pulled her rifle into her shoulder.

"Cool. We're going to push to the bamboo grove by the T-wall."

We had a shorthand, a new language for our squad. Checkpoints were called out at places like the helicopter house, the burned yard, and the yellow school. Hand signals and gestures were replacing speech: a raised fist, two fingers pointing from face to face, arms held out an angle. Our new shared vocabulary.

As I strolled out from under the tree, I could feel my team rising with me, the rustle of their flak jackets, their eyes snapping around. Our senses expanded and merged. Everything I saw was relayed back into the team's consciousness, and they relayed back to me, eyes flashing and fingers pointing. We headed out at a smooth, relaxed pace.

I hopped over a small canal, landing on the soft grass, not yet brown, but not green anymore. The air smelled like cold water. I could feel power rising and flowing through me as I gripped my rifle, feeling the hard plastic through my gloves. Crossing a small street, my team flowed behind me, backing me up. I scanned across a field, feeling Berg and Hannibal's teams converging on the other side like a pincher.

Rolling my neck, I felt the power wash over me. It was like a dark shadow that I could direct, a shadow that could raze fields and level buildings, a shadow of destruction that I could sweep wherever I wanted. I had rifles and grenades and a machine gun at my command. Mortars, rockets, or airplanes dropping bombs if I wanted. I could rain missiles down from the invisible drones. I only had to ask.

The might and the power of the US military was behind me. There was no supervision, no one above me. I was twenty-four, and I walked around with the ability to wipe buildings and people off the face of the earth. All that power was intoxicating. With the radio in my backpack, I could decimate everything in sight. I felt all that power running up my neck and down into my fingertips. I flexed my hand and grinned.

Leaning around the corner of a wall, I popped my head out, and yelled, "Boo!" The children jumped, so I smiled and stuck my tongue out at them. They laughed, stuck their hands out, and asked me for chocolate.

———

One afternoon, Blackwood's squad got into it. Nothing major, a small firefight, twenty or thirty minutes tops. They were becoming more common. Our map in the MRAP was getting a case of chickenpox.

A Weapons Company convoy was in the area. They had set up a snap roadblock. When they heard the contact, they called us up on the radio.

"Hey, Aries II, y'all need a hand out there?" Sergeant Porter, the silver-haired machine gun squad leader from Iraq, came across the radio. I radioed Blackwood to see if he needed help. He didn't.

"That's a negative on the assistance. Just tell your gunners to watch out on the west side of Elephant. Our squad is about four hundred yards off the road."

"Roger. I'll let 'em know. We'll be here if you need a hand."

"Tango. By the way, is this Echo-Five Papa? This is Echo-Four Mike from the 81s platoon."

"Aww yeah, it is. You down there with the Echo boys, huh?" Porter drawled.

"A-firm. If your guys need a break, come on down," I offered.

"Tango. Out."

Blackwood wrapped up his skirmish and finished their patrol. These little attacks kept coming. Not hours-long assaults, just small, quick gunfights. Enough to deaden our fear a little, to make us want to go on patrol so we could get an adrenaline fix. Standing post was boring, and we were all getting used to the high of running and shooting.

Porter and his squad came through a few hours later. I was excited to have some visitors that I knew, instead of Echo guys. I didn't know most of the younger guys in the squad, but I knew Porter.

We offered them chips and beef jerky and Cliff bars. We hid the Pop-Tarts.

"This is where y'all live? A couple'a sandbags and some C-wire?"

I nodded. I felt like a badass; I was finally the warrior that I had always wanted to be.

"Damn, son. Y'all roughin' it out here."

"It's nice," I said. "No staff NCOs, no officers. It's the squad leader's dream."

"I don't know about all that." He ate some beef jerky.

"I heard about Zaehringer," I said. I let it hang in the air.

Porter chewed. "Yeah, that's some shit." He licked his lips and opened his mouth like he was about to say something, but then didn't. I lit a cigarette. He grabbed another piece of beef jerky. It felt like there wasn't anything to say. It felt like there was everything to say. Zaehringer would have said something funny.

"You hear about Bay?" Porter asked.

"Sergeant Bay?" I asked. "No. What happened?"

"Big ole IED. Mashed his legs up pretty good." Porter shook his head. "These MRAPs are alright. Man, I tell you, that was a Humvee, he'd a been gone for sure."

"Shit," was all I said. I thought about Bay laughing and smiling during our CLIC training. It felt like a lifetime ago. "Is he going to be alright?"

"Yeah, think so. Last I heard, at least."

I nodded and took a drag. This was what small talk in Marjah had become, swapping casualty stories like baseball cards.

"Oh," Porter perked up, "I heard about that boy from your platoon that got it, too."

I took a sharp breath and froze. *Shit.* I hadn't heard. I stared at him and could feel the blood draining from my face. My mind started drawing up a list of people I hoped it wasn't.

"Jesus, I hadn't heard anything." I took a drag and glanced around for the other 81s. "Who was it?"

"Hmmm, I can't remember his name."

Please don't let it be Kelly.

"He's one of the ones that come in with you."

Please don't let it be Dolph.

"He's got dark hair."

Goddamnit, don't let be anyone.

"It's . . . it's that strange guy. The one that looks like Johnny Depp." I felt a wave of relief that it wasn't one of my close friends.

"Haley? Kinda short, has glasses?"

"Yeah," Porter held up a finger. "Yeah, that guy."

"Is he okay?" Haley and I weren't close, but he was still a platoon mate, a brother.

"Oh yeah, he's fine. Caught a little through and through in the arm." Porter cocked his head and smiled. "Damn, probably shoulda led with that, huh?" He clapped me on the shoulder. "Don't worry; he's okay."

I felt the tension flood out of me. It wasn't one of my close friends, and Haley was alright. A tingle of relief climbed up the back of my neck.

"Glad to hear it. Any other news from the 81s?"

"Nah, we don't see 'em that often. They're way out west in Bandini."

"Bandini?" I asked.

"Yeah, it's west of Marjah. They're out there with some of our guys. Big place. That's where Zaehringer died." He said it matter-of-factly. I suppose there wasn't any other way to say it.

I nodded. He crumpled up the empty beef jerky bag and handed it to me.

"Well, thanks for letting us hang for a minute. We oughta be heading out before it gets dark."

"Alright. Thanks for swinging through. If you see any of the Weapons Company guys, let 'em know I said hey."

He smiled as he clipped his chin strap back on his helmet. "Will do." He turned around and yelled, "Hey, y'all, let's go! On the trucks!" They loaded up and set off down Elephant, plumes of dust blowing out behind them.

"Why should we help you?" the old man asked as he glared at me. I held his stare. And then I held it for a few beats more. I wanted the rest of the men in the group to see.

"The Taliban were here before you, and they will be here after you leave. How can I make enemies with them?" the old man added, as he held out his hands and gestured to the other men. We were sitting in his courtyard, eight or so men with beards of varying shades of gray, plus Kobe and I. They all started speaking at once, gesturing at each other and me.

"Mmm, they say he is right, Mar-ten," Kobe said, as he leaned over to me. I shifted my legs. It was hard sitting cross-legged with my flak jacket on. I had called this *shura*, this meeting, with the local elders to have a conversation about planting more cotton instead of poppies, but it quickly turned on me. I placidly looked around the circle at the men. Their faces were lined and craggy, angry, and a little fearful. I knew what Alexander would do in this situation, so I grabbed my radio and turned to the air support channel, while I tried to suppress a grin.

"Any station, any station, this is Aries II Mobile. Over."

"Ahhh, Roger. Aries II Mobile, go ahead."

"Hey, I'm in the Lima sector. I was wondering if I could get a show of force over here?" I asked the pilot.

"Roger that. Go ahead and send me your grid," he answered. I passed along our GPS coordinates and explained the situation. He said he'd be there in four minutes. A twinge of excitement ran through me.

I squeezed my watch, started a timer, and turned back to the group. The host had stood up and was giving an impassioned speech. All the other men were looking up at him. I checked my watch: three minutes.

"Kobe, what's he saying?" I asked.

"He says they should all stop working with the Americans. Things were better before the Americans came. You know, this kind of thing."

"Uh-huh," I rubbed my chin and listened to him speak for a bit. "Kobe, I'm going to start talking, and I need you to translate while I talk, okay?"

"Sure thing, Mar-ten," he said. I glanced at my watch: two minutes. I raised my arms and held them out to interrupt the old man. I smiled. When he turned to me, I started talking.

"Before the Americans came here, the Taliban made you grow poppies and took all the money." I stared hard at the old man. "Before the Americans came here, the Taliban would turn the water off to punish you." I went around the circle focusing on each man, one at a time. "Before the Americans came here, there were no schools. But now we're here, and we have dug wells for you, we paved the roads for you, and we built schools for your children." I got to my feet and checked my watch: one minute. "I know things are hard right now, and I am sorry for that, but if you want to get rid of the Taliban, I need you to work with us." I stopped talking and turned back to the host. The men glanced at each other, then turned to me and started yelling and pointing at me again.

Here it comes, I thought.

"Mmm, they are not happy with you, Mar-ten," Kobe said over their yelling. I checked my watch: five seconds. I turned to the south, to see the F-16 come flying in over the treetops. It was so close, it looked like I could touch it. The fighter jet blasted in over the top of our gathering and pulled straight up. It dumped dozens of bright, basketball-sized flares as it rocketed upwards. The pilot punched the afterburners, and the plane disappeared into the sky. The sonic boom crashed through the courtyard, blowing dust, knocking teacups over, and whipping the men's clothes around. It was deafening. Dust swirled all around us. In the quiet that followed, I could hear kids crying and animals bleating through the ringing in my ears.

"And if you don't want to work with us, just remember, he's with me," I yelled, as I pointed to the sky. I could feel the power flowing through my blood as I gripped my rifle. "The next time you think you want to help the Taliban, I suggest you think again." I had a squad of Marines with me and a fighter jet at my beck and call. How dare they question me! The men stared back up at me, fear and terror in their eyes. A screaming child came running into the courtyard and grabbed the host's legs. She pushed her tear-soaked face into his clothes, while he reached down and rubbed her back. The old man stared at me. He wasn't afraid, or angry. Instead, his eyes were round and dark with sadness.

I felt a twinge of something in my chest, something like disappointment, like I had done the wrong thing. But the adrenaline and the power washed it away. I grabbed my walkie-talkie and told the squad to move out.

———

Living on Route Elephant meant that a lot of convoys rolled through. Some were professional. The Weapons Company and Echo Company squads always let us know when they were entering our area, and when they were leaving. They asked if we had any patrols out, so they could let their gunners know. Good guys, team players.

Other convoys didn't call in to let us know. They would blow right through our position, kicking up dust and driving the locals' cars off the road. Once, a turret gunner flipped me the bird as I watched them drive past. Another time I tried to wave down the lead vehicle of a convoy to let them know we had a squad in a firefight. I wanted to let them know so they wouldn't accidentally shoot our guys, but the driver swerved around me and kept heading south. We called them Blue Falcons, because they were buddy fuckers.

. . .

One day a convoy rolled in unannounced, and stopped. It was some bigwig from the regiment. He did an impromptu tour, checking in on the Lords of the Flies. He was cordial enough; most officers are. It's not their job to cuss and chew out enlisted Marines. His high-ranking enlisted men did that for him.

An angry gunnery sergeant pointed out that our mortars were dusty. I pointed out that we were in the middle of a busy road, a road made of dust. Of course, that was no excuse. I followed him around as he pointed out our other deficiencies: trash in the canal, an untidy burn pit, excessive facial hair (Berg), and interestingly, a lack of defenses against suicide bombers. Suicide attacks were uncommon in the Helmand Province, but he wanted us to put in a series of speed bumps in the road. Stacks of sandbags twenty-five, fifty, seventy-five, and one hundred yards out. I ground my teeth to keep from pointing out how that would wreck the traffic flows on the busiest street in Marjah for essentially nothing. If a suicide bomber was rolling up on Aries II, a couple of sandbags in the road weren't going to change anything.

The bigwigs packed up, told us to shave, and headed off, down to the southern part of the city. I hated that garrison Marine Corps mentality. We were out patrolling in one of the most dangerous areas in the world, and all these higher-ups cared about was how often we shaved. I was starting to get sick of how the higher-ups were running things. Mott, however, ecstatically implemented the new changes.

We cleaned the canal and the burn pit, and shaved our faces. We spent the better part of the day paying some of the local kids in Cliff bars to fill sandbags. There was a ten-ish-year-old kid we called Buckwheat that lived next door. He and his friends loved Cliff bars. Once they were done, we negotiated with them—some chocolate for a wheelbarrow—which we used to transport the sandbags and build our speed bumps, twenty-five, fifty, seventy-five, and one hundred yards away from the patrol base. I knelt in the dirt and stacked sandbags with Brown and Demorrow, cussing along with them.

I told them about Nassar in Iraq. If a dump truck full of explosives came rolling in, one hundred yards wasn't going to save anyone, especially when our escalation of force procedures said we couldn't shoot at the vehicle until it was fifty yards away. But that's life. You do it, you complain about it, and it gets done.

The next day, Compton went out to check the sandbags after his squad's post shift was done at two in the afternoon. They were destroyed. Who would have guessed hundreds of cars driving over them would be bad for sandbags? Before Compton and his squad went on patrol, he gathered his guys and replaced the destroyed sandbags.

The day after that, again at two, Compton checked to see which sandbags needed to be replaced. He walked a hundred yards in all three directions jotting down which ones had been burst, crushed, or otherwise squished. His guys filled new ones, put them out, and went on patrol.

The next day, I was up, my turn to check the sandbags after standing post. My guys came down from the trucks and towers. I told them to grab a snack and drink some water, take their armor off for a while. I'd check the sandbags, we'd replace them, and head out. *Rah.*

I walked the north line first, and then the south line. I waved at the north truck and flipped off the south truck, in a friendly way. After that, I headed for the western line, down Route Joanne.

I checked the twenty-five-yard line and jotted down in my notebook how many new sandbags we'd need. Then I went to the fifty- and the seventy-five-yard lines. As I walked down the road, I mentally rehearsed the patrol we were about to do. Checking my notebook, at this point we were looking at fifty-some new sandbags. I headed out to the hundred-yard line and squatted down in the dust.

Reaching out, I wiped the dust off some of the bags, trying to see if they were ruptured or just dusty. As I wiped them off, a sandbag next to me popped. Then another one, the one I had been wiping. Little eruptions of sand sprang up from the sandbags in front of me. I stood up and stared, not understanding what was happening. Everything started to move very slowly. All around me, grains of sand rose into the air and fell back down, like tiny waterfalls in reserve. It was beautiful. Then the noise caught up with me.

An indistinct roar, like traffic on a busy street or the sounds of a city, loud, but in a general way, crashed into me. Sand geysers were springing up from the sandbags and the road all around me. I turned to the south, and things slowed down even more. Across the barren fields, there were twinkling lights spread out along a long wall, fifteen or twenty lights twinkling and flashing at me as the air roared all around me.

I didn't move; I stood there in the eye of a hurricane as the lights flashed and the air hummed. *I see them*, I thought. *The Taliban—there they are*. I could see the pauses between the flashes. *Blink-blink-blink*. I couldn't believe it; I had finally found them.

All at once, the sky ripped in half with gunfire. It was instant and deafening and everywhere. Time sped back up. My brain screamed for me to move. I took a sluggish step towards the canal in front of me, but it was too shallow, only six inches deep—a bad place for cover.

Run! My brain yelled at me, and I took off. I started sprinting back to Aries II as the mud wall to my left exploded and chips and shards rained down everywhere. The fragments bounced off my face, and I breathed in the dust. The dirt in the road danced with incoming fire. My rifle hung at my side as I pumped my arms and ran. I was one hundred yards to cover and safety.

My vision started to tunnel, Aries II stretching further off into the distance as my peripherals closed in. My hearing started to go, a loud humming noise whined in my ears, and my eyesight started to bounce and jostle like a TV that's being carried.

As I sprinted, and my senses started to go, I only had one thought: *I'm going to die because I'm wearing my shitty boots.* It ran through my head five times, ten times, fifty, a million times. The air around me was saturated with bullets and noise and death, and the wall next to me was getting cut to pieces, and I ran and I ran and thought I would die because I was wearing the wrong boots.

As I approached Aries II, Blackwood was standing outside the wire, rifle up and ready, his helmet unbuckled. He was waving me back in, inside some cover. Even up close, he seemed far away, in the center of the dark tunnel. I could vaguely hear the other posts firing their guns.

I ran into Aries II and came to a stop, sucking wind as I frantically checked my arms and legs. *Where did I get hit?* was all I thought, assuming, knowing, that I was riddled with bullets. I could feel my eyes bulging as I patted myself down. I yelled incomprehensibly at Blackwood, barking and sputtering. When I heard the garbled noises coming out of my mouth, I clapped my gloved hands to my face. *Did my jaw get shot off?* I couldn't feel my face. I couldn't feel my hands at all. But when I pulled them away, there wasn't any blood.

Blackwood said, "Holy shit." He grabbed my shoulder and peered into my eyes. "You're good, man. You're good." His voice sounded muffled and tinny.

I took in a deep breath, held it, and slowly exhaled. My vision was coming back. Somehow, I ran down that road through all that fire and was unscathed. I took another breath, and my hearing started to even out. I could hear the Taliban firing away. I turned and pointed back down Joanne.

"We gotta go," I managed. My hands were still shaking, and my breathing was ragged. But I saw them, and I couldn't let the opportunity go to waste.

I walked to the MRAP to get a walkie-talkie. Compton was on the radio with the posts, trying to coordinate fires.

"They're southwest of here, two hundred or so yards south of Joanne," I said, as I climbed the MRAP steps and grabbed a radio out of the charging cradle.

"How do you know?" Compton asked me.

"I got ambushed when I was checking the sandbags," I said as I walked down the MRAP steps, my legs still shaking. As I turned the corner, guys from the other hooch were collecting outside the wire. I gave them the world's shortest brief.

"Fifteen to twenty Taliban, about two hundred yards south of Joanne along the big ratline. Let's go."

Berg and Hannibal ran out ahead, hit the corner of the compound, and plunged into the fire. Berg was only wearing a T-shirt under his flak jack, his stripe tattoos flashing as he sprinted. Gross and I pushed further west down Joanne, to give Berg and Hannibal room to maneuver and so we could provide cover fire.

The two of us posted up behind an old tractor and started scanning. Someone was plunking grenade rounds. I watched a smoke round burst and send up a plume of white smoke. Through my scope, I saw three men with rifles stand up and wave the smoke away from their faces.

"Holy fuck!" Gross yelled. He opened up, sending a flurry of rounds at them, but the smoke enveloped them quickly, and I couldn't tell if he had hit anyone.

As I scanned for other targets, our tractor became a magnet for incoming fire. Rounds pinged off the metal, sending paint chips and bits of metal flying. I glanced at Gross, and he grinned as he looked back at me, and then we both dove off to the side. I hit the ground and started to crawl over to a ditch. This was the biggest firefight we had been in by a mile.

I rolled into the ditch, popped up, and scanned around. I saw Berg and Hannibal sprinting back towards Aries II. It seemed wrong; they weren't the kind of guys to run away from a fight. I took a second glance.

They each had a kid thrown over their shoulders. Berg had Buckwheat unceremoniously hugging his neck, and Hannibal had Buckwheat's little brother. They sprinted back to the corner of the compound and disappeared.

I turned around and scanned back across the field. We were in staggered clumps, hunkered down in the dry canals across the empty field. There were too many Taliban. We weren't making any progress, even as we were dumping ammo at them.

I called Compton on the walkie-talkie. "We're getting bogged down out here. We've only pushed about fifty yards south." I ducked down into the ditch as a tree next to me was shredded by a machine gun. There was no way I was going to be able to run across this field. I started duckwalking through a flooded canal to one that ran north–south. We would have to use that to get closer.

"Hey, Martin, we've got the contractors inbound," Compton came back.

I was confused—who gave a shit about the road pavers right now? "Say again?" I asked over the roar of the firefight.

"The cavalry is coming!" I could hear Compton smiling, even over the radio.

I hit the intersection of the canals and paused, checking on our progress. Jacobs and Brown had pushed the furthest south, but they were still stopped fifty yards ahead of me. I turned around to find Gross when Berg and Hannibal came storming back past me. They didn't stop; they kept running down the canal. As the fire picked up all around them, Berg slid down behind some cover, while Hannibal just crouched. I felt a surge of energy and courage. These guys were fearless.

Right on their heels, two dozen contractors came pouring past me. A blur of white robes, brown vests, and dark turbans, they yelled to each other as they fired their AKs across the fields towards the Taliban. My legs wobbled with relief as I watched them running behind Berg and Hannibal.

Within minutes, the Taliban fled. I was exhausted and struggled to catch up with the contractors' wild charge. When I did, they were all standing around smoking and talking excitedly. I asked Berg if they found anything.

"Nope. Looks like they hopped on their motorcycles once these guys arrived," he said, as he pointed a thumb over his shoulder at our Afghan friends.

"No brass, no blood splatter?" I asked, a note of hope in my voice.

"Yeah, right," Hannibal chimed in. "Those motherfuckers take everything with them. The contractors say they lie on blankets when they shoot, so they can roll up all the brass when they leave."

I stared wistfully at the edge of the compound where I saw their twinkling muzzle flashes. They were right there; I saw them! Now there wasn't any evidence they were ever there at all. Chewing on my lip, I pulled out my cigarettes. The pack was water-logged and ruined from sloshing through canals. I hung my head and turned to head back to Aries II.

When I turned the corner by our compound, I saw Buckwheat and his brother standing there. They looked terrified, their cheeks still wet with tears.

"*Sengay*?" I asked. "How are you guys?" Buckwheat hugged his brother and looked up at me with red eyes and mouth full of missing teeth.

"It's okay. Let's go, little guys," Hannibal said. He waved them over to him, and took them back around the corner to the entrance to their house.

Later that night, when I was getting ready for bed, I noticed some holes in my pants. In the backs of my pant legs, there were little pairs of punctures. I folded the grimy material between my fingers as I lined up the entry and exit holes.

17

NOVEMBER 2010

As Macedonians were killed in battle, Alexander replaced their ranks with locally recruited Persian soldiers. This strained Alexander's relationship with his countrymen, but when Alexander began to stylize himself as a Persian king, adopting their dress and customs, the Macedonians became enraged.

At issue was the Persian custom of "proskynesis," where people would prostrate themselves on the ground in deference to Alexander. For the Greeks, that was an act only performed for the gods, and they saw Alexander trying to deify himself. It caused such fierce internal strife that Alexander was forced to end the practice.

Crack. *Crack-crack-crack.* I ducked down, below the top of one of the last cotton fields. We were in Blackwood's area, to the northwest of Aries II. The last few hours had been a strung-out game of hide-and-seek. We'd receive a couple of shots so we'd maneuver, and then it would stop. When we would get ready to leave, we'd get shot at again. No one was outside. I didn't know the area at all.

"Anyone see anything?" I asked on the walkie-talkie. I poked my head back up and scanned over the tops of the dried cotton plants. There was a building about two hundred yards ahead of us and a thin line of trees to my left.

"Nothing," Berg said.

"Same here," Hannibal said. "Something doesn't feel right."

I felt the same way. Lately, every squad had been getting into it, almost every day now. The patrols got hit, and even Aries II was getting attacked. But this was different. Typically, the fire would come fast and heavy, an immense opening barrage. We would respond and attack back, chewing up ground as we rushed their positions. We'd fight for a while, and as suddenly as it started, it would stop. But this time it started with potshots at Aries II.

"Berg, stay put. We're going to move up this ratline to my west," I said, as we moved north.

"Roger."

I jogged up the thin line of trees, looking ahead. A few months earlier, I would have tried to push through the cotton, but it was too thick and tangled, and I didn't want to get stuck in the field only to have the Taliban open up on us. As I moved, I kept my head down. I had a creeping suspicion we were getting sucked into an ambush.

Ricci, Doc, and Kobe followed me, and we set in on a small canal running down the middle of the cotton field. The building was closer now, less than a hundred yards.

"Alright, Berg, we're set. Go ahead—" *Crack-crack-crack.* The incoming rounds cut me off. I ducked as Ricci started firing off to my right.

"Straight ahead!" he yelled. "Right in front of us!"

I pulled my rifle to my shoulder and peered through my scope. I could see Ricci's rounds impacting the wall of the compound, a little above the cotton.

"I got him! I fucking got him!" Ricci was yelling.

I scanned to the right and the left, and I saw him.

There was a person, running in a crouch, the top of their head barely visible above the cotton. My reaction was instantaneous. I flipped the safety off and pulled my rifle into my shoulder. I swept the reticle of my scope over the cotton and watched their head bob across my line of sight. I started to take the slack out of the trigger. Time slowed down. I could feel my heartbeat in my finger as I gently pulled it back. I slowly exhaled.

Three more steps—my trigger pull was smooth, it was going to be a perfect shot.

Two more steps—I finished exhaling and paused.

One more step—they were almost there.

A long ponytail flipped up. I saw the braid bounce up, long black hair with a blue bow at the end.

I let go of the trigger. Her hair swung down out of view. It was a little girl.

"Ceasefire! Ceasefire!" I yelled, waving my hand in front of my face. Ricci pulled up and echoed my call. I grabbed the walkie-talkie. "Cease fire, cease fire! Cease fucking fire! " I screamed into the walkie-talkie. The other teams' firing slowed down, and stopped. "There's a little girl out there on the west side of that building." No one said anything in response.

"The west side?" Ricci asked.

"Yeah, that corner over there."

"No, he was on the other side," Ricci said, as he pointed to the east end of the compound. I stared at him credulously.

"I'm telling you I got him over there," he said.

I turned back at the compound. No one was around. Everything was still. My legs were shaking, more than usual. I still thought we were getting sucked in.

Rubbing my face, I tried to think. We couldn't flank on the east side; there was a long wall cutting us off. To the west were completely open fields with no cover. It was a shitty spot to be in. Even more reason I thought something bad was about to happen.

I grabbed the walkie-talkie. "Hannibal, take that machine gun and push up as far as you can, while you can still see the front of that compound."

"We don't have anywhere to go unless you want us in that open field."

"Just—" I broke it off. There really wasn't anywhere for them to go. "Alright, come fill in on our position. Berg, we're going to push up to the compound. You guys move alongside us. This is shit. Let's just do it fast."

I let my team know the plan, and we hustled off. As we ran, I tried to stay low, but my legs wobbled and burned. My hands were shaking.

We made it to the compound. Nothing happened. Berg cordoned the east side, while we searched around the front of the compound. No sign of the little girl. No sign of the guy Ricci said he hit. No blood, no shell casings. Nothing anywhere.

I called Aries II and let them know we were headed back.

Back inside the wire, I sat down in the MRAP with Blackwood and told him about the firefight.

"Shit's been getting weird, man," he said.

I agreed, and put another dot on the map.

I smoked a cigarette instead of eating lunch. A few smokes were quickly becoming my go-to meal. I bounced my leg and inspected our firefight map. There weren't any patterns, just a lot of red dots.

"What the hell?" Blackwood asked. He pointed out the front window of the MRAP. There was a small crowd gathered around an old man with a wheelbarrow. I could see two legs sticking out of it.

"Oh fuck," I said. Grabbing my rifle, I hopped out of the MRAP and jogged to the edge of our fence. There was a man, a boy really, writhing in the wheelbarrow. I yelled for Kobe and Doc as Marines started gathering around.

"He say you shot his son," Kobe translated. The old man was panicking. He rubbed his hands together and talked to Kobe in a pleading tone.

"Kobe, was his son shooting at us?" I asked as Doc came running up with his Medkit.

"He say no, his son is a good man."

Fuuuck, was all I thought. I almost shot a little girl, and someone else shot a teenage boy?

We picked the boy up out of the wheelbarrow and carried him inside the wire. His legs didn't seem to be working. We set him down in the dust by the MRAP, behind some sandbags. Doc and Weeks threw on some latex gloves and started working on him.

The boy had two small entry wounds, one next to each of his hip bones by his beltline, but there was only one exit wound. He squirmed around and arched his back while he moaned in pain.

While the others administered first aid, I grabbed the gunshot residue kit and pulled out a swab. Prying his hands apart, I took his right hand in my left, and wiped down his thumb and index finger area. When I let his hands go, he started rubbing them in the dirt. Blackwood glanced at me and raised an eyebrow.

When I sprayed the swab with the solvent, it changed colors immediately. It was a hit—he had fired a gun recently. A wave of relief washed over me. We didn't shoot an innocent kid.

"Hey, Sergeant Mott, he popped on the residue kit." Mott glared at me. He was helping Doc cut strips of gauze.

"Try it on someone else to make sure."

I did two quick tests, one on Ricci and one on myself. Ricci popped. I didn't.

"This guy was the one who was shooting at us," I told Mott.

"I told y'all I got 'em," Ricci said, his arms crossed over his chest.

We called in the casevac nine-line and prepped the same helo landing zone as last time. When the Blackhawk was circling above us, we popped a smoke canister. The helo crew loaded the kid up on a stretcher, and Plant jumped on board as the armed escort. Then, the helo took off in a whirl of dust.

Aries II had its first confirmed enemy casualty. My squad shot someone who was shooting at us. And it felt terrible. I had always assumed that the Taliban were men our age, twenty- and thirty-year-olds, battle-hardened men. Not local teenagers.

I walked back to the MRAP from the landing zone with my head hung.

———

And so it went for the next few weeks. Aries II would take fire, and we would roll out to beat them back. Whenever we were out on patrol, the locals would run inside. Things were getting heavy.

Blackwood and his guys got stuck behind a small shed as a pair of machine guns pinned them down. My squad ran through empty brown fields and rivers of bullets, jumping from cover to cover. One of Compton's teams got trapped on the other side of a compound wall, so he slammed his shoulder into it over and over until it crumbled. We went from occasional firefights to daily firefights, to multiple firefights per day.

Everyone was getting skinny. I was eating less than a single MRE a day, down from two or three. After eating nothing else for months, I couldn't stand the taste. Cigarettes and coffee were the only things keeping me alive.

Staring at myself in the broken mirror that I used to shave, I noticed the dark circles under my eyes. I looked like shit. I could take my blouse off and stand it up. It was so caked in sweat, dirt, and grime that, when I wasn't wearing it, it looked like an invisible man was inside. Everyone's pants were torn. Torn in the crotch and torn in the knees, with strings hanging out from every seam, like fringes.

One day, a retired Army colonel came through on a convoy and stayed with us for a few hours. He was some kind of advisor, and he was horrified by our meager defenses and the skeleton crew that ran Aries II. We laughed and told him that's why he wasn't a Marine.

I took him on a patrol to talk to some farmers. When the firefight began, I gave a pistol to Kobe and told him to watch the colonel.

The colonel freaked out. "Why did you give it to *him?*" he cried out, panic in his eyes.

I gave him a dead-eye stare. "Because I don't know you," I said, and ran off to join the fight.

The colonel called for a convoy to pick him up as soon as we got back. He'd had enough of Aries II.

———

Soon after that, Echo Mobile dropped off some extra water and MREs. We needed ammo and diesel, but they didn't have any with them. Our resupplies were getting further and further apart and we were always running low on fuel. Once we ran out, we wouldn't be able to charge the radio batteries.

Echo Mobile didn't have fuel or bullets for us, but they did have something else. The boy we had shot a few weeks earlier was back. He was in a body bag in the back of an MRAP. I grabbed some guys and a stretcher, and we carried his body to the unused truck that sat on Joanne. We opened the back doors, slid the stretcher in, and locked it back up.

That afternoon I led a patrol back to the compound where we shot the boy. The cotton was cut down and the fields were barren, but otherwise it looked the same. Pockmarks from Ricci dotted the eastern corner of the building. I found the old man, but not the little girl. He was sitting on the ground, shelling beans into a wicker basket. There wasn't any grass in sight.

"We have your son," I told him through Kobe. He stood and clasped his hands in front of him. "You need to come pick him up," I said. His face twisted in confusion.

"Why do I need to pick him up? Why don't you just let him go?" Kobe translated.

I stared at Kobe for a long time, and he stared back at me with his deep hazel eyes. He sighed, looked at the ground, and kicked a clump of dirt. Then he mumbled and told the man why.

The man clutched his hands to his chest. He sputtered and cried a little bit. Thin streams of tears rolled down his cheeks. He tried to say something, but every time he opened his mouth a sob came out. I turned away.

My guts twisted and writhed. I lit a cigarette. A few months ago, I never would have smoked on a patrol. Now I did every chance I got.

It seemed obscene to stand there in front of this crying man—to have the men who killed your son stand there and stare at you and smoke cigarettes. I radioed the squad and told them we were heading out.

As we walked away, I could hear the old man crying. I lit another cigarette and tried not to listen.

When we got back, I gathered the squad for a debrief. We were so dirty, everything was the same color. Our flak jackets and pants and blouses and boots—everything was the color of moondust. Our green helmets were the only spot of color.

I sat heavily on an ammo crate.

"Hey, guys, don't go look at the kid in the MRAP," I asked them. No one said anything. Their eyes—some hard, some empty—said everything. I wasn't sure what to say in response.

"Listen, if this was the other way, if we were Afghan, every single one of us would have done what that kid did. Get a gun and take potshots at patrols."

No one said a word.

"Just," I paused, "don't go look at him. You'll see that shit in your dreams every night for the rest of your life."

I don't know if any of them opened up that boy's body bag. Maybe some of them wanted to stare into the empty sockets of war. Maybe they wanted to see what stares back. I hope they didn't see it.

The next morning the old man came back with some people and the wheelbarrow.

18

NOVEMBER 2010

In 327 BCE, in Uzbekistan, Alexander faced an unreachable fortress called the Sogdian Rock. When Alexander asked them to surrender, the occupants told him he would need men that can fly to take it.

Alexander outfitted his strongest climbers with metal spikes and ropes, and during a dark night, they scaled the cliffs and the walls of the fortress. When they were in position, Alexander's army sent a message to the Sogdians to look up and behold his men who can fly. When the occupants saw Alexander's men on their walls, they surrendered without a fight.

Around that time, Alexander got into a drunken argument with Cleitus the Black, the man who had saved his life at the Battle of the Granicus River. Cleitus hated the way that Alexander was adopting Persian customs, and accused him of forgetting their Macedonian culture. Alexander picked up a spear and murdered his friend on the spot.

Word came down from on high that Aries II would be the furthest southeastern edge of our unit's area of operations. This meant that all our territory to the east and south would be given to a different unit soon. The big blue arrows that generals play with were on the move. The troop surge in Helmand wasn't going to last forever, and they needed to show some successes. An easy thing to point to was the number of battalions needed in an area. So, despite our daily firefights, our area was getting gutted. Now the only area we could patrol was Blackwood's. Incidentally, it was the most violent area.

"This might be the dumbest thing I've ever seen in the Marine Corps," Blackwood observed. "And that is sayin' something."

"How are we supposed to defend ourselves if we can't patrol around our perimeter?" Compton asked Demmingware.

Demmingware shrugged.

"Does that mean that we have to move the guys that live on the other side of the canal? Since that's technically going to belong to the other unit?" I asked. It was a dick question. This wasn't Demmingware's idea. I thought it was just another example of the higher-ups not knowing or caring about what was happening on the ground. They'd rather move some pieces on a map, tell us to shave, and call it a day.

"I'm just passing along what I know," Demmingware said. He ran a hand over his shaved head. Echo Mobile had been getting hit bad recently. Lots of IEDs. He had lost weight over the last few months. That he still made it out to us and put up with our complaining was admirable.

———

To get ready for the change, I started running some patrols through Blackwood's area, to familiarize myself. Most of the squad had been on patrols in that area before, but I hadn't spent much time out there.

One morning, we patrolled around the intersection of Fox and

Joanne. Blackwood's guys called it "the Taliban Market". Apparently, the Taliban would openly hang out at the shops there, drinking tea with AKs and machine guns. It was a kilometer west of us and kilometer east of Typhoon Five. Shows how much they thought about us.

We went early to avoid the Taliban. I wasn't trying to pick a fight with them, just to get a sense of the area. It was cold in the mornings now, and in between planting seasons. Every field was empty and brown. You could see the whole area now, your vision stretching out to ratlines and canals and trees and distant compounds. That also meant everyone else could see us too.

We walked through a farmer's backyard. Chickens scattered, and a small cooking fire smoldered in the gray early light. I said hello to an old man with a white beard. He waved us over to where he was squatting.

"He say, he think Marjah is safe now, that he came back from Pakistan because the Taliban are gone," Kobe said.

I disagreed, but I was happy to hear that people thought that.

"Tell him, I'm glad he has returned home and give him your cell number in case he sees anything suspicious around here."

"He say he has no phone. He is blind."

I stepped closer to the man. His eyes were covered in milky white cataracts. It was hard to tell how old the Afghans in Marjah were. Their life was so hard that by the time they were thirty, they appeared fifty. This man could have been forty, or he could have been ninety. Either way, he was blind, and he had come back to Marjah because he had heard it was safe now.

I thanked him again for coming home and told him to have a good day. Then we set off to the west, so I could check out the Taliban Market before they got there.

An hour or so later, as we were on our way home, Echo Mobile rumbled past us on Route Joanne. We all waved. They waved back. As we were entering the wire, the shooting started.

I turned around and listened, but it was too far away. Somewhere down the road, Echo Mobile was getting lit into. I could hear their .50 calibers cranking away.

My squad poured back into Aries II, and clustered around the MRAP to see if they needed help. Compton raised them on the radio. They had linked up with a patrol from Typhoon Five at the Taliban Market. They didn't need our help.

I rushed through the debrief with my guys as the firefight raged in the background. We all wanted to listen to the radio. It was unusual for the Taliban to attack a mounted convoy. They were getting bold.

After thirty minutes or so, the fight petered out. Not too bad. The Taliban probably decided they didn't want to waste their ammo on armored trucks. I grabbed a bottle of water and made some instant coffee to drink while I smoked a cigarette.

While I was still drinking the coffee, Echo Mobile came back down Joanne and stopped at Aries II. We all went out to see them and hear how the fight went.

Demmingware came inside the concertina wire, his bald head glistening with sweat. He quickly rehashed the firefight for us.

"The damnedest thing happened. One of my guys was holding rear security with his machine gun, and this guy started running at him. Clothes blowing out, waving his arms all over the place. My guy yells at him, and nothing. Then, get this—he takes out a pen flare and shoots it directly into the guy's chest. I watched it bounce right off the guy. He's clearly not stopping. So my guy lights his ass up, ends up practically cutting the guy in half. Didn't even have anything on him. No suicide vest, no grenade, nothing."

"What'd he look like?" I asked Demmingware.

"Serious Hajji, long white beard. Really old."

"Right by Fox and Joanne?"

"Yeah, on the south side of Joanne. He came charging up Fox right at us. Whole convoy of Marines and the fucker came right at us."

A giggled popped out of my mouth. Then a laugh. Pretty soon I couldn't stop. I started laughing so hard my stomach ached. I could feel my eyes bugging out of my head. I was laughing and feeling sick, and everyone was staring at me.

"I talked to that guy an hour ago," I choked out. "He just moved back to Marjah because he heard it's safe now." I tried in vain to suppress another spurt of laughter. "He's blind."

Demmingware and Compton stared at each other as I cracked up some more. I was probably the last person that guy ever talked to. Now he was cut into pieces by a machine gun. I stood up and walked away still laughing. I felt like if I ever stopped laughing, I might have to think about what happened. And if I thought about what happened, I might have to think about the kid. And if I thought about the kid we killed, I might have to think about Haley, and Zaehringer, and Bishop and Bay and Carbajal, and everyone else. And if I thought about them, I might have to think about what was going to happen to all of us at Aries II. So, I kept laughing and tucked the old man deeper and deeper into my mind until I couldn't remember what was so funny.

———

A few days after we lost seventy-five percent of our area, my squad was on post. We rolled out of our warm sleeping bags into the frosty air to suit up for post at four in the morning. It was cold now. During the day, in the sunshine, it felt better. But in the shade, the chill never went away.

I sat in the MRAP, smoked, and read a book under the red light.

Around six, Compton came into the MRAP to get ready for his patrol later. While he and I talked, Hannibal came over the radio.

"Hey, uhh, COC, this is the south post."

"Go ahead."

"I've got eyes on like twelve guys with guns down near the *souk*."

I paused. This had never happened before. "What are they doing?"

"It's weird. They're just standing there, smoking, and drinking tea."

I turned to Compton. His eyebrows were raised. "Contractors?" I asked. He ran out of the MRAP to get Kobe.

"Standby, south post. We're having the terp call and see if that's the contractors."

"Roger that."

I bounced my knee as I waited. The sun was coming up. If those were Taliban, they must be new to the area; otherwise, they would never be hanging out this close to Aries II. I lit another cigarette.

Compton stuck his head in the MRAP. "Kobe says the contractors are in Lashkar Gah today."

I lifted the walkie-talkie to my mouth. "South post, this is COC. Those are Taliban. I repeat, those are Taliban."

Hannibal answered by firing the .50 caliber. *Chunk-chunk-chunk-chunk* came the thudding bass of the big gun.

"I'll grab everyone, not on post," Compton yelled over the firing. I gave him a thumbs-up. "All posts, all posts, if you didn't catch that, south post has eyes on a dozen Taliban down by the *souk*. Sergeant Compton is rounding up everyone not on post to join in. Keep eyes on your sectors in case they're massing for an attack."

I called up to Echo Main to report the contact. As I did, the volume of fire picked up, way up. I moved to the front seat of the MRAP so I could watch. I felt calm as I called over the radio, a raging firefight in the background. My voice was steady as I let Echo Main know what was happening.

"Hey, Martin, Compton," the walkie-talkie said.

"Go ahead."

"We're spread out under the tower, by the other hooch, and behind the south truck. There's at least fifteen of 'em down there. It looks like they're all taking cover behind that short courtyard wall."

"Copy that," I said as I grabbed a map.

I knew exactly where they were. To the northwest of the *souk* fifty yards away was a small ringed yard. The wall was only two or three feet high. We could send a squad out due east of Aries II, and circle down south to the *souk*, completely hidden by walls and buildings. I had patrolled this area every day for months. I knew all the secrets.

"Echo Main, this is Aries II. Over." Again, the firefight crackled and roared behind my voice.

"Aries II, this is Echo Main."

"Roger. We have a squad reinforced of Taliban pinned down. Standby to copy grid." I passed the location along when they were ready. "Requesting permission to push out a squad to encircle them. Over."

"Standby, Aries II. We need to run it up to battalion."

"Copy that. Standing by."

I lit another cigarette and bounced my knee. I thought over my plan. If we followed the route in my head, it would take ten, maybe fifteen minutes to get there. Burn a couple of minutes to set up the squad in the alley. We could pop a flare to let everyone at Aries II know when to stop firing and toss grenades into the courtyard. After those detonated, we'd rush in and clean up. I could feel the excitement warming my arms and legs. After months of being on the receiving end, getting ambushed, hearing trucks get blown up, and watching medevac helicopters flying overhead, this was our chance to even the score.

"Aries II, this is Echo Six," the Echo Company commander said over the net.

"Echo Six, Aries II."

"Battalion says negative on pushing out a patrol. They're concerned about conflicting fires. Over."

I was stunned. They were two hundred yards away from us, close enough to shoot at! Who would we have a conflict with? "Copy all, Echo Six." I ground my teeth together. "Interrogative, if we can't maneuver, can we request fires? Over."

"I don't see why not. Take it up through the Battalion net. Echo Six out."

I threw the radio handset down. This was fucked. I called the battalion fires office on the Notional Boom net, explained the situation, and gave them the grid from earlier.

"Yeah, we can hear you guys getting into it down there," Martinez said over the Battalion net. "Unfortunately, we're denying your request. We can't fire into the neighboring unit's area. Over."

I stared in disbelief at the handset.

"Ahh Roger. I copy that Aries II can't maneuver or fire upon fifteen Taliban that are currently firing at us because it's in the other unit's area. Over," I said, my voice dripping with insubordination and sarcasm. All the officers and staff NCOs in the battalion office would certainly hear this. They would be pissed. *Good*, I thought. *This is insane.*

"That's a-firm, Notional Boom One," Martinez said. "We're reaching out to request a patrol be pushed out." I could hear Martinez's sympathetic acknowledgment of our situation.

The other unit didn't have any patrol bases within three kilometers of us. To think that that was a better solution than having the guys two hundred yards away handle it... My blood pressure was spiking; I could feel the veins in my forehead pulsing.

"Copy all. Boom One out." I threw the handset across the MRAP. It bounced at the end of its cord and swung limply down the aisle, bouncing off my rifle. I opened and closed my hands and tried to calm down. Here we were, trying to take the fight to the enemy, and the higher-ups, safe in their impenetrable base, told us no. I wanted to hit someone.

Boom. The metallic thud of a grenade detonating drew my attention back to the firefight. I tried to see what was happening out the window, but Compton's crew was too far away. The volume of fire was enormous. Hannibal's .50 caliber, medium machine guns, grenades, rifles—it was an amount of firepower we had never displayed before. Whether they were new Taliban or cocky Taliban, they were paying the price now.

Blackwood came jogging up the MRAP. He looked at me and my water bottle full of cigarette butts. I had been chain-smoking for hours now. The burning smoke added to my boiling rage at the battalion leadership.

"Dude, it's wild out there. We're just plastering that courtyard with the grenade launcher. I watched Gross put a machine gun burst through a dude's chest. This is fuckin' nuts."

"It's bullshit that we can't maneuver on them," I said, sullenly, like a petulant kid.

"Huh?" Blackwood said, as he pinched tobacco out of a tin.

I told him about my conversations with Echo and Battalion. He shook his head incredulously.

"What a bunch of cowards." He paused to spit. "But you know what?"

"What?" I asked.

"At least I'm not stuck here!" He flashed a grin with black bits of tobacco between his lower teeth, and then he was gone, back to the fight. I lit another cigarette.

The firefight lasted a little over three hours. I listened to the radio reports from Hannibal as he narrated the Taliban's attempts to escape. From his elevated vantage point, he talked the grenade launcher on to the target. It sounded brutal out there.

The fire ebbed and flowed, but it grew more and more lopsided. By the end, it was only the occasional potshot from Ricci up in the tower. I chain-smoked and fumed.

When it was all over, Hannibal reported only blood-stained grass in the courtyard. I radioed Echo Main to let them know, and I called Battalion to relay the message to the other unit. Turned out they never even pushed anyone out. I was tired, angry, and jaded, and didn't respond.

A few minutes later, a convoy pulled up, coming in from Hansen. They parked in our intersection and dismounted. A sergeant walked up to the MRAP and stuck his head inside.

"Hey, man, just a heads-up. We've got the regimental sergeant major with us. Just so you know."

"Thanks, man," I said dejectedly.

"That was y'all in the firefight, right?"

"Yeah." I didn't want to talk to this fucking guy.

"Damn that was something else. We were listening to it up at Hansen."

I didn't say anything; I just kept smoking in silence. The sergeant looked around for a moment, and then straightened up. I glanced out the back door. A tall man with gray hair and a spotless flak jacket walked up. Must be the sergeant major.

"Morning, Marine!" he boomed at me.

"Morning, Sergeant Major," I muttered back.

"That was quite the firefight down here."

"I guess so," I answered disrespectfully.

He cocked his head to the side. "It was big enough that we delayed our departure because of it."

I lifted my cigarette to my lips, but stopped short of my mouth. I turned to him. "I'm sorry, what was that, Sergeant Major?" I asked, putting my respectful Marine face back on.

"We were in the trucks ready to go, but then we heard the shooting start, so we stood down and waited till it cleared. You guys were really in the shit." I understood that he added that last bit as a compliment, but it sailed right past me. I turned to the sergeant that had come up to me first. They were both standing at the bottom of the MRAP stairs looking in at me.

"You delayed an armored convoy with heavy machine guns because we were in a firefight?" I asked with icy venom in my words and my eyes.

The sergeant shifted his gaze away. "It wasn't my call..." he trailed off. I turned back to the inside of the MRAP.

A massive convoy, with armor and the big guns, stayed safe inside their base, while we ran around and got shot at? They could have driven right up to the courtyard and painted every square inch of that field with lead. My hands started to violently shake. I grabbed the radio handset and started swinging it. I swung the handset, smacking it against the metal walls of the MRAP until it started to crack. I swung harder and harder until it broke into pieces, black plastic bouncing around, wires and circuit boards hanging out.

"Marine! What the fuck are you doing?" the sergeant major yelled at me.

"This chicken shit fucking battalion!" I yelled back, as I threw the broken handset on the floor. "We were out there for three fucking hours! They wouldn't let us maneuver on them. They wouldn't let us fire mortars at them. And then they didn't let a motherfucking convoy come help us!" I was on the edge of tears I was so angry. I could feel my face burn as the rage enveloped me.

The sergeant at the bottom of the stairs was staring, slack-jawed. Even the sergeant major looked shocked. I realized I was standing up, staring down at them and breathing rapidly. I looked down at my hands and saw how hard they were shaking.

"Fuck this," I muttered. I reached out and grabbed the MRAP door handles and slammed them shut.

19

NOVEMBER 2010

In 326 BCE, Alexander headed south of the Hindu Kush mountains and advanced through modern Pakistan and India. There he was stopped by the Indian king, Porus, at the Jhelum River, or Hydaspes, as the Greeks knew it. With Alexander stuck on one side of the river, Porus waited on the other with a similar sized army. But Porus also had about one hundred war elephants.

Unable to cross the river directly, Alexander set off up the river with a small force. They crossed using a wooded island for cover, and raced down the river to attack Porus' flank. When Porus was caught off guard, it provided an opportunity for Alexander's main force to cross the river and attack.

Despite winning, the Battle of Hydaspes would prove to be one of Alexander's most costly battles. He also admired Porus' courage and asked him to serve under Alexander. Porus accepted, and Alexander continued to march deeper into India.

One day, Blackwood's squad got pummeled. They were on their way back from a short patrol, a direct trip to the Taliban Market and back. We listened to the machine gun fire from both sides as they rocked and rolled.

When they got back, Blackwood told me what happened.

"We just posted up in the market there and hung out for a while. I told them to tell the Taliban that we're here, why not come out and fight?" He lit a cigarette. I did too.

"Well, that didn't work. So I grabbed a chair; you know those white lawn chairs?"

"Yeah."

"I just took one from the tea shop and sat down in it, my rifle on my knee, and I said, 'You go tell those Taliban to take off their burqas and fight like men'."

I laughed a staccato, tight laugh. We all laughed like that now; we all laughed from the eyes down.

"Sure enough, when we were leaving a bit later, there they were!" That was him, Blackwood the Brave. He laughed. I laughed. We both lit another cigarette.

———

In late November, Echo Mobile dropped off a satellite phone. I still hadn't gotten any packages from home—no letters, no boxes, nothing. I kept writing letters on MRE boxes that said "No stamp required" and sending them home, into the black hole of no answer. Berg and Hannibal hadn't gotten any mail either.

We only had the phone for a day, and a bit less than twenty-four hours later, Echo Mobile was coming back to pick it up and drop it off at the next patrol base down the line. But life goes on at a patrol base. We still had to go on patrol. We still had to stand post. We still had to repel the attacks. So we fit in phone calls around that and tried to not have our turn be in the middle of the night in America.

During our patrol, I thought about all the things I wanted to talk to my family about. How was the football season going? Did my youngest sister dress up for Halloween? What were their Thanksgiving plans? I also thought about what I would tell them.

I went through the things I could talk about. Firefights? Absolutely not, they still thought I was in intelligence. How dirty we had become? Not a great idea. The netting we put up to keep grenades out of our bedrooms? Nah. My whole world, all the little things from daily life that make up phone calls home were out of bounds. I'd have to think of something.

When we got back from our patrol, everyone was itching to use the phone. You could tell in the way people glanced at their watches and frowned at their friends. My squad's turn was slotted during our post shift at night. It's not very professional to talk on the phone at night during post, but at least my guys would be sure to catch their family during the day back home.

That night, I sat in the MRAP and smoked cigarettes and went from post to post passing the phone along, giving each Marine an hour to use it. We went from the lowest billet up. Leaders eat last.

I sat and thought about my call. I mentally rehearsed laughing at my dad's puns, my "awwws" when my mom said something endearing. I thought about how to keep it light. *"No, I'm doing good, looking forward to getting home!"* And, *"It's getting pretty cold out here."* Little things I could tell them, things to keep their spirits up, things that wouldn't make them cry.

I checked my watch and put my half-finished cigarette into a water bottle and shook it. Heading out to the guard posts, I took the phone from Brown and gave it to Demorrow.

Lately, I had been waking up with a jerk, tangled in my sleeping bag. Morning or night—it didn't matter anymore. I would jerk awake and open my eyes, and my first thought would be, *I wonder if today is the day.* Then I would blink the sleep away, grab my glasses, and try to push it away. The bile in the back of my throat, whispering to me that this might be it... As I shaved, as I brushed my teeth, that voice kept telling me, *This is the last time you'll ever do this.* So I would chug water to push the bile down, and I'd smoke a cigarette for breakfast, and I'd try not to think that that was the day I'd die.

Eighteen hours later, I'd get up, and do it all again.

After Demorrow, I gave the phone to Ricci, and went back to the MRAP. I looked at my dirty hands. My fingernails were always long, they were filthy with the skin pulling away from them. I wanted—needed—to sneak in an "I love you" and "This might be goodbye" into the phone call. Rolling it around in my head, I tried to figure out how to pair that with keeping things light. I made some notes, listing the things to talk about and their angles.

How's the football season going? . . . Yeah? I hear that. I feel like a fifth-year senior, never coming back!

I put my pen down and lit another cigarette. Blackwood and I had been trying to only smoke at the top and bottom of every hour, but it was hard to stick to.

Ricci radioed in that he was done with the phone. I took it to Berg, climbing up the wooden ladder to the small bunker on the roof of the other hooch.

"I'm good, man. You take it," he said.

"Dude, call your dad or something."

"I'm good," Berg said, as he gazed out at the open fields. We sat in silence for a while. Now I understood why he hadn't gotten any mail. I clapped him on the shoulder.

"Alright, man. You need anything?"

"Nah, I'm alright. Thanks, though." He stared out at his sector as I climbed down the ladder, and went across the canal. I climbed on top of the MRAP and pulled the radio handsets up through the emergency hatch, so I'd have them in case anyone called. Dialing my parents' phone number, I listened to the satellite phone trying to connect and imagined the signals bouncing from me, to a satellite, to a gigantic dish, and into the phone lines. It was ringing.

I checked my notebook to go over what I wanted to talk about, and what I wanted to avoid. It rang.

I bounced my foot and wanted a cigarette, but lighting myself up like that on top of the MRAP was an easy way to get sniped. A voice came through the phone. It sounded far away.

"Hello?" It was my mom.

"Hey! It's me! How's it going?" I was so excited to hear her voice. She paused, for what felt like a long time.

"Oops, missed us! Leave a message after the beep." It was the answering machine. My stomach sank, and bile crashed into the back of my mouth.

"Hey, it's Chris. I guess you guys are out or something." I paused. My forehead was furrowing and the space between my eyes burned. "Is anyone there?" I could hear the pleading in my voice. I turned my head. "Well, I hope you all are doing great. I'm doing okay. I just wanted to call and say hi," I put my hand on my face, "and say that I love you . . . and . . . and that I'll be home soon. Okay. Bye." I pressed the button to end the call.

My face scrunched up. It felt warm and painful, but no tears came. I couldn't cry. I couldn't let anyone hear me because I was the tough guy, so I pushed it down; I pushed the sadness down and I let the bile wash over me. I was going to die here. I wasn't going to make it home. It felt strange to accept it. I dropped down into the MRAP and lit a cigarette. My mouth tasted like ash as I let out a shaky exhale.

———

"Did you hear that?" Compton asked me, his head tilted to the side. We were sitting in the MRAP, hanging out.

"Nah, man," I said. "What'd—" He held up a finger and cut me off. He turned his head the other way, towards the back doors. We paused, listening.

"Hey, Jacobs, what was that?" Blackwood crackled over the walkie-talkie.

Compton looked at me. He was worried. "Jacobs, this is Blackwood. Over." I could hear Blackwood running through the walkie-talkie. I stared at Compton.

"What'd you hear?"

"An explosion." The color was draining from his face.

"Jacobs! Jacobs, come in over!" Blackwood was yelling frantically into the walkie-talkie.

I leaned my head back against the seat and took a deep breath through my nose. There wasn't anything we could do, except listen and hope.

"Does anyone have eyes on Jacobs?" Blackwood yelled through the radio.

Compton grabbed the map and started looking for open fields near their last checkpoint. I pulled a blank casevac nine-line card out of my pocket.

"There are two good landing zones, here and here," he skimmed his finger across the shaking map, lightly brushing the lamination.

"Looks good to me," I said. I started writing down the GPS coordinates in the margins of the map. We'd let Blackwood choose. Doing something, even little things, helped keep the fear down. My hands were steady as I wrote.

"Aries II, this is Mobile. Over." Blackwood came over the walkie-talkie.

"Go ahead, Mobile."

"Something happened to Jacobs and Weeks." His voice was shaking. Blackwood the Brave—his voice never shook. "They're both knocked out. Doc is lookin' at 'em now."

"Roger. Solid copy. We have grids for landing zones near your fourth checkpoint on standby."

"Ahhh, shit. Well, we're on the edge of the field south of the long compound."

Compton leaned across me and pointed to the compound on the map. It was right next to a field he had already picked out. "Copy that, Mobile. We've got the grid."

Compton rummaged around on a shelf, and picked up a green notebook. He opened it up to the first page and handed it to me. It was a list of everyone at the patrol base. I scanned the list until I found Jacobs and Weeks, and wrote their battletags on the nine-line card. We had enough information to get the casevac started up.

I grabbed the radio handset. "Echo Main, Echo Main, this is Aries II. Over."

"Arrr-ies II, this... is... Echo Main! Over." The radio operator was joking around, rolling his voice and cadence.

"Standby for casevac nine-line. Over."

"Roger. Standing by." His demeanor immediately changed.

I called in the information we had: two Marines knocked out from an unknown explosion, battletags, LZ grid. It was incomplete, but it was enough to get a bird in the air.

"Hey, Aries II, they're not waking up." Blackwood sounded panicky.

Compton grabbed the walkie-talkie. "Are they breathing?"

"Hey, Doc—" Blackwood cut out. "Yeah, Doc says they're breathing."

"Ask him if they're urgent or urgent surgical," I whispered. Did they have their limbs?

"Mobile, are they bleeding? Do we need to spin up the surgical unit?"

"Negative. No blood, no sign of fucking anything. They're just out."

It sounded strange. As Blackwood got a handle on the situation, I relayed information back and forth between him and Echo Main. The helo was inbound. Echo Mobile was headed our way with some bomb disposal guys, so they could investigate and try to determine what happened.

I listened as the Blackhawk roared overhead. The sun had just set. Blackwood had to cancel using smoke. Instead, he tied a glow stick to a piece of string and spun it around his head to mark the landing zone.

They carried Weeks and Jacobs' limp bodies to the helo, and it took off, racing away in the night sky. Blackwood and his guys hunkered down in the dark to wait for Echo Mobile.

"Aries II, this Echo Six."

I grabbed the green gear. "This is Aries II. Go ahead, Six."

"Roll to tack two." Tack two was the backup radio channel. It was also a way for people to talk in private without clogging up the main channel.

I turned the knob. "Echo Six, Aries II."

"Aries II, that was the most fucked-up nine-line I've heard all goddamn deployment."

My ears turned red, and I felt my face burn.

"Not only did you call it in chunks, it took you over ten fucking minutes to get the whole thing finished."

I didn't say anything. I sat there, feeling ashamed. Compton didn't look at me.

"Well?" Echo Six said.

"Roger, Six," I said, quietly.

"Roger nothing. You better get your shit figured out. If those Marines had been bleeding out, I'd be on my way down there to personally fuck you up. Do you understand?"

"Affirmative, Six." I felt awful. My throat felt raw, and bile seeped into the back of my mouth. I hadn't realized I had done such a bad job.

"Good. Get your shit together. Six out."

I let the radio handset hang between my knees. Jacobs and Weeks made it onto the helo. They weren't bleeding, but we didn't know what was wrong with them. If they were permanently injured, or if they died because I screwed up the nine-line... I let the thought trail off.

Any thoughts I had about being stoic, or heroic, like Alexander, were pushed away by my concern for my friends. I just wanted them to be okay.

Compton reached across me and changed the green gear back to tack one, and walked out of the MRAP. I sat there, alone and ashamed.

———

After that, every day got a little heavier. More close calls, more casualty reports over the radio. With Jacobs and Weeks gone, everyone had to step up. We stood extra shifts on post and took turns filling in on patrols.

Even the firefights felt different. In the summer and fall, things had an ebb and flow. There was a musical element, the crescendo and diminuendo of small arms, the timpani boom of grenades. Between lush fields, we would run and gun and bound with a looseness, like a jazz solo.

But it was winter now. The fields were empty, and you could see for hundreds of yards. We couldn't hide and slink around. Now the firefights had a teeth-gritting quality. We would push and drive and strain while our feet chewed up the soil, but we never seemed to get anywhere. Frantic, mouth-foaming pushes to nowhere.

Before we'd step out on patrol, things were more serious. The joking, laughing, and grab-assing were gone. Pre-patrol briefs were grim. Everyone double-checked their tourniquets.

I used to keep my left hand free, so I could wave at farmers and old men or pull out some candy for the kids. Now I kept both hands on my rifle. Not that there were many kids out anymore.

We'd patrol through brisk mornings, watching the sun come up as the locals started to stir, their cooking fires sending up thin, black lines of smoke. It was hard to avoid open fields, with the crops gone and the next harvest not yet planted. I wanted to stay off the ratlines and roads. So we'd skirt the edges, trying to keep some cover at hand, but staying far enough away to not have to worry as much about IEDs.

I worked the corners of the compounds, using the tall mud walls as an improvised screen. Walking point, I gripped my rifle tighter as I approached. Ten yards before I got there, I turned around and scanned my team. Everyone looking good? How's our dispersion? We didn't need to talk anymore. Hand signals and head nods sufficed. Then I spun back for the approach.

Five yards out, my arm and back muscles tensed as I pulled the buttstock tight into my shoulder. My eyes swept the wall and corners for wires, bulges, anything out of the ordinary. The adrenaline started to come up, just a little, just enough for the colors to pop, for my hearing to get a little better.

Two yards out, staying away from the wall, I started to wheel around the corner, my rifle at the ready as I scanned over it, watching the corner.

One yard—the soil crunched under my feet as I glided forward.

I pulled around and swept the area with my rifle, but there was no one there. A small cook fire was burning by itself a few yards away. My shoulders relaxed as I lowered my rifle. I wiggled my thumb a little; I hadn't noticed it pressing on the safety.

I took a knee and did another scan of the horizon, double-checking, but everything looked clear. I turned around and waved to the rest of the team to set up security. When Berg and Hannibal were in position, we'd push on. In the meantime, I wondered where the people who had been cooking had gone.

———

Blackwood and I were sitting in the MRAP, listening to music and trying to keep warm. In between cigarettes, he turned to me. He opened his mouth, like he was going to say something, but closed it and shook his head. I let the silence hang for a moment.

"What's up?" I asked.

He sighed and looked at his feet. "I don't think I'm going to make it out of here, man," he said.

I stared at him for a moment. His face was taut, and his lips were pursed. He was serious.

I started chuckling. I didn't laugh because I didn't believe him; I laughed because I was surprised it took him so long to figure that out.

He looked at me with his head cocked to the side and scrunched his eyebrows together. "What's so fucking funny?"

"I'm just glad I'm not the only one," I said.

"Huh," he said, and turned away. We were silent for a while. He checked his watch. "Fuck it. Gimme one of those."

I pulled my cigarettes out of my pocket and handed him one.

———

I knelt near a crumbled wall, the rubble spread out before me. We were on a long patrol, a bit north of the Taliban Market.

"Aries II, this is Mobile. Over," I said into the radio. As I waited for an answer, I inspected the area. There was a plow sitting in a field, a half-finished row trailing behind it like a wake. The longer I looked at it, the more the hair on the back of my neck stood up.

"Aries II, Aries II, this is Mobile. Come in. Over," I tried again. Still no response. I started bouncing my knee as I picked up my walkie-talkie. "Hey, Berg and Hannibal, you guys see any people out?" I asked.

"Nope."

"That's a negative. Haven't seen anyone in a while."

Shit, shit, shit, I thought. I bit my lip. I could feel them closing in on us. Despite the bright afternoon sun, it felt like it was getting darker as the fear crept in.

I pulled my backpack off and changed the antenna on the radio. I took the short one off and attached the ten-foot-long whip antenna. Hopefully, it would work. I put my backpack on and tried again.

"Aries II, this is Mobile."

"Go ahead, Mobile," Compton said on the other end.

I let out a breath I didn't know I was holding. "Hey, heads-up. We're having some bad radio contact out here. We're going to push south towards the Taliban Market and then to the next checkpoint. How copy?"

"Solid copy on all, Aries II. Out."

I hooked the radio handset back on to my shoulder strap and stood up. I waved my team on, and let Berg and Hannibal know we were moving out.

As we trudged south, I gazed across the open fields in front of us. There was a small compound to our right, and Berg and Hannibal's teams were both beyond that. We needed to stay on this side of the compound to protect their flank. I looked across the long field with trepidation. We were going to have to go for it.

"Hey!" I yelled to my team. "Push to that ratline across the field. We'll hold there until the other teams are set."

Ricci gave me a long stare, and sighed. I felt the same way.

We fanned out as we crossed the field. I picked up the pace as best I could, but my feet were sinking into the loose soil. I kept looking over at the plow. It was just sitting there, listing off to the side. I ground my teeth together as I walked faster.

We were halfway across the field when I felt my shoulders relax, just a little.

Then the machine gun started firing behind us. *Pow! Pow-pow-pow-pow-pow!* The rounds snapped and whizzed past me. As I spun around, I saw Cantu falling backward. She fell like she was dead.

I hit the ground. The antenna stretched out ten feet in front of me as the air shimmered with bullets. The tunnel vision was immediate. I had to get to cover.

Pushing myself up, the dark soil bunched between my fingers. As I got to my feet, the machine gun roared. After a few steps, I flopped down, the antenna bouncing off the dirt in front of me. I looked to my left. Cantu had rolled on to her stomach. Dirt sprayed up from the field all around us.

"Go!" I screamed at her over the fire, as I stood, took a step, and got back down. Every time I lifted up, the antenna waved around and the machine gun picked back up.

I could see Ricci up ahead, hunkered down in a ditch, firing back. We had to get to Ricci.

I'd get up, take a step or two, and hit the deck. Up and down, up and down, the seconds stretched into hours, and the minutes seemed to turn into days. The field spread out ahead of us, the enemy fire grew heavier, and the safety of the ditch seemed to get further away with every step.

I pressed my body into the dirt and knew this was it. *This is how I'm going to die, buddy rushing across an empty field.* My muscles hummed with life and fear as I braced for the inevitable impact.

I grit my teeth. *Don't stop. Keep going*, I thought. The radio handset swung wildly at my side, as it crackled with traffic. *Don't stop.* The antenna waved crazily above me. Up and down, I kept going.

My lungs ached and my legs burned as they churned up the soil. *Don't stop. Don't stop*, went through my head, like a mantra. I dove to the ground and felt bullets slam into my backpack, and got up again. My legs felt wet and rubbery, but they were still working. I wasn't dead yet. *Don't stop. Don't stop.* Up and down under an invisible scythe of machine gun fire. Up and down.

And after what felt like twenty years, I made it to the edge of the ditch and rolled in. Cantu flopped down right after me. I ripped off my backpack and shoved it away, trying to get rid of the antenna. The bottom of the backpack was soaked from where the bullets shredded my extra water bottles. I patted the back of my legs. They were muddy, but there wasn't any blood.

I grabbed my walkie-talkie and called Berg and Hannibal. They were circling back up. They should be in position at any moment. I lit a cigarette and thought about calling for air support. Clenching the cigarette between my teeth, I pulled my rifle into my shoulder and peered through my rifle scope. There were no good firing positions for the Taliban, except for the section of crumbled wall I had been standing at minutes earlier. As I turned to yell to Ricci, another long machine gun burst rang out. Ducking instinctively, it took me a moment to realize that the rounds were outgoing, not incoming.

"Corporal Martin, we're in position," Hannibal said over the walkie-talkie. I could hear the rest of his and Berg's fireteams firing back at the Taliban.

"Roger," I said. "Keep 'em pinned down while we get out of this ditch. We'll push north to the next ratline." I relayed the plan to the rest of my team as I put my cursed backpack back on, and we scrambled out of the ditch. It was quieter as we made our way across the field, only the occasional suppressing rounds from the other two fireteams.

We swept back through the area around the crumbled wall, but didn't find anything. Once again, the Taliban had disappeared.

Instead of leaving the same way, I switched up our route home to a more defensible path—no sense in getting caught twice on one patrol.

As we trudged home, I thought about the firefight. I had made it across an open field, with a ten-foot antenna waving above my head, while a machine gun did its best to cut me down. It seemed impossible that I was still alive; Cantu too, for that matter. But we were. Just another day for the Marines of Aries II, another routine patrol. This was the thing I had fought and strived for, to be that man in the field, but it didn't feel heroic anymore.

Taking a knee behind a tree, I could feel the cold, wet cloth on the back of my pants press into my leg.

————

The days were short now. Sunrise no longer melted the frost that sparkled on the empty fields. Now it took the weak sunlight a few hours. Sometimes, on clear mornings, the trees and tall grasses along the canal glittered like a million diamonds in the early light. I'd stand at the edge of the wire, smoking and marveling at how beautiful it was.

I tried to schedule more night patrols. It was safer. During the day, there was nowhere to hide when the Taliban came. We still went to their market and told them to take off their burqas and called them bitches. If I was going to die in Afghanistan, I was going to go down swinging.

But we were running out of ammo. Before every patrol went out, the guys on post would offer up some magazines, so that everyone going out would have a full load. Blackwood, Compton, and I noted the shortage every time we called Echo Main. They promised to send more ammo over as soon as they could, but Echo Mobile kept hitting IEDs. We discussed what would happen if we did run out of ammo.

Blackwood started playing the Merle Haggard song, *If We Make It Through December,* all the time. We would sit and smoke cigarettes in the dark, listening to Merle sing about getting laid off at the factory.

When the song ended, Blackwood would put it back on, and we'd light another one.

———

After a tense week, Echo Mobile finally showed up. Demmingware looked like he had lost thirty pounds. All the Echo Mobile guys looked rough. They joked less, and their stares were hard and distant. They dropped off some extra ammo, not as much as we needed, but it helped. They also brought some welcome news: Jacobs and Weeks were okay, and were recuperating at a different base. Everyone was relieved. When we finished unloading everything, Demmingware came up to me.

"Hey, man, you're Corporal Martin, right?"

"Yup," I said as I clapped the dust off my hands.

"Chris Martin?"

"Yeah. Why? What's up?" I asked uneasily.

"Shit," he said, as he glanced over his shoulder. I started to get worried. "Have you gotten any mail lately?"

"No, I haven't."

"Like nothing lately, or nothing at all?"

I turned to Compton. He seemed as confused as I felt. "I haven't gotten any mail this whole deployment."

Demmingware pinched the bridge of his nose with a gloved hand. "Oh man, I am so sorry. There's another Corporal Martin, Chris Martin, in a different platoon. I've been giving all of your mail to him."

I stared at Demmingware.

"He said to tell you that your mom seems like a nice lady, and the cookies were great."

I had to smile at that.

20

DECEMBER 2010

Near the Ganges River, Alexander's army decided that they had had enough. Between fighting Porus' elephants and the eight years of constant war, the soldiers were done. Alexander wanted to continue, and pressed them to join him in conquering all of India, but they refused. Eventually Alexander was persuaded by his closest officers to turn back.

For their journey home, Alexander split his army. Half was to sail down to the Indian Ocean and chart the Persian Gulf by sea. But as punishment for refusing to keep going, Alexander led the other half of the army on a brutal march through the deserts of southern Pakistan and Iran. Thousands of Alexander's loyal troops died of thirst and exhaustion on the march.

The next day we got word that we were leaving. Echo Company was pulling out of Marjah, and heading north to a town called Sangin. The unit that was up there was getting chewed up and needed replacements. When we had landed in Marjah, it was the hottest spot in the country. It was called "the bleeding ulcer of Afghanistan". Now Sangin was popping off, the new worst place to be, and we were headed there. Echo Company, two for two in badass.

A unit from Hawaii came to replace us. The Marines were trucked in a few at a time, starting with officers and squad leaders, then team leaders, and finally the junior guys. One of them brought a guitar, and he would play for us at night. We stood around, listening to him strum and sing as we escaped for a while. He sang about bars and Hawaii and girls. I closed my eyes and tried to remember what the beach was like.

I took out the new officers and squad leaders on patrols to show them the area. As their guys came in, they started leading the patrols, and I tagged along. The last patrol I went on with them, they called an hour-long halt across the street from the Taliban Market. I bunkered down in a ditch, my jaw working furiously as I waited for the shooting to start. Lucky for them, the Taliban never showed up that day.

The night before we left, Blackwood pulled me aside. Our gear was packed, and the new unit was in charge. We were just taking up space until our ride showed up.

"Hey, man, follow me," Blackwood said as he shook a Nalgene bottle. I watched the clear liquid inside foam and bubble. Blackwood grinned.

We headed to one of the hooches next to the supply room. There was a tarp pulled across the opening of the mud-walled room for privacy. A flashlight hung from the ceiling for light. Inside he had stacks of Ramen noodles and a small camp stove. We sat down on the dirt floor, and he opened up the bottle. The astringent smell of alcohol oozed into the dim room.

"My d'ddy sent out a couple of bottles of 'shine," he said, as he raised the Nalgene to his nose and took a sniff. He wrinkled his nose, pulled the bottle away for a moment, and then took a long sip. "Ppftt," he sputtered and blew through his lips before handing me the bottle.

"How'd he get it to you?" I asked as I gently swirled the Nalgene.

"He put in green food coloring and sent it in a mouthwash bottle."

"Nice," I said, as I raised the bottle in a slight toast and took a sip. It tasted like gasoline. My eyes watered as I exhaled and passed it back to him. My throat and stomach glowed in the warmth of the moonshine.

We spent the rest of the night pigging out on Ramen noodles and swigging the moonshine. We reminisced about the firefights we had been in, and cheered to the firefights we would get into in Sangin. Aries II and the rest of Echo Company were the tip of the spear in Afghanistan. We wore our green helmet covers with pride, alone and unafraid at the edge of the world.

———

The next morning, we packed up our gear in seven-tons, and left Aries II. But there was a mix-up. Echo Company was headed to Sangin, but the 81s that were attached to Echo were not. Ricci, Galentine, Gross, and I were staying in Marjah. I watched, crestfallen, as Blackwood, Compton, Berg, Hannibal, and the rest of the guys headed off to link up with the rest of Echo.

Camp Hansen looked different than it had in the summer. There were more towers, more sandbags, more barbed wire. As we rumbled inside friendly lines, I stewed. I wanted to stay with Echo. I wanted to go to Sangin. I wanted to keep fighting. But mostly I didn't want anything to happen to my guys.

The other 81s and I checked in with the Weapons Company staff. They directed us to a bunkhouse that the snipers used. When we opened the door, we all gasped at the brilliant white mattresses. I threw my bags on the floor and hopped onto an empty bed. Sinking into the plush white platform was the best thing I had felt in a long time.

Later, we headed to the computer center, hoping to grab a phone or an Internet connection, but it was closed. Hansen was in River City Charlie, which meant that, someone had been killed or injured, and until their family was notified, no one could use the computer center. Asking around, it sounded like it was always River City Charlie.

So we went to take a shower instead. I undressed, threw on a towel, and strode out into the cold December air. Our flip-flops clapped on the gravel as we headed to the shower trailer. Inside the metal box, pipes fed into small areas curtained off by green camouflage tarps. Water pooled on the plywood floors. A Marine running the trailer told us the rules. Only use the water to get wet and rinse off, and showers were limited to five minutes only. Ricci laughed in the Marine's face.

Slipping into an empty stall, I pulled the tarp door closed. There was a metal faucet on the pipe up above me. It was the kind you hook up a hose to. I turned the red metal knob, and warm water poured down over me. I spun around in ecstasy.

———

After a few days at Hansen, we got our orders. We were heading to Badger, right down the road from Hansen. There were about twenty Afghan policemen there, but since Echo pulled out, there hadn't been any Marines. We would man the mortars there and help the police watch the road for anyone emplacing IEDs. Two other guys from the 81s platoon, Sealy and Martinez, were joining us. It felt like we were all being shipped off in disgrace, hidden away at a small outpost no one cared about.

We rolled out in the predawn light, bouncing around in MRAPs, heading in the opposite direction of Aries II. I wondered how the new guys were doing down there.

Badger was a small, walled compound on Route Elephant. There was an MRAP outside, surrounded by concertina wire and sandbags. Inside the walls there was a tent that functioned as a storeroom, and an ammo supply point that doubled as a bunk room carved into one of the walls. The police lived in rows of tents on the other side of the courtyard.

As the convoy drove away, I looked around. Everything was muddy and gray. It was late December, and cold and wet. We put our stuff away and set up a schedule. I got the night shift on radio watch, ten at night to six in the morning. Once everything was set up, I climbed into my sleeping bag and went to bed.

Things at Badger were simple. We couldn't patrol or do vehicle checkpoints or leave the compound. We were to stand watch and wait for someone to request the mortars—that's it. So we read books, watched movies on laptops, and slept a lot. Late at night, as I smoked cigarettes in the red light of the MRAP, I wondered how everyone was doing in Sangin. I felt like one of the men Alexander sent sailing back, safe and comfortable, while my friends were trekking across the desert, still dying.

After a week or two at Badger, something happened. It's hard to pinpoint if I woke up and things were different, or if it was a gradual realization that bubbled up out of my subconscious. But one day, when I was eating, or shaving, or staring into the distance, my mind tripped over a wrinkle, a wrinkle that wasn't there before. So I stopped and thought it over. *Could it be*? I needed to figure out where this idea came from, because the source of an idea matters.

The source determines the direction, the integrity, even the power of an idea. An idea that comes from a moment of weakness, of temptation, can't be trusted. Rationalizations are flimsy. Every American has decided to restart their diet tomorrow. The same goes for ideas that spring from fear. How many of us have promised to start going back to church if only this one thing goes our way? The source of an idea matters.

So when a small voice in the back of my head said, *I'm going to make it out of here*, I was skeptical. Every afternoon, I still woke up with bile scorching the back of my mouth. Death and dismemberment still flew over us in Blackhawks on their way to Hansen. Explosions roared day and night, while small arms welcomed the morning and bid farewell to the evening. Convoys rolled past us, dragging the burned-out wrecks of MRAPs turned inside out by IEDs.

But that small voice was clear and confident. *I'm going to make it out of here*, it said. It wasn't bargaining, and it wasn't afraid. I wasn't sure I agreed, but I decided to consider it.

———

I sat on the roof of the MRAP, swinging my legs and watching illum rounds float down through the night sky. I had the radio for the mortars clipped to the metal railing behind me. Kelly was firing the illum.

"Rounds out," he said steadily. "Fourteen rounds remaining."

A new round popped in the sky above the old one. Smoky trails from the previous rounds stood out like brown smears against the stars. There were so many stars. The Milky Way stretched across the sky, its whites and yellows and purples spilling and pushing into each other. It was incredible. I leaned back and lay down on the metal roof of the MRAP. The cold crept in through my jacket.

"Rounds out. Ten rounds remaining," Kelly crackled next to me.

I grabbed my walkie-talkie and radioed Ricci in the tower. "Hey, Ricci, wake up the guys. We're going to have a fire mission soon."

"Roger that," he said. There was a brief pause before I heard him yelling, "Fire mission, fire mission, fire mission!" His voice echoed in the otherwise still night. I let the cold ooze into my back as I watched the stars.

I had been keeping track of Kelly's firing, and calculated what we would need to do to take over. After a minute or two, the rest of the guys were on the mortars. I imagined them inside the compound walls, shivering in their sweatpants and flak jackets, yawning in the frosty air. Sitting up, I hopped back down into the MRAP.

"Rounds out. Three rounds remaining," Kelly said.

I picked my walkie-talkie back up and radioed the data over to the gun line. "Gun two up!" came echoing softly down the MRAP's turret. I waited for a moment. "Gun one up!" We were ready to go.

"Rounds out. Two rounds remaining," Kelly said. While he had a moment to talk, I grabbed the mortar radio and called him up.

"Go ahead, Notional Boom One."

"Hey, we're ready to start firing once your rounds are finished. We have approximately forty illum, so we should be able to help out for a while. Break." I unkeyed the handset and waited a moment. "I don't have comms with that patrol, so you'll have to relay any adjustments or instructions over this net. How copy?"

"That's a solid copy on all Echo-Four Mike. Boom Two out," Kelly said.

I lit a cigarette and left it dangling out of my mouth. The smoke rose up and glanced off my glasses. I shook my sleeve back and pressed the button on my watch to bring up a timer. Then I waited.

"Rounds out. Zero rounds remaining," Kelly said.

I pressed the start button and watched the green numbers tick up. Then I picked up the walkie-talkie and told the gunline to load and fire. Once the blast shattered the quiet night, I picked up the mortar radio. "Rounds out. Forty-two rounds remaining," I said. Climbing back on top of the MRAP, I sat there, keeping track of the time, the gunline, and the stars. Every minute, on the minute, we pierced the sky and I watched the illum rounds pop and sway. We were out here making our own stars. I lit cigarette after cigarette as I watched the brilliant white globes rain down over a Fox Company patrol as they searched for a Marine's missing legs.

———

My time at Badger went by in a haze. I'd sit in the MRAP and listen to the radios from night to morning. Then I'd rush back to my cot and undress, before climbing into my filthy sleeping bag where I'd try to shiver myself to sleep before the sun came up. I'd sleep as long as I could, trying to dream my way home.

When I couldn't sleep anymore, I'd get up and find Martinez and Galentine. They had made a frying pan out of cut-up cans and barbed wire. We would squat around a small fire and sizzle slices of Spam over the flames. Then we'd sit around and stare at the fire until it was time for me to go back to the MRAP and time for them to go to bed. And again, and again. We couldn't patrol, and we didn't have visitors. The sky was gray, the soil was gray, and every day blurred into the next day and the day before.

One morning, Ricci woke me up. "Hey, Martin, pack your shit. They're coming to pick us up!"

I blinked up at him, rubbing the sleep from my eyes. He stared at me, a big, goofy grin spread across his face. It took a moment before I understood.

"Holy shit!" I said as I sat up. I grabbed my glasses and hopped out of my sleeping bag.

"Let's get... the fuck... out of here!" Ricci yelled as he whipped the tent flap open and strode out into the morning sunlight.

I got dressed and started packing. Rolling up my sleeping bag, I stuffed it along with some books in my backpack. Everything I had was crammed into a seabag and backpack. Carrying them out into the compound, I put them in a pile with everyone else's stuff. We shook hands and said goodbye to the Afghan police that lived with us. They wished us well. We wished them luck. A convoy pulled up outside, and we grabbed our stuff and left Badger behind.

When we got to Hansen, most of the 81s platoon was already there. Cocagne, Dolph, McVaugh—it was great seeing everyone in one piece. Kelly and Cochran's teams were still with Fox and Golf, but we were told we would catch up with them in Kyrgyzstan. I stood in the smoke pit and asked if anyone had any news about Echo Company. They said three more Echo guys had been killed in Sangin; no one that was at Aries II, but I still worried. I hoped they were all okay.

For the next few days, we took hot showers and ate hot food and slept on mattresses. The Internet was shut down for River City Charlie, but I didn't care. I was happy to be spending time with my friends. When it was time, we loaded on helicopters and flew back to Kandahar. I ignored the door gunner this time.

From Kandahar, we flew back to Kyrgyzstan. Not the way Alexander went, but I didn't care anymore. When the plane took off, no one cheered like we did when we left Iraq.

————

"Get the No. 9; it has the highest percent," Cocagne said. He held up two bottles of beer so we could see. About fifteen of us were standing around the bar in Kyrgyzstan. It was outside, with a broad wooden deck and strings of lights. The bar had plastic menus listing the mostly British and Russian drinks available. We were allowed to have two drinks per day, so everyone got two Baltika No. 9s, for efficiency.

We stood in a shabby line. Our clothes were torn, mud-soaked, and sweat-stained. Some guys had decent haircuts, but most of us had hack jobs from our patrol bases. Our rifles hung off our shoulders and backs, but they felt light without ammo. As each Marine was handed his two beers, he immediately started chugging one as he walked away from the bar. Most of us showed up with an intentionally empty stomach.

Standing on the patio, we drank our Russian beers and smoked American cigarettes. After everyone had chugged their first beer, we were happy and swapped stories. For the first time in months, I relaxed. The alcohol washed over me in warm waves carrying away my stress. The bile started to recede.

The second beer loosened us up, maybe a little too much. There was shoving, threats, and evil glances. People went back to the squad bay and got into fistfights. Our platoon had been split up all over Marjah. We were still friends, but we didn't have a common experience. After living with constant violence, it was hard to turn it off. An awkward glance or an offhand comment was enough to rouse a deadeye stare and sneer, or worse.

Kelly and I tried to lie low. We would spend half the day at the movie theater, watching old DVDs with Air Force jockeys. It worked to pass the time.

Eventually, I went to the computer lounge to send my family an email. We didn't have an exact date for when we'd be back, but I wanted to let them know what we were told. After I sent my email, I didn't know what to do. I hadn't used a computer in months. After thinking for a minute, I pulled up CNN's website to check the news. I wanted to see what they were saying about us. What did the world know about Marjah? I was excited to see what they had to say.

When the homepage loaded, it was full of stories about uprisings in Tunisia, Egypt, and Syria, something they were calling the Arab Spring. I scrolled around looking for stories about Afghanistan, but there weren't any. I checked the archives, but there weren't any recent stories, either. The only stories about the US military were about plans to bomb Libya. I had no idea what was going on. Chewing on my lip, I thought about checking elsewhere, but decided I had had enough, so I closed my browser and left.

That evening, I sat in the chow hall watching the Marines who were on their way to Afghanistan. They were chubby and pink and had clean clothes. I felt bad for them. While I was eating, I could feel their eyes on me; I noticed their whispers and sideways glances. After I finished eating, I went to the bathroom and stared at my reflection in the mirror. There were deep bags under my eyes, and my cheekbones jutted out. I had lost thirty or so pounds. My smile was still there, and my big ears, but something was different. My eyes looked flat. I leaned in closer to look, but people walked in talking and laughing. I turned away, grabbed my rifle, and walked out.

21

FEBRUARY 2011

Back in Susa, in 324 BCE, the rivalry between the Greek and Persian troops was coming to a head. Seeing how tired of war his Macedonian troops had become, Alexander dismissed thousands of them and sent them home. But when he replaced them with Persian troops, his Macedonian men begged to be let back into the army.

In an attempt to unite his forces, Alexander had his Macedonian officers marry Persian women in an attempt to fuse together the competing factions through marriage. After a lavish banquet for his army, Alexander showered his men with gold, silver, and other gifts, and allowed any who wished to retire to head home to Macedon. The Macedonians still disliked Alexander's Persian customs and affectations, but his efforts at reconciliation helped repair the spirit of the army.

Once again, we flew into Cherry Point, up the road from Camp Lejeune. And again, we had to load all our gear into semi-trucks before climbing onto buses. I sat in my seat and bounced my knee. My right hand still held my rifle, my thumb rubbing the safety. It was a hard habit to kick.

Once again, I stared out the window and marveled at how little had changed. The tattoo parlors and pawn shops were still there, as well as the car lots and strip clubs. Same old, same old, except now everything looked brown in the February afternoon.

When we got back from Iraq, I felt offended that the world hadn't changed with us. This time I felt like we had been left behind. The world kept going, having fun, and living, while we were hurting and dying. I closed my eyes and leaned my head against the window; I needed a drink.

We pulled on to the base and drove to the barracks. I stared at the crowd that was waiting for us. It was the same assortment of spouses, parents, and children as last time. Homemade signs and poster board greetings waved above them. I slumped down in my seat, thankful I didn't have anyone coming to see me. I figured I would borrow someone's phone and call home, to check in and let my family know I was back at Lejeune. I wasn't ready to see them face to face yet. I needed to decompress, and get my head screwed on straight, before I saw my family. All I wanted to do was drink a hundred beers and smoke a thousand cigarettes and forget the last seven months.

Once again, we pulled up at the armory and got in line to turn our rifles in. I passed my rifle through the small window to the armorer and let out a deep sigh. All that was left was the march over to the barracks. I walked over to the fence surrounding the armory, and found Cochran. He was with some of the younger guys. They weren't boots anymore. I passed out some cigarettes and lit one for myself.

"I'm telling you guys, it's better if you don't have family coming down," Cochran said, as he rolled his cigarette between his fingers. "You wanna get drunk? You wanna relax? Or do you want to stay in a shitty motel with your family watching TV?" He looked around the group. Some of the guys seemed unsure.

"We're all going home on leave soon, in a week or two," I said. "You'll have plenty of time to spend with your families. Right now, I want to get drunk and tell some fucking war stories."

The younger guys laughed and nodded. Cochran smiled. The line to turn in rifles was almost finished, so we knocked the cherries off our smokes, tucked the butts into our pockets, and headed over to get in formation.

Once again, the company formed up right outside the armory fence. First Sergeant called out the cadence as we marched over to the waiting crowd. The signs and poster board waved harder above the mass of people. As we got closer, I could read some of the signs. I scanned them, pairing the names on the signs with the holders. That must be so and so's wife; that must be what's-his-name's parents. Then I saw a bright green poster board, with bubbly glued-on letters: "Welcome home CM from PA."

Shit, I thought. *Shit, shit, shit.* I glanced down and saw my dad holding the sign. His hair was a little grayer, but he looked the same: a half-smile and big glasses. My stomach boiled with panic. I glanced back ahead as my mind spun.

I couldn't smoke around my dad; he had no idea. And worse, he didn't know I was in the infantry! What was I going to do? I could feel my blood pressure spiking as I tried to think of a plan.

For the last seven months, all I wanted was to hear from my family. It killed me that I never got their letters. But now that I was home, I just wanted—needed—to pickle my brain with alcohol and escape from the world. I wasn't ready to see my dad. I wasn't ready to put on a normal face and try to pretend that I was okay.

First Sergeant called the company to a halt and had us face the excited crowd.

"Weapons Company," he boomed out, "dismissed!" Half the formation sprinted into the crowd as the crowd surged at the formation. There was an explosion of hugs, tears, and smiles. I turned and saw my dad walking towards me.

"Hi there!" he said with a broad grin. "Welcome back!" He gave me a bear hug and clapped me on the back.

"Hey!" I said. "Thanks for coming down." Even if my plans were messed up, I was still touched that he had made the trip down to see me. It felt strange to hug him; I hadn't had any physical affection in a while. We stepped apart and both put our hands in our pockets. I fingered the old cigarette butts at the bottom of my pocket.

"You have any bags that you need to pick up or anything?" he asked.

"Yeah. Not too many, though," I said, as I looked around for my gear. I struggled to think of what to say.

"How was the flight?" he asked while we walked towards the pile of bags.

"It was fine. I slept most of the way. How was the drive?"

"Not too bad. I-95 was terrible but other than that..." he drifted off.

I started looking through the stacks of identical seabags and backpacks. After years of doing this version of finding the needle in the haystack, I could pick out my bags from a mile away. As I pulled out my stuff, Longman walked up to me.

"Hey, man, what are your plans for tonight?" he asked.

"Hanging out with my dad, I guess," I turned to him. "Dad, this is my buddy, Longman. Longman, this is my dad."

"Hi there, how ya doing?" my dad said, as he stuck out his hand. They gave each other a knuckle-popping handshake.

"Doing well," Longman answered, as he pumped my dad's fist up and down. "That's very kind of you to drive down here."

"My pleasure. Not every day do you get to see a bunch of war heroes come home," my dad said. Longman glanced sideways at me as I tried not to roll my eyes.

"Hey, man, we're going to get dinner. You want to come?" I asked.

Longman and I changed into some civilian clothes we had packed away, and headed off to dinner with my dad. He had driven my pickup truck down from Pennsylvania, so the three of us crammed into the cab. As we drove off the base, all I could think was how much I wanted a cigarette.

We went to a Mexican restaurant I liked. When we walked in, everything looked the same: the same sombreros on the walls, the same heavily lacquered tables, the same blue stemmed margarita glasses. Unlike everything else in town, I liked that it hadn't changed. It felt comfortable, like I was walking into an old friend's house.

We sat down at a booth and opened up the tall, laminated menus. The waitress came, and we ordered a round of Modelos. When she asked if we wanted regular or large beers, Longman and I both said, "Large," immediately.

The three of us talked, ate, and drank for a few hours. I sat there, in jeans and a T-shirt, eating chips and salsa, like it was the most normal thing in the world. On the one hand, it was normal. We talked about the news, sports, and North Carolina. We said thank you to the wait staff and used napkins. But on the other hand, my eyes kept moving. I tracked every person that came through the door, every waiter carrying a tray, every customer coming back from the bathroom. The sounds from the road outside rang loudly in my ears. We talked and ate and drank, but Longman and I had another conversation going. We shared glances and nods and kept tabs on everyone. It felt better that way. I don't think I could have sat in the booth without a decent view of the front door.

When we drove back to the barracks after dinner, I was sitting in the middle seat while my dad drove. Longman and I were each six or more beers deep. I needed to smoke something terrible. I tried to bounce my knee, but we were too packed together. We drove through Jacksonville, on the outskirts of Lejeune, and through base security. Longman and I flashed our military IDs as we held up my dad's visitor's pass. We were silent as we headed up the long road to the main part of the base. I was drunk, and the heat was running too hot for three people in the cab. After a few minutes, I couldn't take it anymore.

"Hey, Dad," I said.

"Hey," he said back.

"I'm sorry about this, but I really, really need to smoke a cigarette."

"You need to smoke a cigarette?" he asked, sounding confused.

"Yeah, like right now. You mind rolling down the window, man?" I asked Longman. He pressed the button and rolled the window down an inch or two. I pulled out my pack and a lighter, and in one smooth motion lit up. I took an extra-deep pull on the delicious smoke, held it for a moment, and tried to blow out the window without exhaling on Longman.

We drove for a minute or two, while I puffed away. My dad didn't say anything, and I was drunk enough to not be ashamed.

"I didn't know you smoked," he finally said. Longman turned and looked out the window.

"Yup," was all I managed.

My dad stayed in the barracks with me that night. We got rip-roaring drunk with Blackwood and Martinez. We drank cases of cheap beer, smoked packs of cigarettes, and told wild stories about firefights and close calls and death. I didn't tell my dad I was in the infantry, but I stopped putting up any kind of facade that I was doing intelligence work. I got the homecoming party that I wanted, and it was great having my dad there.

Everyone has a different persona around their parents. You present an image that is more or less in line with who you really are, but it's not all of you. That night, my dad got to see who Corporal Martin, the squad leader at Aries II, was. I'm sure it was surprising, beyond my ability to smoke multiple packs of cigarettes, but he laughed and it seemed like he had a good time with us.

Two days later, I drove my dad to the airport. I was sincerely thankful that he had come down. It was the nicest thing anyone had ever done for me, a twelve-hour drive for a surprise visit. We hugged, and I told him I'd be home soon. Then he headed through security.

Life carried on for our unit. We had short workdays. Platoon formation at seven to do roll call, and then we'd fill out paperwork. Classic military stuff, filling out forms in triplicate—someone always messed up and needed a new form. Classic.

I went to the dentist. She asked me how long I had been grinding my teeth. I told her I didn't grind my teeth; it was probably the stoneground bread I ate in Afghanistan. She stared at me for a long time, her face obscured by her mask. Then she sighed and went back to work in my mouth.

Most afternoons we stood in company or battalion formation for awards. There was an endless stream of purple hearts. Something like a quarter of the battalion got purple hearts.

Some were presented in person, some in absentia, some posthumously. Marines and corpsmen marched to the front in small groups. Some seemed fine, marching up with a straight back, their head held high. Others went slower, walking with slings or crutches, or riding in wheelchairs. One tapped his way up with a red-tipped cane.

After the purple hearts, there were awards for valor: Marines that single-handedly fought off the Taliban, Marines that pulled other people from burning vehicles, Marines that went above and beyond. I stood there, always hungover, as the sun beat down on us and listened to their citations. Blackwood got a medal for directing mortar fire. Cocagne got a medal for bravery. I felt proud seeing my friends have medals pinned on their chests. It was validation. We did it. It was terrifying and awful, but we did it. There was proof.

Eventually, we had a funeral for the guys who died in Marjah and Sangin. Fifteen men in total. The funeral was held in the Lejeune field house, an old school gymnasium with bleachers, wooden floors, and hanging lights in metal cages. We hung around outside the building before it began. Clusters of Marines stood in the parking lot and on the grass, smoking and talking in hushed voices.

"You guys doing alright?" Cochran asked.

"Yeah, I guess so," Kelly said.

I nodded.

"This is gonna be tough," Cochran said. "I remember—"

Boom! Boom-boom-boom! Artillery rounds crunched and thumped in the distance. We ducked. The Marines standing in the parking lot ducked. Hundreds of people all ducked in unison. I crouched down and looked around wild-eyed.

Cochran burst out laughing. "You motherfuckers! Always making fun of me for being jumpy. Well, welcome to the club." He stood back up and took another drag. I pulled out another cigarette.

Our unit filed into the bleachers in the field house. Out on the floor of the gym, there were pictures of all the guys that died on our deployment. Fifteen portraits sitting on black easels arrayed in a curve facing the bleachers. They were smiling in some of the pictures; in others, they were stoic. A few of the guys I knew well: Zaehringer and Jackson, a thin Marine from my boot camp platoon. Others I knew from here and there: Twigg, 'Socks' Sockalosky, Giese, Tate, Htaik, Geary. There were still seven others I didn't know.

I scanned the audience. The families were sitting up front. I rubbed my face and bounced my knee. This was going to be hard.

The chaplain came out, and we all stood as he said a brief prayer for the fallen. I bowed my head and stared at my nicotine-stained fingers. When we sat down, there wasn't any talking or whispering.

They went down the line, reading citations for each of the men that died, where they were from, what they liked doing, who they left behind. I sat there listening and thinking it all seemed so insignificant, so much smaller than what they deserved. I thought about all the fear and pain they went through, and that all they got was a few words in a crumby gym. My face felt red and hot.

I watched as Zaehringer's wife stepped out to receive his picture. I had met her a few times before. She went back to her seat with her in-laws. I made a mental note to go and talk to her afterward.

The gym full of Marines was quiet. Occasionally you could hear someone crying. Wet sobs and hiccups and murmured "It's okay, man," and "Let it out."

When the ceremony was finished and we were dismissed, everyone sat there for a moment. Eventually, in small groups of threes and fours, people started standing up and walking out. Nobody said much. There wasn't much to say.

I sat in my seat and thought about what I wanted to say to Zaehringer's wife, something about how he was funny, and how so many guys looked up to him.

Making my way down the bleachers, I walked along the gym floor, trying to find Zaehringer's family. I spied them near an exit. They were talking to some guys from Weapons Company. It seemed like half of them were laughing and telling a story, while half of them were wet-faced, wiping tears away. I started walking over.

As I got closer to the group, the space between my eyebrows started to burn and I could feel my eyes start to water. I stopped walking, took a deep breath, held it for a moment, and slowly exhaled.

You can do this, I told myself. I took another step forward, then another, but the burning didn't go away. My face scrunched up as my eyes filled with tears. I turned around and walked underneath the bleachers. It was dark and dusty and private. I paced in a tight circle, trying to keep it together, but I couldn't. I bent over double, tears streaming down my face, and I pressed my cover into my mouth so I wouldn't make any noise. Every time I took a wet, shaky breath, it started again. My entire time in, I hadn't cried. Not in boot camp, not on deployments—I was one of the tough guys. But here I was, red-faced and silently sobbing, alone under the bleachers.

I kept thinking about Zaehringer's wife, and Socks and Jackson, and everyone else. I thought about the guys that survived, but had broken legs and punctured lungs and shattered spines. I thought about how I was grinding my teeth and the bile that was always in my throat. I thought about my parents worrying about me, Buckwheat and his family back in Marjah, and about my friends screaming in their sleep. So I pressed my cover harder into my mouth and cried some more.

22

MARCH 2011

Leaving Susa, Alexander marched to Babylon, where he began to plan future conquests. He drew up plans to invade the heart of the Arabian Peninsula, and considered attacking Carthage in North Africa. He was interested in sending an expedition to sail around Africa and developing water-borne trade routes to India. At this point, Alexander had been campaigning for eleven straight years.

When most of the unit went home on post-deployment leave, I stayed on base for an extra week. There was going to be a flood of Marines leaving the unit, and I wanted to get a head start on checking out. Unfortunately for me, the administrative Marines also went home, so I was stuck on Lejeune with nothing to do. I kept myself busy with a rigorous schedule of binge-drinking and binge-watching pirated movies on my laptop.

After days of chugging beer, I decided to switch to something with a little more class, and bought the biggest, cheapest bottle of red wine in the base liquor store. It wasn't until I got back to my barracks room that I realized I didn't have a corkscrew. But instead of walking back to the store, I grabbed my rifle cleaning kit and picked out one of the metal rods that I used to clean my rifle barrel.

I held the rod, about ten inches long and as wide as a pencil, to the cork and raised a boot over my head, ready to smash the cork down into the bottle, when I paused. *Jesus, what an idiot*, I thought. I set my boot down and took the rod over to my sink. I didn't want to get gun oil in my wine, so I washed the rod off with hand soap.

With a clean rod, I again set it on the cork, grabbed my boot and hammered down. The cork pushed a quarter of an inch down into the neck of the bottle. Pleased with my ingenuity, I started swinging harder. With each strike, the cork pushed deeper and deeper, until it was almost free of the bottle neck. I raised the boot and gave one it last vicious swing.

Pop! The cork and the cleaning rod shot down into the bottle, while a geyser of Malbec erupted into my face. I wiped my eyes and looked around. There were purple streaks of wine on the white walls, the linoleum floor, even the ceiling tiles. A third of the bottle had splashed all over me and most of my room. The cork bobbed in the wine with the cleaning rod sticking up like the mast of a ship. I tried to pour some wine into a Solo cup, but the cork kept plugging up the bottle from the inside. Pushing on the cleaning rod was the only way to start the flow. Taking a long drink from my plastic cup, I was glad I had washed the rod.

After I got back from leave, I saw Hannibal, Berg, and Compton a few times, but it was different. We no longer had Aries II to pull us together, to make us close. Without the patrols and firefights, we all went back to being who we were before the deployment, hanging out with old friends. It was strange, talking to them and realizing that I didn't know them, not really, not in any context outside of Marjah.

Even if I fell away from the Aries II guys, it was great being back in the 81s platoon. Most of us were getting out soon. Kelly, Dolph, Longman, Blackwood, Shen, Stapleton—we were all getting out around the same time. Cocagne reenlisted; he was a lifer. We whiled away our days hiding in the barracks, and spent our nights drinking cheap beer.

Our gear had to be washed, scrubbed, and cleaned so we could turn it in. A few guys got some grief that there were bullet holes in their gear. "Can't turn it in damaged," they were told. We existed just to pass the time. Filling out paperwork and attending classes on resume writing until the calendar ticked off the days and we had our freedom back.

In the warm spring evenings, we played horseshoes and talked about what we were going to do when we got out. It felt a little like the end of the school year, when summer vacation is beckoning with its infinite possibilities.

The unit kept moving, though. Training ranges were set up, fitness tests needed to be run, and Marines were getting sent off to leadership courses. Our company commander had us do company runs, over a hundred Marines in green T-shirts and yellow reflective belts running along with the morning sun. At first, the runs were easy, but after a few weeks, he started picking up the pace.

I jogged in the middle of our platoon next to Kelly and watched the sunlight reflecting off the water. As we jogged along, I thought about the last four years.

The younger Marines were running up ahead of me, the red platoon flag waving out in front of them. They reminded me of when I got back from Iraq, growing their hair a little longer and walking with some swagger. The platoon was in their capable hands now.

Cars pulled up at stop signs as we ran past, and our yellow reflective belts sparkled in their headlights. I thought about how hard I tried on the obstacle course in boot camp, and the pain from grinding the hand sanitizer into my bloody palms. Fancy lunches with Colonel Ahmed in Ramadi, and going into wet prison cells. The fleas in Marjah, and leading my first assault through the cornfield. Everything I had hoped to do, wanted to do, strived to do in the Marines, I had done. I had traveled across the world, stood in the fire, and held my head high. I had made my tiny splash in the tides of history.

When Alexander got back to Babylon, he immediately started planning his next campaigns. I couldn't imagine going back to war. I was done. I had had enough.

"Hey, man, I'm out of here," I said to Kelly.

"Wait, what?" he asked, as I slowed down, moved outside the platoon formation, and started walking on the sidewalk.

For the first time in my enlistment, I quit. I had never dropped out of a run, and always finished the hikes carrying extra gear. But this time, this time I was done. I walked on the sidewalk and admired the brilliant green grass. Breathing deeply, I smelled the water and the car exhaust.

In a few days, I would be a civilian again. I had new adventures ahead of me. No more chasing Alexander. I decided to walk back to the barracks. The rest of the company ran on down the road, green T-shirts and yellow reflective belts bobbing in the morning sun.

EPILOGUE

In June of 323 BCE, at the age of thirty-two, Alexander died in Babylon. It's unclear what killed him, but ancient historians say he died of a fever. Malaria or typhoid fever are considered likely explanations.

When he died, he had no obvious heir to the throne. As he was dying, he was reportedly asked to whom should his kingdom go. His answer was, "To the strongest." But within a few years of his death, his empire fell apart, with different generals carving out their own smaller kingdoms.

Alexander has one of the most enduring legacies of any single person. His generalship and tactics are still studied today, and he died undefeated in battle. Many of the cities he founded are still flourishing today, including Alexandria in Egypt, Kandahar in Afghanistan, and Raqqa in Syria. Greek culture and ideas flourished across the Eastern Mediterranean and Middle East for three hundred years after his campaign, giving rise to the Hellenistic Period. He continues to live on in myth, legend, and religion as well, appearing in the Quran and referenced in the Bible.

At the time of his death, Alexander ruled over two million square miles of territory. In eleven years, he conquered an area larger than the Roman Empire at the height of its power. It's unknown how many people were killed during Alexander's campaigns, but when factoring in his battles, civilian massacres, and sieges, estimates range from hundreds of thousands to over a million.

ACKNOWLEDGMENTS

First, I would like to thank my incredible wife for all her support. I couldn't have done it without you. Thank you to my parents and siblings for their support while I was in the Marines. I know you didn't understand why I did it, but you loved and cared for me every step of the way. Also, thank you to Alison Rolf for her excellent editing.

I wouldn't be writing this book—or the man I am today—without the incredible men that taught and shaped me. Thank you to Castillo, Shampainor, Skewes, Tuttle, Cochran, Quinn, Bradley, and my dad.

And to all the Marines and sailors I served with, from boot camp to Afghanistan, Semper Fi. I'm sorry I couldn't fit everyone in the book.

BIBLIOGRAPHY

Arrian. 1971. The Campaigns of Alexander. Translated by Aubrey De Selincourt. London, England: Penguin Classics.

Cartledge, Paul. 2005. Alexander the Great. New York, NY: Random House.

Plutarch. 2004. The Life of Alexander the Great. Edited by Arthur Hugh Clough. Translated by John Dryden. New York, NY: Modern Library.

Romm, James. 2012. Ghost on the Throne: The Death of Alexander the Great. Mississauga, ON, Canada: Random House.

Rufus, Quintus Curtius. 1984. The History of Alexander. Translated by John Yardley. London, England: Penguin Classics.

Stoneman, Richard. 1991. The Greek Alexander Romance. London, England: Penguin Classics.

ABOUT THE AUTHOR

Christopher Martin enlisted in the United States Marine Corps in 2007 and served until 2011. He deployed to both Iraq and Afghanistan as a mortarman with 2nd Battalion, 9th Marines. After leaving the Marines, he attended Denison University, where he graduated Phi Beta Kappa. He currently lives in Colorado.